SPLM/SPLA: History of Liberation

(1983-2005)

David de Bion

A Note from the Publisher

The publisher wishes to acknowledge and thank Dr Douglas H. Johnson for his invaluable help and support for Africa World Books and its mission of preserving and promoting African cultural and literary traditions and history.

Dr Johnson and fellow historians have been instrumental in ensuring that African people remain connected to their past and their identity. Africa World Books is proud to carry on this mission.

© David de Bion, 2020
ISBN: 978-0-6489291-0-9
All rights reserved. No part of this publication may be reproduced, stored in a retrieval system, or transmitted, in any form, or by any means, electronic, mechanical, photocopying, recording or otherwise, without the prior permission of the publishers.
This book is sold subject to the conditions that it shall not, by way of trade or otherwise, be lent, re-sold, hired out or otherwise circulated without the publisher's prior consent in any form of binding or cover other than in which it is published and without a similar condition including the condition being imposed on the subsequent purchaser.
Design and typesetting: Africa World Books

This book is dedicated to
two exceptional mothers and their four sons.
Mama Adhieu Kutwel Anyang and Mama Akoor Deng Nyuon
whose sons had timely died!
And their timely death was a honourable death in history
and despite paying the ultimate price
they never had a decent burial.

Lt Bech Kelei Ayool *aka* Bech Akoor Deng Nyuon
was killed in the battle of Kurmuk in 1989
and his brother Duk Keliei Ayool *aka* Duk Akoor Deng Nyuon
was killed in the battle of Yei in 1990.

Sgt Ngong Bior Alier *aka* Ngong Adhieu Kutwel
was killed in the battle of Juba in 1992
and his brother Captain Alier Bior Alier *aka* Alier Dhieu Kutwel
was killed in Kit during OJS in 1996.

CONTENTS

Chapter 1	Historical Background to the Liberation War (1821-1956)	9
Chapter 2	The Founding of SPLA/M (May –August 1983)	49
Chapter 3	SPLA/M Divisions, Battalions and Their Battles (1983-1986)	60
Chapter 4	Axis Command /Zonal Command (1987-1989)	98
Chapter 5	SPLA/M Campaigns (1989-1990)	125
Chapter 6	SPLA/M's Black Chapter (1991-1994)	138
Chapter 7	SPLM/A's Operations (1995-1999)	160
Chapter 8	The Peace Process (1986-2005)	169
Chapter 9	Glimpse of History of SPLM/A (1983-2005)	184
	Appendix	201
	Bibliolography	203
	Acknowledgements	204

ACKNOWLEDGMENTS

I am indebted to many people who gave their time and experiences during the war to make this book possible. I congratulate also those who advised morally. It is because there is no space I would have written their names all but let me mention few; Cdr Ayiei Manyok Ajak aka Ayiei Magoor, former instructor at SPLM/A Institute of Revolutionary and War Studies in Isoke. Gen Samuel Thiak Ajak, Gen Biar Kuol Ayuen, Hon. Kuol Aguto Akau, Gen Garang Mabil Deng, Gen Machar Akau Machar, Hon. Philip Thon Nyok, Lt Gen Malual Majok Chiengkuac, Hon. Deng Dau Malek, Lt Col Yuot Thuch Pageer and Hon. Peter Atem Ngor, former Red army group leader, for facilitating the research. This book is about Sudan Socialist Union (SSU) 1969-1985 of President Nimieri to National Congress Party (NCP) 1989-2005 and SPLA/M Revolution 1983-2005 to Republic of South Sudan 2011 that brought the concepts described. To some readers, and for still others, the events may be known, but, accepted as something that has to be tolerated with little thought being given to how, it may be made less deleteriously or more supportive to us. Sorry, there remain few things in this book, as they could be able to appear in next future days' books. All in all, this book is a seminal outline of topic for more research and details of the war.

David de Bion,
November 18, 2020,
Juba, South Sudan

CHAPTER 1

HISTORICAL BACKGROUND TO THE LIBERATION WAR

Before narrating the inception of the Sudan People's Liberation Army (SPLA) / Sudan People's Liberation Movement (SPLM) in 1983 as the national liberation movement and its waging of revolutionary armed struggle for twenty-one years, it is aesthetical to stretch back three thousand years into the history of the Sudan to provide the historical background to the war. Beginning around 1000 B.C to 1956 A.D, the history of the Sudan has six major epochs:
- The Tribo-anarchy (1000 BC -1821 A.D),
- The Arab's Migration to the Sudan (700-1200 A.D),
- The Turko-Egyptian Conquest (1821-1881),
- The Mahdist Revolution and State, (1881-1889),
- The Anglo-Egyptian Conquest and The Condominium Rule (1889-1956) *and*
- The Independence of Sudan (1956-1983).

These six epochs and their events and strands exert greatest influence and contribution to/on the cultural, religious, economic and political history of the Sudan. Although, there are, indeed, some positive effects of some episodes upon the Sudanese people in general, it is, however, a different case particularly in Southern Sudan. There were occupations, pacifications and slavery imposed by Turkish and Egyptians, and civilizations introduced by British. This resulted in the uneven development in the country, angering and predisposing the people of Southern Sudan to the path of war. This is why the Sudan had been fighting itself for 38 years, out of 49 years of Independence according to Dr John Garang de Mabior.

THE OVERVIEW OF THE SIX EPOCHS OF THE SUDAN'S HISTORY

TRIBO-ANARCHY, 1000 B.C – 1821 A.D

Tribo-anarchy is the first epoch of Sudan's history. The term "Tribo-anarchy" has no definite etymological origin in English or other classical language, the Greek or the Latin, but it is a label coined herein to describe highest degree of uncivilization that occurred, practiced and existed among the black people at the time. During 1000 BC to 1821 AD, the Blackman race had been chaotic, warlike, and barbaric in the nameless land of darkest skin people, south of the biblical Egypt. Therefore, the concept "Tribo-anarchy" refers to the state of anarchy, lawlessness, barbarism and lack of authority before the arrival of the Whiteman to the Blackman land. As it was in that culture of the time, the strong, gigantic, the richest and the crudest, in wider sense, was the law, the order and the authority itself. This is how and why the proverb, 'strength is bigger than the law' came about. This cruelty had concurrently been happening at the same time that the British philosopher Thomas Hobbes called "the war of all against all" in Europe. This period of anarchy, and tribal wars was exactly described by Mohammed Omer Bashir, a Sudanese scholar in these words:

> The tribes of Bahr el Ghazal and Equatoria were living during the Fung period in a state of anarchy and tribal wars. The strongest tribes prevailed over the weak. The Azande for example, were pressing northward across the Congo- Nile-Divide and absorbing the small weak tribes like Bonga, the Kreish and the Shatt. The Dinka tribes were also

HISTORICAL BACKGROUND TO THE LIBERATION WAR

advancing in the same manner. The state of affairs was only halted by the Turco-Egyptian conquest of the Sudan in 1821.

During that prehistoric, medieval and up to early the 19th Century, the norms of day was that, a given tribe or tribe A could unjustifiably attack the weak neighbouring tribe B. It was a time of the clan against clan, section against section, family against family. The five brothers, for example, could rob cows of the two brothers. Two brothers could rob the goats of one son in his family. The classical story of time occurred at village, in what is the present Bor, Jonglei state, South Sudan. As the habit of hunting, two men beat a hunting drum at dawn, about three hundred men gathered. As the sun was rising up, they moved to the nearby village, where they found a cattle camp of about fifty herdsmen. When herdsmen asked them, where they were going with spears and dogs, they replied that they were hunting. The herdsmen showed them the forest where buffalos, elephants, antelope were present and in abundance. The hunters left for the forest. After a short time, they returned running toward the cattle-camp, shouting "white buffalos", and begun spearing the cattle, killing several cows. The owners of the cows, who were few in numbers and who were afraid of hunters, were shocked and filled with wrath.

"Why are you killing our cows?", they asked the men.
"We are hunting", the hunters replied
'Then, why are killing our cattle, "
"Hahaha, are these your cattle", they mocked, " we thought these were just white buffalos"
"You did badly, why can't you go to the bush", another herdsman lamented.
"What if the thorns go and pierce our feet", one of the hunters contemptuously replied.

As the herdsmen were complaining, one hunter turned, hit the head of goat to death with big stick. When he was asked, why he was killing the goat, he responded, 'I thought it was a reed buck'. The fifty men feared the 300 hunters and kept quiet. The hunters skinned the cows and cut them to pieces of meat and left for their village. Nothing the owners of cows could do because they would be killed for birds as their banquet by strong 300 men. This was the time, where there was no police or government, where one might go and open the case against any wrongdoer.

THE ARAB'S MIGRATION TO THE SUDAN

The Arab's migration is second epoch of the Sudan's history. The Arab began coming to the Sudan around 7th century A.D as traders. They started arriving to the land of the Black people from 7th to 12th century A.D. They came through two routes, Egypt and the Red Sea, with goods like salt, clothes, beads, and hoes, which they bartered with ivory, ebony, gold and ostrich feathers from black man. When Arab traders returned to Arabian Peninsula, they talked of land of the black people. As the time went by, the medieval Muslim geographers gave the name 'bilad al sud' to the nameless land of the black man. And this was how the Sudan was named by Muslim geographers as historians, Holt and Daly wrote, "The medieval Muslim geographer, gave the name, bilad al-Soudan, to belt of African territory to the south of Sahara Desert. In the more restricted sense of the territories lying southwards of Egypt[2]".

Slowly by slowly, the trade between the Bilad al Soudan and the Arabian Peninsula was booming and flourishing. Arab begun settling in the new land, since the black people were rural, who wore animals' skins or walked naked, they liked Arabs and welcomed them because of their salts, beads and clothes. The arabization of the North Sudan resulted from the penetration of region by tribes, who had already migrated from Arabia to Upper Egypt. After the collapse of the kingdom of Al-Muggura, there was nothing to prevent the steady immigration of Arab tribesmen... Islamization, al beit it first of a very superficial kind, must have accompanied this population movement and the intermarriage of the Arab with the native people[3] When the Arab migrated into the Northern Sudan, they found four territories Nuba, Fur, Soba, and Funj. Some of these kingdoms collapsed of the natural causes. Arab Inter-married with them created the new tribes. Islam and Arabisation which were monolithic in nature assimilated other cultures and religions. The effect of Islamization and Arabization was one of the causes of the war.

HISTORICAL BACKGROUND TO THE LIBERATION WAR

THE TURKO-EGYPTIAN CONQUEST (1821-1881)

The Turko-Egyptian Conquest is the third epoch of Sudan's history. Egypt was a province of the Ottoman Turkish Empire in 1820's. The Ottoman had been governing the Middle East and the Arabia peninsula. Muhammad Ali, who was the Vassal-Governor of the Ottoman Sultan in Egypt decided to send expeditions to Sudan on personal, private mission. He sought to conquer the Sudan for two reasons: (1) to eliminate the Mamluk and (2) to restore the trading relation between Egypt and the Sudan, which existed before but was lost after sometime. In describing Muhammad Ali's motive of invading Sudan, Holt and Daly summed it up ; "By Massacre and proscription, he [Muhammad Ali] had succeeded in 1811 in breaking their power in Egypt, but a remnant of the Mamluk had escaped beyond his control and established themselves in the pretty state of Dongola [in Sudan].[4] In achieving that goal, Muhammad Ali sent his armies and conquered Sudan, he killed some of Mamluk, his armies took some prisoners of war and others surrendered themselves and honourably returned to Egypt. After he had destroyed Mamluk, restored trade between Sudan and Egypt. The business resumed. As time went by, the mode of the trade changed from good commodities to human commodities because Africans were apelike and idle. By virtue of African apelikeness and idleness, Muhammad Ali introduced slavery in Sudan, at the time when slavery was lucrative business in Arab World and Europe. And this was how the evil slave trade was started by the barbaric Turkish in the Sudan and until it was abolished by the half-barbaric British Empire at the fall of 19th Century. The Turkish, Arabs and Europeans had sold hundreds of thousands of South Sudanese into slavery during the Turko-Eygptian rule. Actually there are no statistics available about how many Southern Sudanese were sold into slavery at time. However, historians Mathew LeRiche and Mathew Arnold stated that hundreds of thousands were sold: 'As Richard Gray, a prominent scholar of Southern Sudan notes, 'by 1883, it was estimated that about ten to twelve thousand slaves were annually imported into Egypt[5]".

SPLM/SPLA: History of Liberation (1983-2005)

THE MAHDIST REVOLUTION (1881-1885)

The Mahdist Reovolution was fourth epoch in the Sudan's history. As the Turko –Egyptian administration had been doing injustice to the Sudanese people through oppression, misrule, corruption and highest taxes. The Sudanese revolted under Mohammed Ahmed, who proclaimed himself as the Mahdi or the Expected One to his followers the Ansar. The Ansar fought the Turks and Egyptian capturing towns including Khartoum and declared the theocracy. Holt and Daly narrated the rise of Muhammad Ahmed and his rebellion in the Sudan: "the father of independence [Muhammad Ahmed was] a nationalist leader, who united the tribes [northern tribes] of Sudan by an Islamic ideology, drove out the alien rulers and laid the foundation of a nation state[6]. The Mahdist Ansar fought under a slogan "kill the Turks and cease to pay taxes". In that war, the Ansar killed the English Vassal – Governor of the Sudan, Charles George Gordon on January 25, 1885. After the fall of Khartoum, The Mahdist also briefly extended their rule to Southern establishing garrison at Rajaf in Southern Sudan. During the five years of the Mahdist administration, slavery intensified in the Southern Sudan, here, the Northerners exhibited the counterpartness to the Turk and Egyptian by selling many Southerners into slavery. There were schools now in North to enlighten them about modernity. Mahdist like Turks and Egyptian never established a rule and delivered the services, like education in the South, which kept South backward. All in all, the Turko-Egyptian rule was oppressive and enslaving one, and this was why it was overthrown.

ANGLO-EGYPTIAN CONQUEST, 1889-1956

Anglo-Egyptian Conquest was the fifth epoch in Sudan's history. Sudan was strategically and politically invaded by joint forces of the British Empire and Egypt in 1899. The invaders were commanded by British Lord Kitchener. There were five reasons of the conquest: (1) recovery of the lost province of Egypt which is the Sudan, captured by Mahdist Ansar forces and established theocratic Mahdist rule (2) revenging the life of Charles George Gordon, who was killed by Mahdist soldiers (3) to acquire Sudan as a British colony as a part of expansionist policy of its empire. (4) to stop the slavery in the Sudan, which was epitome of evil of the nineteenth century (5) to prevent France from taking Sudan as it colony; this was to stop France from controlling the Nile. The conquest happened at time, the Ottoman Turkish Empire that was ruling Middle East including Sudan became 'the sick man of Europe'. It was declining or disintegrating, meanwhile British Empire was taking over the Middle East as shown by its occupation of Egypt in 1882. After the famous Battle of Omdurman, in which Mahdist Ansar forces were defeated, an agreement on how to govern Sudan by Britain and Egypt was designed. Holt and Daly wrote on this deal:

> With neither annexation by Britain nor incorporation under the Khedivate, a suitable solution to the problem of the Sudan's status [was adopted], Cromer devised a hybrid form of government, which appeared both to honour Egyptian claims and to safe guard British interest. This solution was embodied into the Anglo-Egyptian convention of 1899, which came to be known as the condominium agreement since they created a theoretically joint Anglo-Egyptian sovereignty over the Sudan. British claims were openly based on the right of conquest while Egyptians were defined by reference to certain provinces in the Sudan which were in rebellion against the authority of his Highness the Khedive. The agreement stipulated that the Egyptian and British flags should be flown together in the Sudan[7]

In fact, Egypt's participation in governing of the Sudan was insignificant because Egypt was already British Colony of its own. Egyptians were, on one hand, British servants in their own country, and on the other hand, they were masters or partners governing the Sudan with Britain. During condominium rule epoch, 12 major political events took place in the Sudan; The Establishment of Effective Government, The Passports and Permits Ordinance, The First Southern Policy, The Independence of Egypt, The Graduates General Conference, Advisory Council, Second Southern Policy, A Call for Trusteeship in Southern Sudan, Sudan Administrative Conference, Juba Conference, Cairo Agreement, Torit Mutiny.

SPLM/SPLA: History of Liberation (1983-2005)

Establishment of Effective Government

The establishment of effective Government was the first political event of the Anglo-Egyptian rule and of the fifth epoch of the Sudan's history. The Condominium rule had, for the first time, established the effective government encompassing the whole Sudan. During the tenure, nine strands or policies took place or introduced. These were aimed at delivering services to the people or disseminating western civilization in the country. These were the enacting of laws, introductions of policies, and formation of political and cultural organization and the guarantying of independences to both Egypt and the Sudan. It is the Condominium Rule that demarcated and drawn up the map of the Sudan. The Governor-General was heading the administration as Holt and Daly described, how the government was set up and how it worked:

> Within the Sudan- the central government was divided into the major and several minor departments. Dominating this structure were three secretaries, civil, legal and financial …. The most important of three, the civil secretary headed the civil service and acted as liaison officer between the central and provincial governments… The country was divided into provinces, the number and boundaries which were altered through the years. Each was headed by a governor (mudir) responsible to the governor –general through various departments. Provincial districts (markaz) were in the charge of British inspectors (Mufatish) whom from 1922 were called district commissioners. A district comprised a number of sub-Districts, over each of which presided a mamur. This class of official was largely made up of Egyptian, though a policy of sudanization gradually introduced educated Sudanese as sub-mamur from 1915 and as Mamurs shortly thereafter. Thus provincial and central administration was British in the higher ranks and Egyptians (and eventually Sudanese) in lower[8]

Independence of Egypt, 1922

Independence of Egypt was second political event of Anglo-Egyptian rule. Egypt as colonial master in the Sudan and colony of Great Britain in its own country got its independence in February 1922. After this the Egyptian officials and soldiers were removed in the Sudan service. It became irrelevant in the Sudan affairs although it remained legally a partner in the Condominium. At the time, the Sudan Defence Force (SDF) was created to replace the outgoing Egyptian soldiers. "In February 1922, The British government issued a declaration of Egypt's independence"[9]. Southerners were indolent at the time, otherwise, they would have been contaminated and influenced by the Egyptian independence and demanded for their own independence too. This was greatest missed opportunity.

The Passports and permits Ordinance (1922)

The Passports and Permits Ordinance of 1922 was third political event of Condominium rule, the fifth epoch of Sudan's history. The Sudan Government passed many laws in including The Passports and Permits Ordinance (1922). This ordinance was meant to restrict the movements of people between the South and North. Southern Sudan was declared as the Closed Districts. Northerners were required to use passports to come to South. Traders were given trading permits with the expiring date. Northern soldiers were evacuated and the Equatoria Corps comprised of Southerners only was established in December 7, 1912.

> The adoption of indirect Rule had an even greater significance in Southern Sudan than in the north... from the early days, the condominium had sought to limit the spread of Islam in the South and certain steps had been taken to achieve this. After the war, this object was pursued with great urgency imbued now with dogmatic dictates of Indirect Rule. The Southern governors' meeting in 1922 proposed leaving the administration in the hands of native authorities under the British supervision. But often such authorities did not exist. Where tribal organization no longer exist, it might still be possible to recreate it under the provision of the passport and permit ordinance of 1922, the South was declared as a closed district resulting in the progressive exclusion of northern traders and limitation of southerners travelling to the northern to find work. Beginning in 1922, chief courts (lukikos) were established under the guidance of British official[10]

This was the first time the British recognized southerners and enacted the law in their favour as the colonial masters and the civilizer as the time.

The First Southern Policy (1930)

The First Second Policy of 1930 was the fourth political event of Condominium rule. In 1930, the Sudan government came out explicitly declared the policy on Southern Sudan; the policy stipulated there should be non-Arabic speaking staffs whether administrators, clerks and technicians, there should be control of immigrant traders from the north. English had to be the language of communication. The chiefs were ordered to stop their Arabic names and Arabic dressing was also banned. The cardinal aim of this policy by the British was to advance the national interest of the Southern people socially, economically and politically. This policy was at the best interest of the ignorant, uncivilized Southerners.

The policy of the government in Southern Sudan is to build up a series of self–contained racial or tribal units with structure and organization based, to whatever extent the requirements of equity and good government permit, upon indigenous customs, traditional usage and beliefs[11]. The policy was to promote the African customs, traditions and belief

The Graduates General Congress (1938)

The Graduates General Conference was fifth political event of Condominium rule at work. It was an organization of northern Sudanese founded in February 1938, its members were educated Sudanese students and Trade Union members. Though formed as social and philanthropic in nature, the members started to engage in political activities and in the matters of Public interests and concerns.

Ismail Ashari was its first secretary general. The Graduates General Conference was first northern entity to oppose a policy that only served the interest of Southern Sudan as one of its memoranda shown. In 1942, it issued a memorandum that called for...demanded the abolition of the Closed Area Ordinances, lifting of restriction on traders and the movement of the Sudanese within the Sudan, the cancellation of subvention to the missionaries and the unification of education syllabuses in the northern and southern Sudan[12] In April 1942, the congress wrote another memorandum of the most political one, with twelve demands.

"The primary demands was for the issue, on the first possible opportunity by the British and Egyptian government, of a joint declaration granting the Sudan in its geographical boundaries, the right of self-determination."[13]

In 1940s, the Congress broken up, through this factionalization, two political parties emerged in the Sudan. In 1943 the Ashigga under Azhari emerged as the first genuine political party in the Sudan favouring Union with Egypt. As a response to this development, moderate supporters of Sayyid abd al-Rahman al Mahdi established in 1945 the Umma, as a political party favouring the complete independent of Sudan[14].

By 1945, two political parties had emerged; the National Unionist Party (NUP) and the Umma party. The NUP led by Ismail al Azhari advocated the Union of Sudan and Egypt, The UMMA party backed Sayed Abdur Rahmad al –Mahdi championed unqualified independence[15]. The two wings of the politically minded class were broadly identified as favouring either an independent Sudan to be achieved with British cooperation (the Sudan for the Sudanese) or Union with Egypt (The unity of the Nile Valley[16] At time, Still Southerners were unconscious of their nationality and nationalism, as the Northerners asked the two alternatives, they would have asked for Southern Sudan Independence too. This was second miss opportunity.

The Advisory Council, 1944

The Advisory Council was sixth political event of Condominium rule at work. In 1944, the Advisory Council was instituted by the government. It was a de facto parliament at time; the government formed it due to the growing Sudanese nationalism. The Government decided in 1944 to establish an Advisory Council for Northern Sudan alone. The South was excluded from the Advisory Council and although the civil secretary made a broadcast trying to allay the fears that behind the ordinance there is no hidden secret policy to split the Sudan into two[17]. Here the British harboured the idea of separating the South from the North, and there was no zeal on the side of Southerners to re-echo the British ulterior plan for the South. "In 1944 the Civil Secretary, Sir Douglas Newbold put forward for the first time three alternative for the south. 1. Integration of the south into the north 2. Integration of the south into East Africa.[3] Integration of parts of the South with the North and the other parts with East Africa[18]. These were perfect premises, if it were not inexperience of Southerners; they would have drawn up their own conclusion by taking up the best alternative either the independent Southern Sudan, or integration with East African or Northern Sudan. This was the third miss Opportunity. This advisory was created after the Government fell out with Congress. The Government sought to create the broad –based body to negotiate with because the British Government announced the independence of the Sudan already. The Advisory Council set up the committee to organize the Administrative conference

The Second Southern Policy, 1946

The Second Southern Policy was seventh political event of Condominium rule at work. During the years 1940s, the first Southern Policy as practiced came under criticism from different quarters both public and private. It was attacked by the northern political parties and Egyptian government. Southern Question dominated the negotiations that took place in Cairo and London among the three entities; Great Britain, Egypt and the Northern Sudanese. As it was revealed by the secret memorandum of Civil Secretary on the new, second Southern policy circulated among the Government officials on December 16, 1946, Mr J. W Robertson wrote:

> Whatever may be the final effect, inside the Sudanese of the present treats, negotiations, it is certain that the advance of the Northern Sudan to self-government, involving the progressive reduction of the British executive authority and public canvassing of the Southern Sudan question will be accelerated. It is therefore essential that policy for the southern Sudan should be crystalized as soon as possible.[19]

Here the Civil Secretary was asking the British administrators views on the new and Second Southern policy. At first, the three alternative solutions for the Southern Question were provided but now the two alternatives were dropped and one was chosen as shown below.

Policy of the Sudan Government regarding the Southern Sudan is to act upon the facts that the people of the southern Sudan are distinctively African and negroid but that geography and economics combined (so far as can be foreseen at the present time) to render them inextricably bound for future development to the middle-eastern and Arabicized northern Sudan and therefore to ensure that they shall, by educational and economic development, be equipped to stand up for themselves in the future as socially and economically equals of their partners of the Northern Sudan in the Sudan of the future. The biennial report to this Britannic Majesty's Government is due early next year. Subject to your comments on this letter, I propose to advise his Excellency that in His Excellency's next report he asks his Britannic Majesty Government to approve that two of the alternatives... he ruled out as a practical policy at the present time.[20]

The two alternatives ruled out were integrated with East Africa or partly with each.

A Call for Trusteeship in Southern Sudan

A Call for Trusteeship in Southern Sudan was eighth political event of Condominiums rule politic of the time. Instead of the immediate unification between the Southern and Northern Sudan, according to Civil Secretary J.W .Robertson, most British administrators called for trusteeship in Southern Sudan.

B.V. Marwood, the Governor of Equatoria reacted by rejecting the immediate unification of South and North, and he proposed a period of trusteeship till the South is fully enlighten about its rights and about the advantages and disadvantages of unification. Mr Marwood explained:

> The proposed line offers a via media- eventual link-up with the north but a period of tutelage till the South can stand on its own feet. The word partnership is used but as Mr. Owen has pointed out you cannot have a partnership between a boy of 12 and a man of 40. The line I propose to take is to accept in the main civil secretary's contentions but to press for safeguards and periods of Trusteeship, till the South is vocal and knows its own mind.[21]

J.H.T Wilson, who was a District Commission of Jur River District, rejected the unification the South and North and he proposed the federation between the South and North, also he tried to allay the fears of Northern that British wanted to grant independence to the Northern but continues to colonize the South, in his letter to Deputy Governor of Wau on 2 January 1947, he wrote:

> In my opinion it is right that it should be decided NOW to cast the lot of the South with the North. I regard it as of importance that our target in the South should be federation with the North as partners on an equal footing in the self –governing Sudan of the future in the same way as we regard our target in the North as a self –governing Northern Sudan within 20 years ....A statement should be made by the British Government that Britain has no intention of colonizing the southern Sudan...If in practice, at the end of 20 years, the South is still immature and requests the present administration to stay for its protection, it should do so until such time as the South can take its place as a partner alongside the north.[22]

In summary of opinions expressed, proposals and comments made by British administrators in South, one thing was clear in their point of views, the British administrators were all unanimous on the need to safeguards the interests of South and assurance that the British administrators would continue to administer the south until it was able to stand on its feet for the first time the idea was put forward that the south should in the future have regional autonomy or be federated with the North.[23]

Sudan Administrative Conference

Sudan Administrative Conference was ninth political event of the Condominium rule. As agitation and nationalism and call for independence intensified, Sudan Administrative conference was set up to deal with the question of associating the South with Central and local government. The conference recommended that the South should be integrated with the North and be represented in the proposed Legislative Assembly.[24] The Southern Sudanese were not invited to attend this conference... The conference dismissed as irrelevant the argument that the South was more backward than the north.²⁵ The British administrators in the South rejected the resolution of the conference as unacceptable and instead they called for Administrative Conference and Advisory Council for the Southern Sudan.

> When the minutes of the conference were published, fourteen British Administrators in the South signed a letter addressed to the Civil Secretary expressing their dissatisfaction with the recommendation and calling for the institution of an administrative conference for the Southern Sudan. Their main contention was that the future of the South was being discussed by wrong men in the wrong milieu. They suggested the formation of a Southern Advisory Council for safeguarding the interests of the South and demanded assurance that legislation affecting the Southern provinces passed by the Northern Assembly would not apply to the South, save with the approval of the Governor – General after consulting the Southern Advisory Council. The fourteen British rebels came to accept regionalism or federation as the only right policy which would protect the interest of the South²⁶

Northerners affirmed the British government decision to unite the South with the North by the new and second policy. The British administrators tried to incite the Southerners to supplement their efforts of rejecting unification by calling for Southern Administrative Conference and Advisory Council, but, Southerners were uninformed and indolent in their behaviours. This was first time the Northerners took political decision of uniting the South and North independently, and second time of making a decision of uniting South and North after civil secretary memorandum on Southern Sudan. There was no Southern national fervour at the time that British administrators would stir up. In order to allay these fears and gauge the views of Southern Sudanese, the Civil Secretary agreed to hold the proposed conference and Juba Conference was held.

Juba Conference 1947

Juba Conference was tenth political event of the Condominium rule. As the result of the fourteen British administrators' criticizing and rejecting the

Civil Secretary memorandum of December 16, 1946, uniting the South with the North (which was purely British Government decision, because of Suez Canal issue), and the Sudan Administrative Conference recommendation that reaffirmed and legalized it (new and second Southern policy in the Legislative Assembly ordinance (which was purely the Northern Sudanese decision), and the British administrators demanding of the setting up of the Advisory Council to Southern province and the institution of Administrative Conference for Southern province, the British government accepted the grievance of the administrators and called for conference that was held in Juba and became known as Juba Conference of 1947. The Juba Conference was held on June 12-13, 1947 for three political and administrative reasons: (1) to gauge the views of Southern Sudanese (2) to allay the British administrators' concerns (3) to ask the Southerners whether they can send representatives to the proposed legislative assembly in Khartoum or not. The conference was attended by seventeen traditional chiefs, educated southerners, six Northerners, six British officials.

In the broadest sense of the word, the British Government was testing the water by gauging the views of the Southern Sudanese. This was to evaluate the level of threat that might be posed by Southerners, if their demands are not met. Also, the British government was fact finding out whether there was a coherent or natural relation between the British administrators' positions and the Southerners', in rejection the unification of the South and North.

In fact, the British administrators, who had the Southerners in their heart called Sudan Administrative Conference's resolution as bad deal for the Southerners, in their conclusion, they said 'the future of the South was being discussed by wrong men in the wrong milieu'. Before the Juba Conference started, the British administrators orchestrated how the Southerners would argue their position, inculcating them with schemata of their historical and political positions. 'British administrators did a great deal of canvassing before and among the Southerners to support the idea of an Advisory Council for the South'. Because of that canvassing, on the first day, the Southerners spoke against the unification of South and North, as they were induced by the British administrators. On the second day, they changed their position and spoke in favour of unification of South and North Sudan.

HISTORICAL BACKGROUND TO THE LIBERATION WAR

Here the question arises up, 'What was the reason why Southerners changed their minds?' The answer is as Beshir put it 'The change in attitude of certain educated Southerners who first spoke against any participation in the legislature Assembly and later changed their minds was due to the effect of Mohamed Saleh Shingetti, a Northern member of the Conference[27]. Mr. Shingetti bribed the Southerners to send representative to the Assembly in Khartoum. Some unconfirmed sources said 'each uneducated chief was given 100 Pounds. This amount could buy 40 cows at the time. Since a bull was bought at 3 pounds and heifer at the 1 pound. 'We are forcibly buying bulls from the Dinka at 3 pound '. Also, Mr Shingetti gave educated Southerners more than 100 pounds and promised them a promotion in the next civil service. When the meeting opened on the second day, the Southerners were speaking of sending representatives, which exactly the opposite of it before. The two British administrators tried to incite the Southerners by reminding them of how Northerners enslaved and mistreated them during slavery time. This historical reference brought Mr. Shingetti and Mr. Marnood head to head in exchange of acrimonious statement. Mr. Marwood, one of British administrators, questioned Mr Shingetti on why he refused the Advisory Council for the South and he put it like this. "Judge Shingetti had not yet given any convincing reasons why the first step of an advisory council which had been found necessary in the North should not be equally necessary in the South.'[28]

Mr. Owen, another British administrator, revisited the history of slavery in order to arouse the feeling of Southerners against Northerners but the Southerners were not irritated, he asserted;

> Southerners are still suffering from the sins of Zubeir Pesha and the slavers. The sins of the fathers shall be visited upon their children even unto the third and fourth generation. He said that the South had not forgotten the days of oppression even if the North had done so, and even today the Southerners view was dominated by the fear and suspicion. He concluded that the southerners would never willingly join until the later should prove by their acts not merely by their words, that they had undergone a change of heart.[29]

SPLM/SPLA: History of Liberation (1983-2005)

This heart-breaking historical evidence never received any applaud from the Southerners; Southerners had remained indifferent despite the fact that they were given a historical reference how Northerners had enslaved them. This terrible let down the two British administrators, who stood up to oppose the unification of South and North.

Mr. Shingetti who already won the Southerners to his side, responded to the Mr. Marwood and he said:

> Northerners had no desire to dominate the South. They maintained that the country was one and the policy of this council was made in Khartoum, so the northerners wanted the southerners to join with them in the formation of policy for a whole country. Mr. Owen had referred to the slave Trade ...but he felt bound to the point out that the British had their time been the biggest slave trader in history. The West Indies were populated by Africans who had been enslaved in the past by the British but with the growth of public opinions, the British had come to realize the evils of the slave trade. What had happened in England had now happened in the Northern Sudan where it was fully realized that under this Government slaves had been introduced into Sudan and Abyssina.[30]

The Juba Conference concluded with five resolutions which included; (1) Southerners wanted United Sudan (2) Southerners wanted to participate in the proposed Legislative Assembly, etc. At the end of conference; British administrators were let down and disappointed by Southerners. Southerners lacked the national fervour. After this Juba conference, the next event was the Cairo Agreement

Cairo Agreement, 1953

Cairo Agreement was eleven political event of Condominium Rule. After the Juba conference, two agreements were signed in Cairo both of which were dealing with how the three countries, Britain, Egypt and Sudan should have the future relations. Although Sudan was united in Juba Conference, Southerners were not invited to attend these discussions. There was struggle between Britain and Egypt, Britain wanted to remain in the Southern Sudan and give independence to North while Egypt wanted one united Sudan. In those negotiations Southern Sudan was traded off by Britain with its usage of Suez Canal. The export of slaves from South Sudan remained undisturbed even after slavery was abolished worldwide and Sudan was under the British during the condominium rule (1889-1956). The reason for the continuation of slavery in the Sudan was to appease the Arab Muslims 'compromising with believers over the barbaric pagans '! It was on same compromise that South Sudan was handed over to Arabs of Khartoum in 1956 in exchange for the use of Suez Canal [the continued use of Suez Canal by British was exchanged from Egypt with unification of the Sudan] as Bol Makueng argued in his book, South Sudan: Handbook of Nation and State Building. On October 12, 1954, an agreement was reached, which called for the self –determination for the Sudan. This agreement has followed another agreement on January 10, 1953. A transitional government would be set up for three years, whereby the governor- general would be assisted by five members; two from Sudan, One Egyptian and one Britain and one Pakistani.[31] "No southerner, for example, was invited to attend the historic discussions which took place in Cairo between the Sudanese political parties and the Egyptian government. The absence of the Southerners, from the discussion was seen as a proof of a desire to belittle the South and ignore its demand.[31] Out of 800 posts, only four went to Southerners

> When the result of the Sudanization committee was announced in October 1954, Southern suspicion, nurtured over fifty years, turned into hostility. The Sudanization committee in the best traditions of the British Civil service allocated jobs and made promotions in accordance with seniority, experience and qualification.... four Southerners were appointed assistant district commissioners and two as mamurs, these were the highest posts allocated to Southerner but it was also looked upon as a changing of one master for another and a new colonization by the North.[32]

Torit Mutiny 1955:
An Attempt to Rewrite the Rules in the Middle of the Game.

By 1955, many events had taken placed either unnoticed or noticed by the Southerners. Some Southerners participated consciously in the decision of these events. These events were; the Second Southern Policy, Sudan Administration Conferences, Juba Conference and the Cairo Agreements. As time went by, Southerners realised that they were doing mistakes because they were severely feeling the negatives effects of these event. In the broadcast sense of the word, Torit Mutiny occurred because of four reasons: (1) rewriting the three sets of rules. As the one Sudan was now playing by now the rules and policies provided in the Second Southern Policy, Sudanese Administration Conference, Juba Conference and the Cairo Agreement, Southerners mutinied to reverse all recommendation and ordinances that were set out in the three events. (2) Equtatoria Corps refused the orders of transfer to the north (3) Killing of striking workers of Zande Scheme by the Northern policemen (4) Disappointment on the Sudanization Committee "Following the months of unrest during which in July 1955, striking workers on the Zande Scheme were shot down by Northern troops attempting to disperse them, the Equatoria Corps of Sudan Defense Force refused the orders in August.[33] "The culmination of the events was mutiny by Equatoria Corps in August 1955. 261 Southerners and 75 Northerners were killed in the disturbance that followed.[34] After Mutiny, some were arrested and some escaped to the bush. Some political decisions were taken to solve the Southern problem, Northern political parties agreed to a federal solution for the Sudan.

SUDAN'S INDEPENDENCE (1956)

Sudan's Independence was sixth epoch of Sudan's history. Sudan got its Independence on 1 January 1956, from Anglo-Egyptian rule/the Condominium or more correctly from Britain. Ismael Al Azhari was the first Prime Minister of the Republic. The independent Sudan was the sixth epoch, which has its own episodes and events. Election of 1958, Formation of Sudan African Closed District National Union (SACDNU), Anya Nya I, Southern Sudan Liberation Movement(SSLM), Addis Ababa Agreements (AAA), Akobo Mutiny, Jonglei Canal Protest, Wau mutiny.... among others.

Elections of 1958

Following the independence, an election was held in 1958. All Sudanese political parties including Southerners contested, Federal Party, one of existing Southern political parties contested and won seats in parliament. On 5 July, Abdallah Khalid, Secretary General of the Umma Party was elected Prime Minister over Azhari by a vote of sixty to thirty–two.[35] A New parliament was sworn in Khartoum. In this Legislative Assembly, the Southerners asked for the federation promised to them as safeguard to interest before independence. On the morning of 17 November 1958, only a few hours before parliament was to reconvene to discuss the federation of South, the army took control of key three towns. Major General Ibrahim Aboud took over the power in military coup suspending the Parliament and declared the state of emergency. This was deliberate attempt to disrupt the parliament and declare the federal status to Southern Sudan. As the result of the dissolution of Parliament, all Southern members of parliament went to exile in Uganda, Congo and Kenya.

SACDNU/ SANU: ANYA NYA POLITICAL WING

In 1960s, a genuine Southern party was formed in exile. Political events in the South were taking new turn. The army's repressive measures in the South drove thousands of Southerners outside the Sudan into Uganda, Kenya, Ethiopia and Central Africa Republic (CAR).

> In 1960, for example, something in the nature of large scale migration began out of Equatoria into Uganda and Congo. Leading educated Southerners abided-parliamentarians fled the country. The exiled formed an organization; the Sudan Christian Association and the Sudan African Closed District National Union (SACDNU). SACDNU's leading members were; J.H Oduho (President, former member of Sudan parliament, William Deng (SG, former Assistant District Commission) Marko Rume (VP, Ex MP) Safarino Lohure (Ex-MP, President of liberal Party), Ferdinand Adyang (Ex-MP, Valerio oregat (Treasurer) Jame Wek Athian (Ex-MP), Aggrey Jaden (Deputy SG) Akuot Atem de Mayen, Alex Modi Yango, Pancransio Ochieng, Philip Palek Lith, Basia Rinzi, Ex-Chief, Nathaniel Oyet, (Ex-MP).[36]

SACDNU changed to Sudan African National Union (SANU) in 1963. The objectives of SANU was to solicit international military, diplomatic, political and moral support and to sensitize the national opinion back home

Anya Nya I: SANU's Liberation Army

On 30 July 1963, the SANU formed its military wing, and calling it the Anya Nya, "Snake Poison". As the Southern Sudanese veteran political Gale wrote in his memoirs:

> On July 30th, 1963, the President Joseph Oduho Aworu summoned George Kwamai Akumbek and Pankrazio Ocheng to an urgent meeting. In attendance were Joseph Lagu Yanga, military specialist, Paterno Atari.... Today we were to give a suitable name to our armed forces, which we were intending to launch on the eighth anniversary of the August 18th, 1955 Equats (sic) uprising.[37]

After long discussions, many names were suggested; at last the meeting resolved the military wing would be called Anya Nya. The Anya Nya declaration read, 'Our patience has come to an end and we are convinced that only the use of force will bring decision... from today onwards we shall take action...we shall give no mercy and expect none...etc.[38]

Elijah Malok Aleng described how the Anya Nya was formed his memoirs too.

> Major Yasia Lukajo and Captain Davis Dada opened up military camps in Yei District, while Captain Bernadino Mou Joul, opened up another military camp between Yambio and Tombura Districts. At the end of May 1963, the three above mentioned officers reported to the party leadership that the first batches of troops were not only ready for graduation but were also ready for deployment in the war front. There was very high degree of patriotism and self-sacrifice among all the elements of the newly born liberation army, which giving a rosy and glowing accounts of high morale and discipline among the troops.... Maj. Yosia Lukajo who was the most senior officer in the briefing team, concluding his statement by saying" Mr. President, Excellences, the members of the National Executive Council the first troops of the

national army for the war of liberation which we proposed to be called Anya Nya are now ready for instructions. He stood at attention and saluted the president of the party Mr. Joseph H. Oduho. This turned out to be a historical moment, a southern army officer saluting the Southern president of a party[38]

From there, the Anya Nya I started attacking garrisons of the of the Sudan army. Their ultimate aim was to defeat the Sudan's army in the battlefield.

Southern Sudan Liberation Movement (SSIM)

SANU continued to fight for the liberation of Southern Sudan at the political frontline while Anya Nya I on the war theatre, difference emerged in both political and military wings. Mr. Oduho fell out with William Deng Nhial the Secretary General of SANU, and William Deng defected and returned to Khartoum, Elijah Malok wrote:

> Unbelievable on 16 August 1967, a military coup d'tat took place within the Liberation movement at about noon that day in a small village of Owiny ki Bul bordering Uganda but inside Torit District, Colonel Joseph Lagu who, was until then the chief of staff of the Anya Nya army announced before a group of Anya Nya young trainee officer that he has taken over political authority of the movement and from then on, he would be both chairman of the movement and the commander – in-chief of Anya Nya forces.[39]

After few days, Lagu formed a new political wing of the Anya Nya I forces called the Southern Sudan Liberation Movement (SSLM). The war of Liberation was fought under: SSLM until Addis Ababa agreement was signed in 1972. Veteran Journalists Arok Madut Arok wrote "The Anya Nya guerrilla forces launched as early as 1964 had by 1969 degenerated into seemingly tribally based bush governments under various war lords, each threatening to do away with the other.[40]

SPLM/SPLA: History of Liberation (1983-2005)

Addis Ababa Peace Agreement 1972: The Blank check

In May 1969, General Jaffer Nimiery took over power in a military coup and he promised to end the war in Southern Sudan by granting their autonomy or the regional government. This made the SSLM under Joseph Lagu negotiated peace with him. The Addis Ababa Peace Accord between the Sudan Government and the rebel Southern Sudan Liberation Movement (SSLM) ended the civil war that raged in the Southern Sudan for seventeen years.[41] Actually, this agreement was a blank check because it had no guarantee or mechanism to ensure its implementation in spirit and letter. Also it did not address the root causes of the fundamental problems of the Southern Sudan.

High Executive Council

Addis Ababa Agreement (AAA) allowed the formation of the regional government of the Southern Sudan, which was vested in the High Executive Council (HEC), responsible for the police, prisons and wild rangers. Molana Abel Alier was appointed the president of HEC and he formed his cabinet in Juba. This mark the beginning of peace in Southern Sudan after seventeen years of war. This time the development started in Southern Sudan for the first time since Turco-Egyptian Conquest.

Jonglei Canal Crisis (1974)

After the AAA, Southern Sudan had been peaceful from 1972 to 1974 until; the time when the government announced the digging of Jonglei Canal. The Jonglei Canal stirred up a lot of protest all over the South. The protest against canal started with school children in Juba and Malona Abel Alier described:

> It extended to the towns of South in particular Malakal, Bor, Torit, Yei and Wau. More school children and other youth went on to the streets of Juba. There was more destruction of the property and some of the Police who were on standby near schools were assaulted and injured. It was in the midst of this confusion that a young officer shot a school boy by a stray bullet further away from the riots. By the end of that day, two school boys were dead from bullet wounds.[42]

HISTORICAL BACKGROUND TO THE LIBERATION WAR

Akobo Mutiny: A Flight without Captain

On March 2, 1975, the absorbed Anya Nya I forces mutinied in Akobo, killing their commander Abel Kuol. The main reason of Mutiny was their refusal to be transferred to the North, where they would have to be integrated into the national army. The integration process did witness violent incident which put agreement (AAA) to a severe test.... reactions to the idea of fusing two warring armies of yesterday into one national army of tomorrow., picked out the many notable occurrences are the incidents of Juba(1974), (Akobo 1975).[43] In March 1975, hurried moves towards the integration of the Anya Nya I into the army, again contrary to the provision of Addis Agreement resulted in an armed rebellion in Akobo by some of the absorbed Anya Nya fighters.[44] The mutiny in Akobo was led by junior and non –commissioned officers who included Corporal Peter Bol Kur, Lieutenant Vincent Kuany Latjor of Signal personal, Corporal Gordon Koang Chol, a prison officer. Corporal James Wutjong, Majiek Gai Teny. Most of these officers were from Nuer tribe. These officers would have formed a strong liberation movement, unfortunately they failed to form a formidable movement because they were not educated and did not have a strong leader, and this made them a flight without a captain.

Wau Mutiny 1976: The betrayal of Comrade -in –Arms

In 1976, the absorbed Anya Nya I officers and men in the Southern Command planned to go back to the bush and wage the war of Liberation again. This plan was circulated in Bahr el Ghazal. All officers agreed to desert with their men. Captain Aguet Awan deserted with his forces as planned; however, his co-conspirators did implement their part of the plot. Abel Alier narrated how the plan was done:

> "Benjamin Bol's letter from Wau to Joseph Oduho in Juba.... It unfolded a plan for general desertion by the absorbed forces, back to the forests. According to this plan, arms and ammunitions were to be taken from stores of absorbed forces to the forest and buried in safe places. Deserters and political leaders would replan the rebellion.... Aguet was probably aware of and party to the plan for mass Anya Nya Desertion.

SPLM/SPLA: History of Liberation (1983-2005)

On the evening of 16 February, Capt. Aguet slipped out the barracks with his whole force[45].

After Captain Aguet Awan was never followed by his comrades-in-arms. Attempts were made to persuade him to return, but he refused, ending with his killing of Emanuel Abur Nhial aka Abur Matung, Captain Kucha Dengadek Akau by forces of Captain Aguet Awan, he was arrested and executed by firing squad. Therefore, Wau Mutiny, particularly Aguet Awan was betrayed by his comrade-in-arms.

Unconstitutional dissolution of Assembly

In 1980, President Jaffer Nimiery unconstitutionally dissolved Southern Peoples Regional Assembly as well as the government. He dismissed the president of the High Executive Council. 1982 was bad year for Southern Sudanese as Lam Akol put it:

> The year 1980 started rather harshly for southern Sudan. February saw the coming into force of the "High Executive Council and Regional Assembly Act 1980" issued by Nimieri and on the basis of which he dissolved the high executive council then under the presidency of General Joseph Lagu. This Act practically replaced the Self-Government for Southern Provinces Act 1972.[46]

This was the part of wider political acts of dismantling Addis Ababa Agreement, which provoked Southerners overwhelmingly.
Redrawing of the Sudan

A new map of the whole Sudan was redrawn up in 1980. In this map, some parts of the Southern Sudan that are fertile and has oil were curved out and added to the map of northern Sudan. Lam Akol clearly gave the background to new map:

The people's National Assembly was discussing the Regional Government Act 1980 for the division of Northern Sudan into six regions. A map attached to the bill show the borders of new regions also showed some parts of Southern Sudan adjacent to the North added to the latter [Northern Sudan].[47]

This redrawing of the map and annexation of fertile land and oil rich areas to North caused protests in Southern Sudan, as Abel Alier revealed:

Officials in Khartoum had attempted to transfer the rich oil, agricultural and grazing lands of Upper Nile and Bahr el Ghazal province to the Northern provinces merely by redrawing the map. Boundary changes brought the South especially students and school children to the streets...... Discoveries of another oil field north of Unity Field revived the boundary disputes. The new field is near the boundary between Bentiu Area Council and Southern Kordofan. The central government and Southern Kordofan authorities maintained that the new oil with its first well Igligli was within Kordofan. Our view was that it was within Bentiu area Council.[48]

Building of oil Refinery in the North: 1980

When the government decided to build oil refinery in Kosti instead of Bentiu, where oil is drilled. This was opposed by many southerners. It was later decided to abandon the Kosti refinery and pipe the crude oil to Port Sudan for export.[49] This angered many Southerners.

The Division of Southern Sudan

President Nimieri proposed in February 1981 to divide Southern Sudan into three regions. Mr. Nimieri unveiled this plan in speech to the Sudan Society's Union Conference in Khartoum. In December 1982, President Nimieri asked the High Executive Council (HEC) to recommend to him division of the South, which he said, should be known publicly as 'decentralization' since the word Division was inviting a lot of violent protest.[50] There was confusion among Southern Sudan as revealed in SPLM Manifesto:

> Division of the South into more regions in order to weaken the South through divide and rule. This policy was supported by part of the Southern elite that saw benefits in a divided South and opposed by those who saw losses. The same politicians changed sides several times within a day in support or in opposition to redivision of the South, depending on changing fortunes as which side was seen to be winning.[51]

SPLM/SPLA: History of Liberation (1983-2005)

Low Intensity War of Anya Nya II

Before SPLA/M, Anya Nya II was waging a low intensity war of liberation in Upper Nile and Bahr el Ghazal. Anya Nya II (AN II) was formed in 1975/6 as a result of Akoba Mutiny led by Commander Gordon Koang Chol. AN II was fighting smallest guerrilla warfare of attacking passengers travelling between Nasir and Akoba. They were coming from bases in Itang and Bilpam inside Ethiopian border. The AN II received 80 guns for the first time in its history from Sudanese opposition leader Sadiq al Mahdi through Libya. Through these guns AN II killed a Sudanese army Major Ansar. By 1982, there were many different groups of Anya Nya II fighting in different parts of the country under different leaders. In Bahr el Ghazal, Anya Nya II was under the leadership of Commander Paul Malong Awan, in Upper Nile was under Commander Daniel Deng Alony, and in Bentiu was under Commander Bol Nyawan. Another group of freedom fighters was in Boma. At the same time another group of Southern rebel was under Commander Lakuryang Lado, Pagan Amum and Ngacigak Ngaciluk slipped in to the bush in 1982. Their organization hit the news, when it launched the daring attack on Boma Mountain in July 1983 and seized some foreign tourists.[52]

BOR MUTINY: AN ACCIDENT THAT REDRAWS THE MAP OF THE SUDAN

Bor Mutiny of May 16, 1983 was an accident that redrawn the map of the Sudan forever. It was not it, but became it, the all and the end of the liberation struggle. Honestly, it was not a planned liberation war, but it actually became the liberation war that liberated Southern Sudan and changed the borders of the Sudan forever. It was a fighting between Battalion 105 (that was comprised of Southerners only) and the Sudan army. To the Sudan government, it was a mutiny, to the Southerners, it was an uprising. Bor Uprising as it is called and judged twenty-one years later on, was the totalization of vision, sacrifice, martyrdom, hunger and thirsty by Southern Sudanese.

Historically Battalion 105 was one of the six battalion formed out of screening, reorganization and absorption of the ex-Anya Nya I rebel forces as stipulated in (AAA), that ended seventeen-year civil war in 1972. At the time, Anya Nya I soldiers of Jonglei province were assembled in Malek, 20 kilometres south of Bor District. At the time of absorption, Battalion 105 had the parade of 1000 men in formation of the five companies'. The companies were stationed at five different barracks. By 1980, the first company was deployed at Sudan-Ethiopia border town of Pochalla, commanded by Major Kerubino Kuanyin Bol. The second company was deployed in Pibor commanded by Captain David Riek Macuoc and Captain Peter Panom Thapiny. The third company was in Yei commanded by Captain Martin Manyiel Ayuel, (this company was transferred from Bor to Yei as the part of Southern regional integration before national integration, because the composition of all the Battalions were on ethnic basis). The fourth company known as the Mauna, the specialized company was transferred to Bentiu commanded by Captain Benjamin Nyakot Biar. The fifth company, known as the Headquarters Company was in Bor, Malual Chat Barrack, headquarters of Battalion 105, and was commanded by Captain Bullen Alier- Magardit and Captain Wilson Kur Chol. The Battalion 105 Commander was Colonel Stephen Ogut Buong, (though some sources erroneously claimed that Major Kerubino Kuanyin Bol was the commander of Battalion 105)

This is how the mutiny unfolded, by 1982 the General Army Headquarters in Khartoum had finally given the order of transfer of the 6,000 absorbed Anya-Nya I forces to North, whereby they would eventually be integrated to the national army. Indeed, this transfer and integration plan was long due since 1975, when it was suspended after it resulted into mutinies in Akobo (1975) and Wau (1976).

In the same way, the Ex-Anya Nya I forces refused the transfer to North in 1975/6, the same way, they refused again the transfer to North in 1982/3. Anyway, it was not all Ex-Anya Nya who refused the transfer but some of them especially Battalion 105. In 1983 there was a revolutionary situation in Southern Sudan, because, there were labyrinths of problems, conflicts, disagreements and discontents. These problems were at different layers of the society, first, there was a problem between the South and North, and this was the problem between President Nimeiri and Southern Politicians, second, there was a problem among the Southern themselves, some Southerners were talking of what they called "Dinka domination" which brought Kokora, and third, the problem of Battalion 105 refusing the transfer to the North.

The root cause of these problems was no other than President Nimieri, who had already cultivated jealousy and hatred among Southern Sudanese through the policies of his ruling party, the Sudan Socialist Union (SSU). The SSU government proposed division of Southern Sudan that had caused a dangerous debates and campaigns. An intensifications and ripening of these debates was manifested by vilifying songs of Kokora, that is "Dinka Turjuo, Dinka Mapi"

Here President Nimieri was the one holding the power from above and Battalion 105 and Southerners in general were opposing him from the base. When Battalion 105 in Bor had refused the order of transfer to the Northern completely that were sent to them through the radio message. The Southern Command in Juba decided to send the delegation led by Brigadier General James Loro in February 1983. The delegation arrived to Bor and went to the barrack. As in the army conduct of business, a parade was called in Malual Chat; James Loro officially briefed the soldiers about the order of transfer. He told them, they would leave for North in two phases. Bachelors, who are not married should leave first by river barges, phase two, would be the married ones. In rarest show of indiscipline, the soldiers asserted to James Loro, "they will not go to north come dusk, come dawn, come dry season, come rainy season over and over again and again". After the soldiers had refused that they were not going to North, James Loro returned to Juba

The second delegation that went to Bor was led Brigadier General Musaicl Al- Nueri, Division commander in Malakal, who flew to Malual Chat Barracks in Bor with Captain Salva Kiir of Military intelligence, Brigadier Al-Nueri travelled there, to reorder the transfer of the soldiers to North. The whistled was blown, the parade stood. Al-Nueri cleared his throat and regave the order, 'Attention' he called out, "you are transferred to North; therefore, you salute the orders. The soldiers kept quiet. "Are you with me?" The soldiers kept quiet. It is military ethical duty to salute the orders as the sign of acceptance, discipline and submission.

HISTORICAL BACKGROUND TO THE LIBERATION WAR

When the soldiers were refusing and showing insubordination, Captain Bullen Alier Magardit, the commander of the company, requested al Nueri to give them a break in order to go and have a chance of talking to them alone. Al Nuer agreed and the soldiers were fallen out of the parade. In their private parade, a committee of seven Non- commissioners' officers (NCOs) was instituted as follows; Sergeant Major Reuben Thiong Tat, Sergeant Major Yusif Kiir Tang, Sergeant Garang Ngang Abui, Corporal Manyiel Kueth Makuei, Sergeant Manyang Agok Aliet, Lance Corporal Herjok Akuom Magun, Corporal Malith Lual Jok. Since there are no always first organising committees of rebellion, this committee became in disguise as first organizing committee of the rebellion. '(S)oldiers and workers do constitute the first organizing committee of the rebellion.'[53] There was a great interest in what was happening, all politicians, intellectuals and students were all behind Battalion 105 in secret. This committee of NCOs as the mouthpiece of other soldiers; prepared and gave reasons, why they refused and defying the lawful orders; (1) they said, there has been no school for children since 1972, and schools were expensive in the North (2) they said, they have the extended family, they were taking care of them, and when they would have gone to the North, it would be difficult for them to support them (3) they said, their wives don't know or speak Arabic, how they would communicate when buying food in the market (4) they said, there has been no new recruitments into rank and file, this mean, you were ill-intention against them (5) they said their rank had been frozen since 1972, there had not been promotion for 12 years (6) they said, they had not received the new uniforms and guns since 1972 .

The reasons were presented to Brig. al-Nueri, in this response, he said, 'you will be given new gun as soon as you arrive in Shendi, and you have not been promoted, because, you have been failing the promotion examination. At last al- Nueri returned to Juba without agreement whether the soldiers were going to the North or not

Another team of officers from Malakal also arrived to Pochalla in March 1983, they announced the order of transfer to the soldiers. The message of transfer enraged the soldiers terribly. And a dog fight was slightly missed when Sergeant Major Paul Garang Deng- Amuor, heckled the speaking officer and asked him" what is that behind?", he asked as he was pointing at bush. The officer ignored him, in highest degree of contemptuousness, Paul Garang pulled up his G3 Rifle and he cocked it. His other colleague intervened immediately and holding him up. The officer hurriedly closed the parade and he ordered them to put all their grievances and reasons of why they refused the transfer in writing and they returned to Malakal. Garang testified later he would have gored open the stomach of Arab woman's son and he ran to the forest if he was not held up by anyone.

In March 1983, Bor had become an epicentre of the military crisis, puzzling, disturbing and felonious to hear of soldiers disobeying the lawful order. This was tantamount to treason, punishable by death or long term prison sentence. The army general headquarters in Juba was pondering and deducing of what action to take on indiscipline soldiers in Bor. There was a talk of military action being planned. This talk of military action against soldiers in Bor, irritated some politicians and members of parliament from Jonglei. They concerned themselves with issue of Battalion 105 for the number of reasons; (1) Most of the soldiers were sons of Bor (2) if the fighting breakout as it was being speculated, it was their children, who would be affected by the outbreak of violence. In the light of above reason, politicians and MPs, were formed into committee and sent to Bor to persuade the soldiers to obey the orders and leave for North. A last delegation that went to Bor was formed and led by Maj. Gen. Sadiq al Banna, Journalist Arop Madut wrote about it:

> The drama created by the salary issue had already caused dangerously commotion in Bor.... Gen. al Banna organized a meeting which brought all MPs of Jonglei province and other senior military officers Major Gen. Soro Sinvinco, Masaid al- Nueri and Major Arok Thon Arok. Al- Banna disclosed that commotion in Bor had become a security concern to the authorities. He wanted the MPs from Jonglei that unless they convince the soldiers in Bor to obey the lawful order from their commander, they would be held responsible. After a heated argument the meeting resolved that a committee to handle the standoff to be chaired by Dhol Achuil Aleu, the Vice President, Philip Obang, Minister of Education, Abdel Latif Chual Lom(MP), Elijah Malok (MP), Sameul Gai Tut, Akuot Atem de Mayen, Gen. James Soro and al-Nuer and Major Arok Thon Arok.[54]

HISTORICAL BACKGROUND TO THE LIBERATION WAR

After the committee was formed Al Banna informed President Nimieri, the commander –in-chief to approve the committee, to grace it, President Nimieri sent Colonel John Garang de Mabior to represent him in negotiating team. Historians Le Riche and Arnold narrate how Colonel John Garang was sent by President Nimieri:

> The SAF began to reoccupy Bor with the aim of arresting Kerubino while Southern Political figures tried to negotiate a deal... Garang, then visiting the region, secured a place on a negotiating team attempting to deal with unrest in Bor mid-May.[55]

The negotiating committee led by honourable Dhol Achuil arrived to Bor and went to Malual Chat barrack. Col. Garang did not go with them, he met Kerubino Kuanyin separately. He told Kerubino to accept the orders and go to North, but Kerubino told him that he would be arrested as soon as he reached Shendi. Col Garang said ok let see what the government would do. In fact, the meeting between Garang and Kerubino took place at Bor Hospital Staff Guest House (the SPLM office now in Bor). There was no minute of that meeting recorded. Garang abstained himself from the negotiating committee, he never went to Malual Chaat even for fear that intelligence would implicate him to the Mutinee. The committee went to Malual Chaat, after long deliberation there was no breakthrough therefore, the committee flattered the Battalion 105 that your transfer to North is cancelled and your salaries of January, February, March and April would be paid. The committee returned to Juba and made their report of finding to the army headquarters.

At this time Col Garang went to Langbar, where the loyal soldiers were staying. Ideally, Col. Garang as the most educated man had been harbouring a vision to liberate the Southern Sudanese, but he highly kept it secret, for fear that, it could be detected by State security apparatus. He knew how the security was tightest and toughest in Khartoum at time and how Southerners were untrusted. As he later revealed to Dr Francis Mading Deng in 1986. When Mading asked him, why he did not tell him about the liberation, when they were in Khartoum, Garang replied, it was a "well- guarded secret".

In Bor, the situation was very intense, people talked of rebellion everywhere; in schools, tea place, randaya, open places where the local brewery called merrisa abiiit was drunk. Some women sung the song of rebellion as they were grinding the halt-germinated ban of sorghum as yeast for merrisa or white brewer. The song goes:

> Our Southern's army have refused to go to the North
> The South has refused going north
> They say going north
> Is better going to the bush
> Going to Shendi
> Is better going to Bilpam
> And join the Anya Nya II

As battalion 105 remained adamant, about 400 soldiers unexpectedly arrived at Malual Chaat in March led by Major Zain, an Arab northern Sudanese. This shocked 105 men.

"Where are you coming from? Why are you coming?", asked 105 officers

"We are coming from Juba", answered the soldiers

"What is the mission you came here for?" asked 105

"We don't know our mission; we were ordered to come"

Why do you come to the barracks without informing us?

"We are just told"

"Where is your departure order?"

"There is no departure order"

"Therefore, you are sent to arrest us?"

At last, Battalion 105 gave these soldiers the ultimatum of 3 hours if they didn't leave, they would fight. Tension within Malual Chaat reached the office of commission, so Commissioner Anei Kur had to rush in and took the new soldiers to Langbar and stationed them. The war was avoided that day by Anei Kur Agol.

It became clear that soldiers in Malual Chaat would be attacked anytime. The turning point came on May 14, 1983, an intelligent officer

HISTORICAL BACKGROUND TO THE LIBERATION WAR

came from Langbar to Bor Town to gather information, about what was going in Malual Chaat, and he was shot and wounded by soldiers of 105. This officer was taken to Bor hospital, some soldiers from Langbar were guarding at the main gate of the hospital. 105 hit men came inside through fence of the hospital and one of them passed through the latrine hole, the latrine was oldest types where they put bucket behind and removed, and he entered with a pistol and shot dead the wounded man.

On May 16, 1983, Battalion 105 was attacked at 5:00am by the army from Juba, the fighting continued up to 3: pm. At this time four solider of Battalion 105 were martyred and seven wounded, including their commander Kerubino Kuanyin Bol. The soldiers of 105 killed were; Corporal Maker Jol Deng, Private Sgt Deng (Shoki) and the wounded were; Gabriel Gatkueth Bol, Corporal Mun Kun, Private Gai Dui, all wounded and other soldiers arrested were taken to Juba for detention. In Juba, some of wounded and detainnees were killed, for example; Guet Awar Ayuel, Ajang Deng Adieer, Yai Ngong Yai, Garang-Korok and many others .

At 5:00pm, the loyal Sudan army soldiers contained the situation and established the control over Bor town. Battalion 105 had withdrawn to rural Bor. Commander Kerubino Kuanyin was escaped by canoe to Aguetdhier in toc, about 25 kilometers north of Bor. The rest of forces went to Macdeng, also North Bor, they spent a day at Macdeng, in morning of May 17, and they confiscated a truck of Dirot Company, and drove to Panyagor where they looted some Northern Arab shops. Some of Battalion 105 soldiers scattered around Bor, since 99% of them was from Bor District.

Col. John Garang de Mabior left Bor on May 17, 1983. He took a car of Dr. Kuckon Pac, the Director of Bor Teaching Hospital, he told officers at Langbar and former Vice President Abel Alier that he was going to bring his family from Baidit. Garang drove to Panyagor the same day.

Since the mutiny was unorganized and spontaneous event, Col Garang as the most educated person and the veteran of the first Anya-Nya war, he saw an opportunity in this mutiny, whereby he would realize his long undisclosed vision of liberating South Sudan therefore, Garang went to the bush. He spent a night in Payagor, he left in the morning, travelling with him in the car were; his wife Rebecca Nyandeng and two sons, Mabior and Chol and four other men, Mabior Kuir Maketh, Cagai Atem, Maker Deng

SPLM/SPLA: History of Liberation (1983-2005)

Malou, Atem Kuir Garang. Before he left Panyagor, he wrote a letter and gave it to a business man, Kon Nuul, to give it to Kerubino if he comes.

At Duk, he found some soldiers of 105, among were Captain Wilson Kur Chol and Captain Alier Mangardit and many non-commissioned officers. He called a shortest meeting and he told them, "We are going to Bilpam". This was the first time, Garang talked publicly about the liberation war. He left immediately, he knew, he might be followed from Bor or intercepted from Malakal because he had not returned to Bor as he said it.

John Garang travelled through Waat till he spent the night at Gakyom Village on Sobat River opposite Ulang town, in morning, he left the car there and he walked toward Bukteng. He crossed Akoba River into Ethiopia. He went to Marol –Gauang, where he found Anya-Nya II soldiers under captain Gatjiek, who welcomed Garang warmly. John Garang stayed with Gatjiek for many days.

On 6 June 1983, the company of Battalion 104 under William Nyuon Bany rebelled in Ayod and moved to Bilpam direction. In 1975, when some soldiers of Battalion 104 mutinied, killing their commander Abel Kuol in Akoba, the headquarters of Battalion was relocated to Nasir

At Marol, many soldiers, students, intellectuals and politicians began arriving. Event of May 16, acted as the whistleblowing for the frustrated, discontented South Sudanese with president Nimieri and his Sudan Socialist Union (SSU) policies. Among the politicians who arrived were Honourable Uncle Akuot Atem de Mayen, Samuel Gai Tut, and William Abdhalla Chuol Deng-Luth. Among the soldiers were; Lt Colonel Francis Ngor Maciec, Captain Salva Kiir Mayardit, Sergeant Garang Deng Beny, Sergeat Kuol Mayen Mading, and Sergeant Panchol Majak. This group moved to the Ethiopia's border where Garang was airlifted to Itang

There are two competing accounts on how Garang got in touch with Ethiopians. The first account says as Garang was on his way to Ethiopia, Major Arok Thon Arok contacted the Embassy of Ethiopia in Khartoum that Colonel Garang is at border, therefore, the Ethiopia government ordered the governor of Gamballe region to locate him, as they were searching for Garang, agent was sent to Itang, this agent got lieutenant Anyuat Achiek, prison officer, who defected in 1982 from Nasir. Anyuat given AK47 rifle in order to guard himself from Anya-Nya II, he went to border to search for Garang. He came to Marol, where he found Garang, he went to border and reported it at police post at Burabii border. The police at Burabii gave information to the government of Gambella through Radio message and Anyuat was sent to Marol to go and tell Garang to come to Adura-Thiajok area, because Marol was far and deep inside Sudan.

The second account said, Garang came to Ethiopia border, and wrote a message to the Ethiopia authorities and the message was sent at the police post called Katiba and helicopter flew in and took him to Itang.

Notes
1. Beshir, 1960, London p. 10
2. Holt and Daly, 1961, UK p. 1
3. Ibid p. 21
4. Ibid p. 41
5. LeRiche and Arnold, 2012, London p. 8
6. Holts and Daly p.77
7. Ibid p.78
8. Ibid p.102
9. Ibid pp.105-106
10. Ibid p.126
11. Beshir p.119
12. Ibid p. 126
13. Shimanyula, 2005, Nairobi p.1
14. Holts and Daly p.127
15. Beshir p.61
16. Ibid p.61
17. Ibid p.119
18. Ibid p.120
19. Ibid p. 123
20. Ibid p. 124
21. Ibid p. 125
22. Ibid pp.64-65
23. Ibid p.65
24. Ibid p.65
25. Ibid p.65
26. Ibid p.140
27. Ibid p.141
28. Ibid p. 141
29. Holt and Daly p.137
30. Beshir p.71
31. Ibid p.64
32. Holt and Daly p.139
33. Beshir p.73
34. Holts and Daly p.146
35. Beshir p.83

36. Gale, 2002, Lou, South Sudan pp.235-236
37. Ibid p.237
38. Malok 2009, Nairobi p.41
39. Ibid p.46
40. Arop, London p.5
41. Malok p.80
42. Alier, London pp. 240-241
43. Ibid p.169
44. Akol 2009, Khartoum p.2
45. Alier p.78
46. Akol p.1
47. Ibid p.1
48. Alier pp.258, 289
49. Akol p.4
50. Alier 274
51. SPLM Manifesto p.9
52. Akol p. 4
53. Sartre pp. 519-520
54. Arop p. 10
55. LeRiche & Arnold p.62

CHAPTER 2

THE FOUNDING OF SPLA/ SPLM, MAY-AUGUST 1983

THE GENESIS OF THE PROBLEM

It started with lawful demand of the first war (Anya Nya I War)
In which, world leaders demanded Northerners to give back land of Southerners
The war repeated itself because the Addis judgment [peace agreement] was not executed

- SPLM Muor Muor Division morale song

The fundamental problem of Southern Sudan, as it manifested itself in Bor uprising on May 16 1983, laid its origin in the abrogation of the Addis Abba agreement (AAA) of 1972, signed between the Sudan government of President Jaffer Mohammed Nimieri, and the rebel movement of Southern Sudan Liberation Movement (SSLM) / Anya-Nya I forces of General Joseph Lagu Yenge. That agreement granted the regional autonomous government, vested in the two branches of the High Executive Council (HEC) of Southern Sudan and the Regional Peoples' Assembly in the South. The Anya Nya I forces, in accordance with accord were also

47

SPLM/SPLA: History of Liberation (1983-2005)

absorbed into the national Army, becoming instantly the Southern Division with its general headquarters in Juba, the regional capital.

In a secret introspection, the Anya-Nya I officers and many other observers, evaluated the Addis Abba agreement negatively, seeing it as total 'sell-out' in the first place. They said, according to them, it was shallow with no security guarantee in whatsoever side, claiming the agreement itself was not their own making, but rather, it was dictated to them by the refugee and other stakeholders, who were believing the war was too long and wanted nothing rather than peace. In that way, there were many core issues and demands that were compromised by Southern Sudanese in the interest of ephemeral peace, and losing sight of original, desired, ultimate objective of liberation of Southern Sudan, on which the war was fought upon.

Although, AAA was treacherous as a such as they were calling, it was, however, not absolutely as they thought it to be, the agreement, through half of its eleven years from 1972 to 1978, had provided a number of dividends to Southerners, bringing some developments to Southern Sudan for the first time. During those years of peace implementation, Southern Sudan quickly flourished economically. Many projects were planned and started; Mangalla Sugarcane Plantation, Yirol Sim-Sim Project, Tonj Kenaj, Patalaga Tea Plantation, Renk Agricultural Projects, construction of Juba Bridge, construction and establishment of University of Juba ...etc. Above all else, oil discovered in Northern Upper Nile, town of Bentiu by Chevron Exploration Corporation in 1978, that discovery boasted the Southern economy. Many Southerners, during that peak of economic success, finished their education as it is shown by great numbers of graduates, who joined the SPLA in 1983, compared to the Anya Nya I that had no single PhD holder in its rank and file. This economic development in the South was envied by the Northerner elites and their political parties. In 1978, this jealousy Northern groups, that is, both the ruling SSU party and the other opposition parties met at retreat in Port Sudan. In that retreat, the opposition leaders told President Nimieri that before, they had been trying to overthrow his government, but then as they called him, they were not coming to depose him still, but, however to reveal something that went wrong and to advise him on it wisely and accordingly. They told him that he made a terrible and regrettable mistake by signing the Addis Abba agreement (AAA) with the Southerners, and as the result of the AAA, Southern Sudan was developing quickly and sooner than later it would outperform the North in development and political consciousness, and they would be powerful and would remove all leeway we were managing them. In responding to them, President Nimieri asked them about what he should do. The parties hinted out to him two strategies: (1) to dissolve the regional assembly in order to create a political vacuum and crisis in South (2) divide the South into three regions to weaken the unity in Juba (3) dismantle the agreement politically and military slowly.

President Nimieri bound by their advice, he unconstitutionally dissolved regional Assembly and the Government in 1979, plunging the region into power struggle among the politicians. He also unveiled a new map, annexing the fertile land and oil and other mineral rich areas in Bahr el Ghazal and Upper Nile to the North. In 1978, he authorised the digging of Jonglei Canal, which was benefiting Egypt and the North in irrigation and disadvantaging the South by drying up the Sudd Marshes (one of the eight modern world wonders). As it was orchestrated in the retreat, the proposed division of the South Sudan to three provinces of Equatoria, Bahr el Ghazal and Upper Nile was rejected by some and accepted by some, sparking off the hottest debate and sowing the seed of hatred between Equatorian and people from Bahr el Ghazal and Upper Nile regions, and resulting into notorious, dishonourable and divisive politic of Kokora, and the platitude of, 'this is Juba Na Bari, go to your homes' was everywhere. By 1982, President Nimieri had started abrogating the AAA, he was, at the time, propagating derogatory, vilest statements about the agreement, rubbishing it, in most of his political speeches. These speeches were relayed and re-echoed by the many political commentators and the editorial pages of the newspapers, in one of his speeches, President Nimieri was quoted as saying 'Addis Abba agreement was neither Bible nor Quran, it was made by people and could be unmade by people, it can be done away with'. President Nimieri was pragmatically not implementing AAA in letter and spirit, but rather, he was only implementing the minor provision and ignoring major ones, in doing this, he intransigently frozen the rank of the absorbed Ex-Anya Nya I officers. Based on his policies of dishonouring the agreement, there was no reasonable promotion of officers or recruitment of new soldiers into the Southern Division, except for the few officers, who passed his so-called promotion examination, in which 99 per cent of officers of Anya Nya I failed. If you failed the examination, you were automatically discharged and retired. In fact, all ex-Anya Nya I officers were destined to fail because they were illiterate. As the result of this policy, only 12% of Anya Nya I officers were promoted in the period of 12 years, this lucky group included John Garang, Kerubino Kuanyin among others. All these policies of SSU worsened the frustration and discontent among the soldiers, politicians, intellectuals, students and all masses of Southern Sudan.

In 1983, President Nimieri drew finally his last scrabble letter of the abrogation of Addis Abba Agreement, which was the transferring of Battalion 105 to North. Unfortunately, his finger was cut off by the edge of the drawing board, spilling the blood over his hand, Mr. Nimieri, like a toddler, fainted, and raving after resuscitation, like a drunkard with his constitutional powers for the use of legitimate force, he hastily attacked Battalion 105, culminating into incident of Bor- the Mutiny. Bor Mutiny was phenomenal event that compelled the rebellions and precipitating the war, as the only political solution to the problem of the Southern Sudan's backwardness.

By June 1983, all Southern Sudanese, from all segments of the society; politicians, soldiers, teachers, students…etc, had gathered in Itang refugee camp. Itang was a camp combining the refugee of former Anya Nya I, who rejected the Addis agreement of 1972 as well as the families of Anya Nya II, who mutinied in Akoba in 1975. Among the very important people, who gathered were; Colonel Dr. John Garang de Mabior, Honourable Akuot Atem de Mayen, Lt. Col Samuel Gai Tut, Lt Col. Abdallah Chuol Deng, Justice Martin Majier Gai, Captain Salva Kiir Mayadit and so forth. The exodus of the Southern Sudanese to Ethiopian border was spontaneous organization. As people were becoming many, the Ethiopian government wrote a letter, instructing the Southern Sudanese to organize themselves. Because there were different groups present in Itang at the time. Among them were; Anya Nya II soldiers, the new arrivals of officers from Sudan army and other politicians. The three groups were nationally obliged to form one political and military organization.

At this time the Ethiopian government had changed its old position of refusing to support Anya Nya II for eight years. It was claimed later on, that the change of mind from Ethiopians Derg regime of President Mengistu was after, they heard in the news of Colonel Dr. John Garang's defection from the Sudan's army, in that context, the Ethiopians were hoping of the new approach to the war in the Sudan.

When Akuot Atem heard of letter instructing Southerners to organize themselves, he called for the first meeting, which he himself chaired. In that meeting, Col Garang raised the point of information to him that the meeting to organize and form a new movement should not proceed ahead because the two most important people (VIPs) or the popular agitators, who started rebellion were coming on the way. These VIPs on the way were; Major Kerubino Kuanyin Bol who was still healing from a gunshot wound. At the time he was hiding with forces at Toc (swarm) in Bor area. Major William Nyuon Bany who also defected from Ayod with Battalion 104. Akuot and other attenders agreed to Col Garang's suggestion and the meeting was called off and postponed it.

As members were waiting for Major Kerubino Kuanyin and Major William Nyuon, there was too much talk of, who should be the leader, everyone was canvassing and steering of how to become the leader. This prompted, the Ethiopian government to send a second letter inviting five men to visit Addis Abba for two reasons: (1) interviews about what you want in Ethiopia (2) to meet president Mengistu. The five men, who were flown to Addis Abba on this invitation were; John Garang, Samuel Gai, Akuot Atem, Martin Majier and Salva Kiir. In Addis Abba, first, they were individually interviewed about, what they were after in Ethiopia, second, they were also asked individually to write a concept paper of what each one was standing for. When the results of both oral interviews and concept paper writing were announced, there was an emergent of two objectives. Akuot and Gai jointly wrote a concept paper that propounded the fighting for independent Southern Sudan as their objective, while Garang wrote he wanted to fight for the liberation of whole Sudan as their objectives.

Colonel Dr. John Garang won both oral and written interviews. He was the only person with PhD certificate among the Southerners. In fact, he was liberal and socialist in his approach to the problem of Sudan. During the oral and written interviews, he was giving scenarios, issues or problems in the Sudan, and he clearly provided, how these problems should be resolved.

On the other hand, Akuot was conservative, radical and narrow-minded in his approach to the problem, he portrayed the problem in country as the 'Southern problem' as it is called by the Northerners, in this way, he did not win the Ethiopian support.

Finally, at the end of visit to Addis Abba, John Garang won the support of the Ethiopians, because of his individual praxis in presenting the problem of the Sudan as a whole. John Garang became favourite candidate for the leadership of the would-be movement, because, he was elucidating the problem of Sudan in speech and in writing. He was secretly anointed and confirmed the leader of the movement, but, the Ethiopians were technical and cunning in their approach, they temporalized the declaring of Garang as the leader of movement, to demonstrate they were free and fair, and not interfering in the work of their protégés. After knowing, 'who is who?' and 'What ideology and objectives, he is fighting for', the Ethiopians sent back the five men to Itang in order to go and organize themselves into one military and political organization. The Ethiopian government sent two platoons of soldiers, one to provide security for all. Another platoon to guard Colonel Garang alone.

When Akuot and Gai saw Garang being guarded by the Ethiopians soldiers, they realized that something was wrong, and this troubled them very much, Col Garang had the power of Ethiopian soldiers now, they said. To balance the power, they went and contacted Anya Nya II in Bilpam, they talked to them, that they should be their political leaders and to represent them in the up-coming meeting of formation of the new movement. By this virtue, Akuot and Gai became Anya Nya II members, when they were actually flew to Gambella from Thiajok with Col Garang together. They were not Anya Nya II members completely. In fact, they were one group with Garang, a group that defected to the bush after May 16th incident in Bor, while Anya Nya II had already spent eight years in Bilpam.

While at that same time, inside Sudan, Battalion 105 and 104 met at Pantiop area and they finally marched to Itang in early July. Since the group in Itang was waiting for them, their arrival was a celebration. No sooner had Major Kerubino Kuanyin and Major William Nyuon reached Itang with forces, than the meeting was called immediately to discuss, deliberate and decide on the four agenda: (1) the formation of the liberation movement (2) the definition of the objectives of the movement (3) the naming of the movement (4) the election of leader of the movement. As the members were deliberating, discussing, proposing or opposing and seconding on the four agenda. Two controversial and divisive issues sprang up: (1) the problem of the method (2) the leadership and power struggle. By the look of it, during the meeting, it was clear that all Southerners had already factionalized themselves into different groups and allies. It was found out that John Garang allied himself with soldiers and officers of Battalion 105 and 104 of Major Kerubino and Major William respectively. While Akuot Atem and Gai Tut had allied themselves to Anya Nya II forces. In the proceeding of the meeting, the beforehand functionalization and alliances were immediately reflected in the speeches, and point of views articulated on the subject of deliberation. John Garang, Kerubino Kuanyin, William Nyuon were now on one side while Akuot, Gai and Chuol on the other side.

In the first meeting at Itang Primary School, it became clearest, that Bor Mutiny was unorganized and spontaneous incident, which it had no leader who was organizing it. This was so, because Major Kerubino Kuanyin Bol, Captain Bullen Alier Nhial-magardit, Captain Wilson Kur Chol, Sergeant Major Reuben Thiong Tat, Sergeant Major Yusif Kiir Tang, Sergeant Garang Nyang Abui, Corporal Manyiel Kueth Makuei, Sergeant Manyang Agok Aliet, Corporal Herjok Akuom Magun, Corporal Malith Lual Jok and their 120 men of Battalion 105 were "popular agitators but not leaders of the revolution. (S)oldiers and workers do constitute the first organizing committees of rebellion"1. (A) Beginning of universalisation, these other exploited men appeared to them representative of all exploited people"2. Since exploitation of Arab was one immediate cause of the war, other exploited men, who were not part of Battalion 105 that fought on May 16 came in and were now competing, quarrelling over the leadership.

These other exploited men, who became the representative of all exploited were; Lt Col Abdhalla Chuol Deng Luth, Colonel Dr John Garang de Mabior, Honourable Akuot Atem de Mayen, Justice Martin Majier Gai, Honourable Samuel Gai Tut. By that time Kerubino Kaunyin who actually mutinied in Bor became just popular agitator not the leader.

In founding process of the movement, the problem of the method of liberation came about like this. According to Anya Nya I veteran politician Akuot Atem, in his managing outlook of the political and military situation of the country, he proposed, the name of the new movement to be founded, would remain the old name of old movement of the first civil, that is SSLM/Anya Nya II. And given, the fact that, they were many factions, they would add one word to the old name, "united", therefore, he argued that the official

name would be United Southern Sudan Liberation Movement (USSLM) and Anya Nya II forces remained its military wing. Akuot also said the objectives would remain the fighting for independent Southern Sudan that is separation. Akout's conception budded from rationalization, he argued Southerners wanted to liberate themselves from North islamisation and arabisation. He drew his conclusion from pure reasons without considering experiences of past, without considering other factors like the current affairs in the region, for example, the foreign policy of Ethiopian government towards Sudan or Sudan's foreign policy towards Ethiopia. Akuot and his allies Gai and Chuol believed in the righteousness of their cause, and therefore, they could use force only to achieve their objectives without craftiness and diplomacy.

On the other hand, Colonel Dr. John Garang opposed Akout's line of reasoning, he propounded a movement would be founded on the new basis, given a new name, not the Anya Nya I ones. The movement would be founded on the new objective and aims, and therefore objectives had to be the liberation of whole Sudan, from Nimule in the South to Halfa in the North, from Homesgresh in East to Gennan in West. Employing empiricism in his approach, Garang argued from his past experience of Anya Nya I war, he said, when Southerners fought for the liberation of Southern Sudan as their objectives, that objective separation itself, had antagonized them in the eyes of other marginalizes Sudanese. All backward regions of Sudan never sympathize with the South or its cause, and they ganged up with the minority ruling Arabs cliques, who were even oppressing themselves like the Southerners, to fight the Southerners. And indeed, these other Sudanese who are oppressed, too, would fight the Southerners willingly without knowing that, they are also oppressed and backward like the Southerners. These are Darfur, Nuba and Beja people. Garang said they would fight for the whole of Sudan, so that they would gain support from other Northern Sudanese and the international community. Garang was drawing up his conclusion, after he juxtaposed between Old Anya Nya I and the new movement about to be formed, he clearly hypothesized on the course of action that the new movement would take. He knew the mentoring government of Ethiopia could not support the separatist. He had also a good background of geopolitics of the region, where Sudan was supporting Eritrean separatist in Ethiopia. Looking from that perspective, Ethiopian government would not support secession in the Sudan but would only support the liberation movement that would maintain the unity of the country, because Ethiopia could not oppose it division to two countries and agreeing in dividing the Sudan into two countries, that would be a contradiction in term of its foreign policy.

The leadership power struggle also arisen likes this; Samuel Gai proposed Akuot Atem to be the chairman and this was seconded by Abdhalla Chuol. Gai and Chuol supported Akuot to be chairman because of two reasons (1) his age and past experience and (2) his seniority in Anya Nya I movement. Major Kerubino Kuanyin proposed Garang to be chairman and this was seconded by Major William Nyuon, Major Kerubino and Major William supported John Garang to be chairman, because of two reasons: (1) Garang was the most educated man, who had a PhD among all Southerners in Itang and (2) he was most senior officer in army, a colonel by rank, not because of the so-called underground movement as many sources falsely claims.

In July 1983, the two camps of Akuot and Garang, and their respectively allies, were bogged down in irreconcilable disagreement on objectives and ideology of the movement. Many meetings were held, but there was no leaping forward. The second, the third meeting were held but the two factions still disagreed. The third meeting almost turned violent because

SPLM/SPLA: History of Liberation (1983-2005)

Gerang's group ushered in Ethiopian communist oriented languages, they described the Anya Nya I as the job-seekers and politicians as bourgeoisies. When news of the disagreement, differences, leadership wrangling reached the Ethiopian government, President Mengistu sent his envoy, General Mesfin, the chief of military intelligence, to come and mediate the talk. In the fourth meeting, the acrimonious argument continued, Samuel Gai Tut, a graduate of Beirut university, who was competent and good orator in Akuot's faction out-bursted an exclamation in Nuer Language, 'kany piny ke mijak ke Beirut, engo mee gor ke Garang gar?", which can loosely be translated, 'I jump out of plane from Beirut with white and red coloured degree certificate, what does Garang want people?" (This is common culture in Dinka and Nuer, if you are annoyed and you want to fight or attack someone, if you first mention the name of the pet bull as a sign of approval), Gai banged the small wooden table at the Itang Primary School and he lit up his cigarette and walked out of the meeting. The fifth and sixth meetings were called, all attended, but Akuot and Gai boycotted.

After the deepest conflict of interests, or point of views, diversity of tendencies, personality conflict, secret rivalries, contradiction, incompatibilities, boycott and absence among the Southerners, the Ethiopia government intervened and decided to arrest Akuot Atem de Mayen, Samuel Gai Tut and Abdalla Chuol Deng on the BEHEST of Colonel Dr. John Garang de Mabior. The information of their arrest was leaked to them. Thus, Akuot, Gai and Chuol called all the Anya Nya II soldiers and others and they fled to the Sudan-Ethiopia border.

After Akuot and his group escaped to Sudan, John Garang as leader proceeded with reorganization of the group. Through his individual praxis, he called a meeting at Itang Primary School, which was attended by 77 officers, Non-commissioned officers and politicians and intellectuals. The officers and NCOs were from organized forces of the Sudan, that is army, prison, and wild life, who were supervised by General Mesfin fused and formed the national liberation. In this meeting around mid-July, the Sudan People's liberation Army (SPLA) and its Sudan people's Movement (SPLM) was founded by 77 men. The prominent figures among the officers who founded SPLM/A were; Colonel John Garang de Mabior, Major Kerubino Kuanyin Bol, Major William Nyuon Bany, Captain Salva Kiir Mayardit,

Martin Majier Gai, and Joseph Oduho Awero. Major Arok Thon was not in that meeting; he was still being investigated in Khartoum over the May 16th mutiny in Bor

1. Notes
2. 1.   Jean – Paul Sartre,Critique of Dialectical Reason, Translated Alan Sheridan-Smith, Edited by John Ree, Editions Gallimand, Paris, 1960 p.22
3. 2.   Ibid p.21

CHAPTER 3

SPLA DIVISIONS, BATTALIONS AND THEIR BATTLES, 1983-1986

BATTALION 105/104:
THE NUCLEAR OF LIBERATION MOVEMENT

In late July 1983, the SPLA/SPLM had started groundwork for the Liberation war. It began by initiating and adopting the two immediate tasks: (1) the organizing of fighting forces (2) the writing of the Manifesto. SPLA, the military wing, had initially started organizing the remnants of former Sudan People's Defence Force (SPDF), those were the former Battalion 105/104, and others deserters from other Battalions, the prison servicemen, game warders and policemen into a combined, new formation known as New Battalion 105 and 104. These two Battalions were put into training in Itang. Some specialize units were nominated out of them. These units were; Air Defence, Combat Engineering, Combat intelligence (CI), Signal, Artillery Units. All the specialized units received their training in Itang except Air Defence that was taken to Addis Ababa for training, where they were introduced and trained, how to operate and fire the Surface to

SPLA DIVISIONS, BATTALIONS AND THEIR BATTLES, 1983-1986

Air Missile (SAM 7) anti-aircraft. In Addis Ababa, the Air Defence was trained for solid 18 days only.

As the soldiers were under training, John Garang was busy in Addis Ababa writing the manifesto with Justice Martin Majier Gai. The manifesto was written with help and expertise of Ethiopia Workers party (EWP), the ruling party, of the mentor of SPLA, President Mengistu Haile Mariam. The manifesto was entirely the internalization of the Marxist-Leninist literature of the EWP. After the manifesto finished, Col. Dr John Garang de Mabior, the Chairman and Commander-in-Chief of the SPLA/SPLM, published it on July 31st 1983 (this was the day of it printing and publishing, it was not the day SPLA/SPLM was officially launch as the movement). In the manifesto, the objectives, missions and vision of SPLA/SPLM as the national Liberation Movement were spelled out as the extract below from the SPLM Manifesto showed:

> In the Northern backward areas, the old CNF (Congress of New force, which includes the Fur, Nuba and Beja) took advantage of the political crises in the Sudan and Organized African- based coups against Khartoum. One of these was led by Lt. Col. Hassen Hussein in 1975, and later developed into guerrilla movements led by people like Lt. Col Yacoub Ismael and Major Zekaria Abdhalla. The battles of Bor (Commanded by Major Kerubino Kuanyin), Pibor and Ayod (Commanded by Major William Nyuon) caused wide spread desertions in their units of Southern command and in Northern Sudan, and an Exodus of refugees to bordering Countres. Element of the Military and political organization [above] have established the Sudan People's Liberation Army (SPLA) and Sudan People's Liberation Movement (SPLM). Although the movement has started by necessity in South it aims eventually at engulfing the whole country in socialist transformation. The SPLA is fighting to establish a united socialist Sudan, not a separate Southern Sudan. The immediate task of the SPLA/SPLM is to transform the Southern Movement from a reactionary Movement led by reactionaries and concerned only with the South, jobs and self-interest to a progressive Movement led by Revolutionaries and dedicated to the socialist transformation of the whole country. It

must be reiterated that the principle objectives of SPLA/SPLM is not separation for the South. The South is an integral and inseparable part of the Sudan. Africa has been fragmented sufficiently enough by colonialism and Neo- colonialism and its further fragmentation can only be in the interest of her enemies. The separatist attitude that has development in the South since 1955 has caught the imagination of the backward areas in the Northern. Separatist Movements have already emerged with guerrillas fighting in Western and Eastern Sudan. If left unchecked, these separatist movements in the South, East and West coupled with the stubborn determination of a repressive minority clique regime in Khartoum to hang on to power in the Sudan at all costs will lead to the total disintegration of the Sudan. This imminent latent and impending disintegration and fragmentation of the Sudan is what the SPLA/SPLM aims to stop by developing and implementing a consistent democratic solution to both the nationality and religious questions within the context of a united socialist Sudan. A general strategy to transform the Southern Movement into a genuine liberation movement .... Consists of the following highlights;

(a) Establishment of a Sudan People's liberation Army (SPLA) and Sudan people's liberation (SPLM) to wage a protracted armed struggle.

(b) Early determination of the correct leadership of the SPLM, so that the movement is not hi-jacked by counter revolutionaries

(c) Maintenance of contact with the enemy through guerrilla harassment and semi- convention engagement in order to maintain the momentum of war. Initially the practice of engaging the enemy on en mass must be avoided. The war will be protracted because of the present size of the enemy and that of the SPLA. The power of SPLA will grow from the small nucleus it is now to a conventional force that will be able to destroy Sudan's reactionary army.

(d) The SPLA must regroup the scattered fighting forces in Southern Sudan, win their confidence, give them further military and political training and through war and correct conduct win the confidence and support of masses of the people.

(e) In order to be able to regroup and politicize the fighting force effectively, the SPLA shall need to establish its own progressive camp apart from those of Anyn-Nya II which are more or less tribal and sectional camps. The SPLA will then work to win the confidence of Anyn-Nya II force and bring them under SPLA command.

(f) Establishment of an effective propaganda machinery to involve as many masses of the people as possible. This will include among other method of propaganda and agitation, the establishment of an SPLM radio station

(g) Establishment of political office in all countries to pursue external contacts for military and other assistance such offices will, of course, be under the supervision of SPLM Headquarters.

(h) Establishment of an Institute for Revolutionary War Studies in a liberated area for training political and military cadres. These cadres will be drawn from the many students, workers and officials who have left or will leave towns for the bush. Officers and other ranks who desert Sudan's reactionary army will be screened and required to attend this institute for political orientation and refresher military training.

(i) Transformation of the fighting Units in the field into organic Units of the SPLA. The trained cadres from the institute for revolutionary war studies shall take over these units and impact their revolutionary knowledge and practice to all under their commands.

(j) Politicization, organization and militarization of the peasantry shall follow as areas become liberated.

(k) Contacting opposition groups in both North and South with the view of forming a united front with these groups, provided that leadership of such a front remains and progressive.

(l) Finally, it shall be necessary to seek and obtain intellectual, moral, military and other material assistance from any country or international organization that is, sympathetic to the aims and objectives of SPLA/SPLM .... Conclusion and prospect for the future... The SPLA/SPLM is convinced of the correctness of its socialist orientation. The SPLA/SPLM program is based on objective realities of the Sudan and provided a correct solution to the nationality and religious questions within the context of a united socialist Sudan thereby preventing the country from an otherwise inevitable disintegration. The SPLA/SPLM will learn from the accumulated bitter experience of 17 years of war by Anya-Nya I, more years by Anya-Nya II, the several coups attempts (1971, 1975, and 1976) and the present revolt in Southern, Western and Eastern Sudan. Finally, the SPLA/SPLM is convince that the necessary internal and external conditions exist to enable it to transform the Southern Movement from a reactionary into a genuine people's liberation movement that will spearhead socialist transformation of the Sudan, beginning in the South where peripheral development and dependency relations are weakest and spreading to all part of the land. Equipped with correct theory and practice determining to persist in the struggle and armed with material moral and organizational support of the masses of the Sudanese people the SPLA will surely win. Long live the unity of the Sudanese people. Long live the SPLM. Long live SPLA. Victory to the SPLA and therefore to the Sudanese people.[1]

After the publication of the SPLM Manifesto, Chairman John Garang distributed it to some embassies in Addis Ababa. He also secured guns and ammunitions in Addis Ababa, and came to Itang. In Itang, the two Battalions 105 and 104 were graduated in August 1983. The two Battalions had the manpower of 1,227 soldiers, starting from John Garang to the last soldier. Battalion 104 has three companies, the first, the second, the third company which were commanded by; Lt Gatkueth Badeng, Lt Gatwic and Lt. James Kailei Tang respectively. Battalion 105 has also three companies, the first, the second and the third company, which were commanded by; Lt. Paul Garang Deng-amuor, Lt Manyang Agok Aliet, Lt Manyang Kiir. At that time, as SPLA/SPLM had been organising itself after Akuot Atem and Samuel Gai fled, John Garang had also been requesting the Anya-Nya II forces in Bilpam to join the SPLA organization process in Itang, but, its leader Gordon Kong Chol had been refusing to join and come under

SPLA command. In resolving the pending issue of the nagging Anya Nya II forces in Bilpam, John Garang ordered immediately two Companies of Battalion 105 and 104, to attack Bilpam. Bilpam was attacked, dislodging Anya-Nya forces of Gordon Koang in October 1983. Two days, after dispersing of Anya-Nya II, John Garang flew to Bilpam by helicopter, and establishing Bilpam the SPLA/SPLM General Headquarters. Itang was left as a refugee camp because SPLA/SPLM did not want to mix the military affairs with refugee affairs in Itang. During the inauguration of Bilpam as the SPLA/SPLM headquarters, Sergeant Yusif Keer Tang, who was one of the popular agitators in Bor revolutionary was executed by firing squad, he was accused by the SPLA/SPLM leadership of collaborating with Anya Nya II, it was allegedly said that, by the time, the SPLA was planning to attack Bilpam, Yusif Keer alerted the Anya Nya by writing a letter to them, which was caught on its way to Bilpam.

Shutdown of Bucket-Wheel: The First SPLA Mission in Sudan.
In its new headquarters of Bilpam, the SPLA sent quickly Colonel Majur Nhial Makol with 51 soldiers to Sudan to shutdown Jonglei Canal project. The closure of Jonglei Canal was the first mission of the SPLA, after its formation, on the Sudan's soil. The aim of shutting down the Bucket-Wheel, the biggest excavators that was digging Jonglei Canal, was to hit the heart of economy and infrastructure of the country. Jonglei canal was defined in the SPLA Manifesto as one of the causes of the war. It is claimed that, it was dug to benefit Egypt in rising up the water level of the River Nile, improving its irrigation, but drying up the Sudd marshes that feed cows and animals in Southern Sudan. On September 24, 1983, SPLA attacked Poktap, arresting workers of CCI, including 8 white men and taking radio communication systems. The news of arrest was broadcasted in the International media including, BBC Focus on Africa. Col. Majur Nhial reported to John Garang, he had accomplished the mission successfully and he was holding the eight foreigner captives with him. Garang ordered him to bring them to Bilpam. Unfortunately, there was a foul play between Col Majur and certain Lt Sebit, the intelligent officer of contingent force. It is allegedly said, an intelligent agent from Sudan army in Bor contacted Sebit and bribed him, without knowledge from Majur.

SPLM/SPLA: History of Liberation (1983-2005)

Under unclear circumstance, a helicopter flew in, landed and air-lifting the eight foreign workers around Duk area, four days after their capture. It was announced by Sudan government that the abducted engineers of Jonglei canal project were rescued and freed by security forces from unknown hostage takers, because the SPLM/A was not officially launched. Lt Sebit escaped to Bor after he was accused of bribery and pending arrest anytime. This incident brought Lt. Col Majur and the SPLA/M leadership into a problem, Majur was recalled back to Ethioipia and ending up in the SPLA jail for few years, accused of failing the SPLA first mission.

Attack on Malual Gohoth: An official launch of SPLA/SPLM.
In October 1983, Battalion 105 and 104, moved from Bilpam in Ethiopia to Thiajok in Sudan .Thiajok is a small village at the Sudan-Ethiopia border, there, a plan to attack on Malual Goath was designed. As it was defined in the SPLM Manifesto, there were seven real and potential enemies of the movement, identified as follows: (1) Sudan's reactionary army (2) the Northern Sudanese bourgeoisie and bureaucratic elite (3) the Religious fundamentalists (4) the Anya-Nya II reactionary army (5) African and Arab reactionary countries (6) imperialist countries. Based on the definition of the seven enemies, the SPLA/SPLM declared the war on the Sudan's reactionary army in August but delayed the declaration of war until November 1983. Throughout October, the cloud of war was hanging low and aggressively on the heads of the Sudan army, imminent and inevitable. The two bulls of the Sudan; the army and the rebels were subtly preparing themselves for a show down in the battlefield; they were evilly eyeing each other, with fullest fury and venom. The fever of war was fogging in guts of everyone, rumours of the preparation going to and fro between the army and rebels.

On morning of November 16, John Garang, William Nyuon, Salva Kiir, and the other officers and men, were busiest, cleaning their guns. At one o'clock, the boxes were opened and magazines loaded with ammunitions. At dawn of 17 November 1983, there was rattling barrels and whistling of bullets in air, finally attacked Malual Goath, the first of its kind in country since the May 16, jumpstarting the revolutionary war at last, between the Sudan army of Field Marshal President Jaffer Mohammed Nimieri, and the rebel SPLA of defected officer, Colonel Dr John Garang de Mabior. It was solemn moment in the history of the Sudan because its two biggest bulls of elephant had banged their horns. And the smashing of their horns through barrage of bullets was heard around the world. Within few minutes of the battle, the miasma of blood was smelled by intransient oppressors in Khartoum, before it was announced over the radio stations. Within 20 minutes of killing and wounding, Malual Goath was captured by SPLA and occupied it for 4 hours, before they tactical withdrew.

Reorganizing after battle, SPLA had suffered 20 causalities, among them, Lt. Pareng Koi Katjang, becoming first ever officer to fall in war. Since the attack was well coordinated, in evening, Col Dr. John Garang announced it over the international news, that he had founded a national liberation movement called the Sudan People's Liberation Army /Sudan People Liberation Movement (SPLA/SPLM), which had attacked Malual Goath garrison on 17 November 1983.

After SPLA had withdrawn into vicinity, a helicopter came to take the wounded, Comrade Garang Akok Adut shot it down, making Garang the first ever sharp shooter of Southern Sudan. The shooting down of helicopter by newly founded rebels, shocked political and military establishments in Khartoum, curling up their hairs in fear and anxiety, and forcing them, to ask themselves many questions about the credibility and capability of the Southerners to shoot down.

At that time, the name Anya-Nya II was informally used by the soldiers to call each other until the attack Malual Goath, when the name SPLA/SPLM was unveiled. Two days, later on, the mantra 'SPLA Oyee' and 'Comrade' were also introduced, in meeting on November 19 in Thiajok as new political and socialist expressions.

The Mobilization of Dinka Bor cattle camp youth

By November 1983, there were three events happening simultaneously: (1) Chairman John Garang went to launch the movement by attacking Malual Gohoth (2) Kerubino Kuanyin was training the students, who later became Jamus Battalion in Bilpam (3) Captain Cigai Atem with platoon of 51 soldiers, most of them, Dinka Bor went to their home area Bor for mobilization of the recruits. Through funniest deception Captain Cigai and his team of officers; Lt. Herjok Akuon Magon, Lt Awuou Aluong among others succeeded, by mobilizing about 8,000 cattle camp Bor youth.

Captain Gigai Atem and his team of Political commissars had tricked and hoaxed the Dinka Bor cattle camp youth into the SPLA/SPLM, by telling them to go to Bilpam to get guns in order to come, and protect their cows from rustling by the hostile neighbouring tribes of Murle and Toposa. This message came at the backdrop of different Murle and Toposa attacks on cattle camp in Bor. Indeed, Bor youth were provoked by offensive attacks by Murle tribes on Nayac cattle camp in Gog area on July 1, 1983, killing 38 men and taking about 2000 cows. On July 15, 1983, Anyidi cattle camp of Palek was raided by Murle, killing 113 men, but taking no cows. On July 17, 1983, Toposa and Rwoto tribes attacked Paluer cattle camp of Abii, killing 40 men and taking no cows. These attacks on Bor cattle camps prompted the youth, to accept the words of SPLA/SPLM political commissars as truth messages. Bor cattle youth massively rushed to Bilpam, to acquire guns and coming back to protect their cows from other tribes. The cattle camp youth marched to Bilpam in thousand, two brothers or three brothers, would leave their cattle to the sisters and young brothers, and left for Bilpam, hoping to return after two months, but, it later took them 9 months to return home, as freedom fighters, not cattle herders anymore.

Attack on Nasir Town

On December 12, 1983, the SPLA attacked Nasir town, the second attack of its kinds on the Sudan's soil by SPLA. The sand model of the offensive was designed at Mandeng Village. Major Salva Kiir was the operation commander and Colonel John Garang, the supervisor of the offensive. The SPLA captured, and occupying it for one day, before withdrawing back to Mandeng Village. In that battle, SPLA had suffered 10 casualties among them was Corporal Agok Adier Ngoon. Concealed properly in Mandeng Village, a helicopters gunship was flying over the village to Nasir. SPLA sharp shooter, Garang Akok Adut shot down that helicopter. When three helicopters came to see the wreckage of ill-fated helicopter, another helicopter was shot down again by Garang Akok. The shutting down of two helicopters caused a great fear among the Sudanese people and began to realise country was really at war.

After the Nasir operation, John Garang, William Nyuon and Salva Kiir returned to Bilpam. Battalion 105 and 104 remained at the Thiajok. John Garang took Garang Akok Adut, the sharp shooter, who shot down three helicopters, to president Mengistu of Ethiopia. At a dinner in the state house, Dr John wonderfully narrated to President Mengistu and his generals at dinner, how their trained Garang Akok shot down three helicopters, which were flying at 10, 000 feet above sea level. Flabbergasted by the achievement of two week trained air gunner, President Mengistu commended, honoured, described and marked Garang Akok Adut as the first black man to shoot down a plane. This is so because, some planes were shot down in Angola's war but were shot down by Cuban sharp shooters not Angolan.

Jamus Battalion: The Tip of Iceberg

When John Garang, William Nyoun and Salva Kiir, went to attack Malual Goath and Nasir. Lt Col Kerubino Kuanyin Bol was organizing and training the students and other intellectual, who were named Jamus Battalion in Bilpam. Jamus means Buffalo in Arabic. It was the first SPLA trained army, having 1200 soldiers and graduated in December 1983. It was divided into two contingencies. Jamus – Malakal and Jamus-Wau. When Jamus Battalions was graduating in December 1983, Tiger and Timsaa Battalion were being organized and trained.

Jamus–Wau forces were sent to Bahr el Ghazel for a recruitment mission. They were two companies, led by Lt. Col Kawac Makuei Kawac, assisted by; Lt. Elijah Hon Tap, Lt Faustino Puok, Lt Victor Bol Ayolnhom and Lt Ayuen Alier Jongror among others. It was the first SPLA column to enter Bahr el Ghazal region. They left immediately for Bahr el Ghazal. As they were crossing the River Nile, they met a steamer called Busta at Watkec, they destroyed it, killing people in barge, despite the fact that, it was not military target. After that attack, they proceeded ahead, passing on the revolutionary messages. The youth accepted and massing up in thousand to join the SPLA. They went to the end of Bahr el Ghazal, which is Aweil area, where they blew up Aweil Bridge, destroying it completely. Their recruitment mission was successful, recruiting 8,000 cattle camp youth of Dinka Bahr el Gazal who became the Muor Muor Division. Among

SPLM/SPLA: History of Liberation (1983-2005)

officers, who went to Bahr el Ghazal, Faustino Puok Tang was killed in action becoming the second officer of SPLA to die in the war.

In January 1984, Major Arok Thon Arok came to movement after he was released from jail. When he arrived at Bilpam, the SPLA/SPLM HQs, he was added to be the fifth member of Political Military High Command (PMHC), he was put number five in hierarchy, although, he was senior to Kerubino Kuanyin, William Nyuon and Salva Kiir. That planted seeds of discontent between him and the other four members, leading later to his arrest.

Jamus – Malakal was commanded by Lt. Col Kerubino Kuanyin Bol, the deputy Chairman and Deputy Commander in Chief, and assisted by; Captain Wilson Kur Chol, Lt. Maduk Yaung, Lt Bullen Ayuen Mabior, Lt Reuben Thiong Tat. The force had carried out a series of guerrilla warfare in Upper Nile, attacking Canal Mouth on Sobat River, Akoba, Ayod and Poktap. In an attack on Poktap Lt Akuany Makoi was killed. These series of attacks by Jamus, Battalion 105 and 104 forces on the Sudan government in Upper Nile, closed down the evacuation of the Jonglei Canal project and its staff. In attack on Canal Mouth in January 1984, many SPLA soldiers were killed, including Martyr Falata Thichot and Thawan Pargol Alany, who was a best footballer player in Merik Football Club in Malakal. After the hit and run warfare on many enemy garrisons, Jamus Battalion returned to Bilpam for reorganization.

Moonlight Brigade: The Beacon of Liberation

Whereas Battalion 105/104 and Jamus were enthusiastically mobilizing and recruiting the youth in Bor and Bahr el Gazal areas, Tiger and Timsaa Battalions known as Moonlight Brigade were under training in Bilpam, preparing for war at the front line. Tiger and Timsah were mostly Nuer of Anya-nya II, who stayed behind, when their leaders; Akuot, Gai and Chuol fled to Sudan. They had the parade of about 1800 soldiers, all from Nuer except about 800 Dinka and Shilluk.

Tiger Battalion

Graduating in April 1984, Tiger Battalion was led by Lt. Col Salva Kiir Mayardit, assisted by Captain Paul Dor Lampur, Captain Awiec Bak, Lt Garang Mabil Deng, Lt. Taban Deng Gai, the political Commissioner, Lt

SPLA DIVISIONS, BATTALIONS AND THEIR BATTLES, 1983-1986

Wilson Deng Kuorot aka Deng Wek, Lt Ayuen Alier Jongroor, Lt Aluk Akec, Lt. Aret Jok Yuot. Lt. Majak Agot Atem, Lt. Akuoc Miyong. Lt Kur Nathan Garang. From Bilpam, they moved to the foot of Pochalla. Before, they could reach Pochalla, some soldiers rebelled, killing Captain Awiet Bak and five other soldiers, at dawn in Tedo area, and left and joining the Anya-Nya II. These soldiers were of Bentiu Nuer origin, they all left for Bentiu. Tiger later attacked Pochalla and withdrew back, besieging it. Two Mig jet fighters came to attack Tiger; one of jets was shot down by Lt Akuoc Miyong, making him the second sharp shooter to bring a plane after Garang Akok. In attack of Pochalla, 15 comrades were killed, including two officers; Lt. Aluk Akech and Lt. Aret Jok Yuot. When Tiger withdrew from foot of Pochalla, Sudan People Defence Force (SPDF) ambushed them at Ajuera area where they killed more 10 soldiers including; Lt. Chol Angui and Lt. Kur Nathan Garang Awer.

Timsah Battalion:
The sister Timsah Battalion was led by Lt. Col Arok Thon Arok and assisted by Major Thon Ayiei Jok. Companies and platoons commanded by some officers who included but not only; Lt Mayen Lual aka Mayen Akoba, Lt Manyang Kiir, Lt Chol Deng Alak. It attacked Pibor and tactically withdrawing to rural Bor, because their ammunitions finished. Timsah arrived at Anyidi area, spent some days at Achol base, and proceeding to Yuai through Duk. At Yuai, Timsaa met Tiger, where they reorganized again; one company composed of soldiers of Dinka went to Bare el Ghazal with Captain George Kuec. This company attacked Thiep police station in Warrap area, becoming the second SPLA expeditionary force to arrive in Bahr el Ghazal after Jamus soldiers. While other soldiers of Nuer origin were put under the command of Major Paul Dor Lampur, and went to Bentiu, where they closed down Chevron Oil Exploration's operation in oilfield.

Koryom Division: The Trailblazers
Upon the accomplished mission of Captain Chagai Atem and his team of good propagandist of the political commissars, Dinka Bor cattle camp youth began arriving at Bilpam in December 1983 to January 1984. The only reason influencing them to leave their cows and trekking for 18 days

SPLM/SPLA: History of Liberation (1983-2005)

or so to Bilpam was to acquire guns for tending their cows and protecting them from Murle's and Toposa's attacks. Captain Cigai Atem went to Bor in December 1983, started telling people about the guns at Bilpam. The news of guns in Bilpam came against the backgrounds of Murle and Toposa attacks on five cattle camps of Anyidi, Paluer, Amou-Meth, and Nayac in South Bor and Wunlit of Ajoung in Twic area. No sooner had they arrived, than the SPLA/SPLM best, persuasive, oratory political commissars came to address them. Using a mid-sentence and Orwellian style of communication, the political commissars disorient them, after disorientation, they brainwashed them, after brainwashing, they politicized them. After politicization, they instilled, inculcated and incited the war fervour into them, their minds, their blood and their spirit. One of the propagandists told them, 'SPLA/SPLM has not called you to come and take guns and go to protect your cows from Murle. Murle is not a problem, the problem is the Arab. It is the Arabs who have committed two virulent, felonious crimes (I) they took your land and subjugated and enslaved you and (2) they give guns to your brothers Murle to go and kill you. Therefore, your enemy is the Jalaba in Mading-Bor. SPLA/SPLM have called you here to liberate your land from Arabs. The Arab had killed 29 chiefs in 1967 in Bor Chief Alier Leek, Chief Jogak Deng, Chief Ayom Dor, Chief Athui Madol, Chief Malual Kang, Chief Bul Koch, among others, isn't it? They killed the chiefs; all you knew this tragic event, weren't you? All these chiefs are your relatives, either through paternal or maternal relation. To free yourself and your people from the Arab's subjugation, injustice, oppression and enslavement, is only objective, mission and goal SPLA/SPLM call you to Bilpam', the political commissar harangued in front of the recruits until they were converted, accepted and shouted, 'Revolution! Revolution! Death to Arab! Death to Bourgeoisie!

Few days passed, Colonel Dr. John Garang de Mabior the Chairman and Commander in Chief of SPLA/SPLM came to Bongo, addressing the 8000 recruits, he predisposed them to the revolutionary armed struggle, he said 'Arabs especially President Nimieri has grabbed your land and, is occupying it now, and above all else, Mr Nimieri has sold your water to Egyptian people. This is why Egypt is digging Jonglei canal, this canal will take all water in the toc where you graze your cows during dry season, and because of canal, toc will dry up, your cows will die of thirst and hunger, because there will be no "agou" or the grass in the toc. The land of the living man can't be taken away from him and he keeps quiet, unless he is a coward, are you cowards? "No, No, No" they thunderous murmured. Garang congratulated them for heeding the call of war. He named them Koryom Division. Koryom means "locust" in Dinka language.

When they heard of the news of the liberation war not the guns for tending cattle which they were coming for, some recruits began escaping and returning to Bor. These escapees were attacked by Anya-Nya II on their way back to Bor. The rebellion within the rebellion of about 400 soldiers of Tiger Battalion at Tedo, Anyuak area, marked the beginning of another war within the war. That is the war between the SPLA and Anya-Nya II inside the Sudan. There was now a military confrontation between SPLA and Anya-Nya II. At the time, Anya Nya II had sworn to block the SPLA forces that were either leaving or going to Bilpam. In training centre, Koryom had been facing by the three problems (1) unintended outcome, because they were tricked by SPLA leadership (2) starvation, they suffered a hunger they never experienced in cattle camps (3) torturous physical exercise. These three bad conditions in Bongo forced some Koryom members to escape, but, they were forced to return to Bilpam by Anya-Nya II and Nuer civilians who were attacking them on the way with spears. This, too, prevented Koryom members, who were not convinced of the war objective to stay in training against their will. Despite the challenges, problems and uneasiness in the training, Koryom was trained for six months and successfully finishing the training, were divided into two Brigades, I and II.

Koryom I: The First Brigade

As a result of May 16th 1983 Bor and Ayod coup de grace by some of 105/104 Battalion's companies, who lastly went into bush, and who were followed by the students in whole Southern Sudan, forming already Jamus, Tiger and Timsah Battalions. Thence, these three Battalions had made a waves of liberation war in the South. Little by little, a huge number of students, cattle camp youth, and intellectuals from Greater Bor and Panarou also went into bush now formed a division named Locust (Koryom). The first brigade of Koryom was graduated on September 3, 1984, composing of the four Battalions; Zindia, Cobra, Raad and Rhino. For worst or for better, the graduation was marked with firing squad of men, who were accused of different crimes; the executed men were Comrade Lakurnyang Lado, the leader of Southern Sudan Liberation Front (SSLF), Comrade Dr Juach Kerjok, and Comrade Engineer Manyang Dieu. Comrade Lakurnyang Lado was accused of refusing to dissolve his movement and come under SPLA/SPLM leadership. By refusal, he was accused of dividing people, by forming different movement. On the other hand, Juach Kerjok and Manyang Dieu were allegedly charged of being agents sent by the Sudan's government. "Fraternity has to be imposed by violence"2, thus, Lakurnyang and other men were violently executed to impose fraternity. The men were executed before the troops, as mean of nurturing bravery in themselves, and getting used to, seeing of the dead persons.

At the time of graduation, Koryom forces had already accepted the timely death in the war, with its highest price of dying, wounding and blood shedding. In celebrating their self-sacrifices, some bards among them, immortalised those ideals in composing the revolutionary songs, which were sung daily at 3pm, over the Radio SPLA, the voice of Sudanese revolutionary armed struggle. The famous songs of glorification, honour, courage and heroism were; *Wenu Nimeiry ya Jama*, in Arabic which means, 'Where is Nimerri brothers?', '*Ke theer cii ro beer nyo*', in Dinka language which means, 'Things cannot and will not ever be the same again', *Shalla Abiu Adiu talaga*, in Arabic which means 'Even my father will deserve to die by my bullet'. In response to these revolutionary songs in press conference in Khartoum, President Nimerri contemptuously and belittlingly asked, 'they are there in the bush and they are singing, 'where is Nimerri?' when they left me here in Khartoum, tell them, I am still in Khartoum, where you left me, it is you, whom I shall ask, 'where are you?'. Actually they are there in the bushes, where do they sit and eat, if really their parents really die by their *talaga* (bullet) as they sing it. They are *Majanien* (mad men). They are '*shamachi*' meaning those who were sniffing the grease oil in gutters and garbage.

The rest of forces reinforced Battalion 105 and 104 under Comrade William Nyuon, fighting the Anya Nya II forces of Abdhalla Chuol around Thiajok area. The four Battalion of Zindia, Cobra, Raad, Rhino marched into Sudan, crossing through Nuer Gajak areas, where they fought bitter war with the Anya-Nya II forces, who were armed by president Nimieri in Malakal.

At Lou-Nuer areas, Lt. Col Arok Thon Arok, a member of permanent Political Military High Command (PMHC) of the movement, took over all the command of the four Battalions, although; each Battalion has a commander separately. Commander Arok Thon was the supervisor of all operations. During rebellion of AN II that resulted in fighting and property destruction from Gajak Nuer, this outraged Nuer people and they refused to contribute food to the SPLA, prompting SPLA to loot for food from the Nuer community in 1984. When the news of fighting between the SPLA and Anya Nya II broke, President Nimieri mockingly laughed and said again, "Southerners did not go to bush to liberate themselves from Arabs as they claimed in beginning but to discipline themselves, to determine, which tribe is strongest, which one is the weakest, therefore,all those self-destruction are our guns, if they go and kill themselves, it is achieving our objectives of destroying the SPLA, if they are killed by snakes in grass, snakes are our guns, if they are killed by thorns in bushes, thorns are our guns, if they are killed by hunger, hunger is our gun.

Raad, Cobra, Zindia and Rhino battalions arrived at Bor in December 1984, although, they were sons of Bor community, people were scared, demoralised and intimidated by their wildest behaviour of grabbing and looting food in the villages. Within 30 days, SPLA soldiers ate tens of thousands of goats and sheep in whole villages. In those days, the elders and chiefs were gossip-mongering against the SPLA soldiers, they could remark, 'these boys deserted and ran away in Nyinthar Malual, where they were to fight the enemy and they are meandering and looting in the village here. Look! Two soldiers can kill a goat, give it to lady to cook, when they come to eat, they don't finish to eat it all, or some time, they don't even come back to eat it'. People were surprise by the careless, unusual and stranger behaviours coming from Bonga with their sons. They expressed doubt, about their ability to liberate the country, as they were claiming.

Rhino Battalion

Rhino Battalion was led by Lt. Col (PSC) Martin Makur Aleiyou, and deputised by Captain Pagan Amum Okiech. It has six companies; the first, the second, third, the fourth, the fifth, the sixth company, commanding the companies and platoons were; Captain Andrew Anhiem Aliet, Lt Johnson Jok, Lt Kelei Riak Makol, Lt Akuei Deng Akuei, Lt Maluk Mou, Lt Majok Solomon, Lt Marial Chanuong Yol, Lt Paulo Aguto Ngong, Lt Zechariah Aguto Ngong, and Lt Deng Kuot Gut, Lt Ateny Ajak, Lt Chier Akuei Ajou, Lt Biar Kuol Ayuen, Lt Daniel Abudhok, Lt Thuryin Mayen, and Lt Justin Jok.

In September 1984, Comrade Martin Makur Aleiyou with his men crossed the border from Ethiopia to Sudan, from the east westward. Along his journey, his men and he had three difficult problems; (1) attack by Nyagate or Anya –Nya II forces of Akuot Atem, and Samuel Gai (2) heavy military equipment carried by the heads (3) long route to Bahr el Ghazal. The objective and mission to Bahr el Ghazal were; (1) to engage the enemy in wandering guerrilla warfare of hit and run tactics (2) to spread and advocate SPLA/SPLM policies, propaganda and mobilization, so that capable men join the training. On the way, the attacks, carrying on heads of ammunition and ambushes laid by AN II almost failed the advance and mission of Rhino, AN II had made several attempts to fail the mission, but Rhino defeated them and the mission went forward.

Ambush at Panwel

On 23 December 1984, things changed for the better, those bad Bongo boys, as they were called by the community, clashed and annihilated the convoy of Mazalat (Special Forces) in Panwel. The Battle of Aguer-Koi started like this. Two days before Rhino could cross the River Nile and celebrating the Christmas in swamp (toc). First Lieutenant General Hamed Mohammed Sadiq el-Banna, commander of Southern Command in Juba, sent two companies, from Sudan Jamus (not SPLA Jamus), to reinforce and reopen Juba-Bor road after its closure by SPLA activities. In the evening of December 23, Lt. Deng Akuei and Lt. Deng Kuot Gut laid a furious, hand to hand ambush at Panwel, near Aguer-Koi cattle camp. At 3:20pm exactly, the two companies bounced into an ambush. Rhino and other men from Zindia, opened fire on them, the fighting lasted for 3 minutes. The Jamus soldiers, who were bravely decorated as thaka Sudan, were defeated shamefully, running into Panwel's bushes in disarray, hyenas and birds danced and ate their meat. The SPLA destroyed two Saladin tanks and four Lorry-trucks. The defeat of this big force of Jalaba, changed the perception of community about the Koryom soldiers, whom they were calling deserters and eaters of goats and sheep within 30 days. After that battle of Panwel, there was greatest glorification of the SPLA soldiers by elders and chiefs in the villages, they said, they had the right to eat goats and sheep now. They are real heroes, and they will, indeed, chase away the Arab from Southern Sudan.

The Battle of Yirol

After this battle, Rhino still followed its instruction towards Bahr el-Ghazal. In the swamp (toc), soldiers celebrated two events, the victory over the Sudan army and the Christmas, the birth of Lord Jesus Christ. Rhino moved to the vicinity of Yirol town, meanwhile the Radio SPLA, the propaganda machinery of movement, broadcasted the battle of Aguarkoi very well, and the presence of the forces at Yirol area, convincing Captain Marik to defect from Yirol and joined Rhino. Yirol army garrison was situated at the east mouth of Greater Bahr el-Ghazal. Makur Aleiyou had been cajoled at the time by the new defected Captain Mariik to attacked Yirol. Although Comrade Makur mumbled something about being busy and disavowed, he ordered the attack on Yirol on en masses, at conventional one not guerrilla one according to SPLM Manifesto Chapter 8. Captain Marik then had to command 408 men to the Battle for Yirol. At 4:00 am, Rhino force poured broadsides after broadside into the enemy. The battle commenced at 4:00am. The smoke of gun powder was so thick; only the flames coming out, from and between the fighters that was seen sparkling and vanishing. After about a half hour, the gun's sound ceased, ammunitions had finished, Rhino had tactically withdrawn to the bush.

When the parade for the reorganization of the members who were lost was done at 3pm in afternoon, it was confirmed four officers were among the martyrs Captain Marik himself, Lt. Bol Kuch, Lt. Majok Sudan, Lt Maluk Mou and Sergeant Major Wal Ajieth Agot and 30 other men were killed in the battle of Yirol. Rhino withdrew in disarray, leaving all wounded heroes behind, who were later summarily executed. In fact, Lt Col Makur was blamed for attacking a big garrison like Yirol in conventional manner, which was not the aim of the SPLA/M at the time. The aim was to attack in small number and big numbers in self-defence. Makur confirmed his disavowed plea. Rhino evacuated Yirol and one company was left, to lay besiege on Yirol. The (Sudan army) remained in Yirol until its evacuated in October 1986, because hunger and wave of fear sent by the newly SPLA reinforcement to area.

Zindia Battalion

It was led by Major Peter Panhom Thapiny, it had been attacked by Anya-Nya II several at Yindit area, however, it repulsed attacks. The aims of AN II were not clear, 'what were they fighting for?' This was why SPLA was demonizing them as "Nyagate". The etymology of the word "Nyagate" 'is not clear, some claimed it to originate from Dinka, others from Nuer or Shilluk. If it is of Dinka origin then, it means an insect called "Gate" that bites hen. These insects can also always bite people in persistent and disturbing manner in which the AN II was attacking the SPLA. It could attack now and then.

In the labyrinth of the AN II ambushes, Zindia had vigorously penetrated through and triumphantly arriving in Bor area, where Comrade Arok Thon took over the command, as it was ordered by the SPLA/M leadership in Bilpam, and moving to Equatoria for recruitment and mobilization of the civilian's population to support the war effort. Comrade Arok with Zindia trekked from Bor through the forest of east Mangalla garrison, entering into eastern Equatoria region.

They went through villages, and attacking police station at Lokirili area. Killing some policemen and proceeding to Owiny Ki Bul. earlier in December 1984. Before one Company of Zindia participated in the Battle of Aguar-Koi, that was first its military action against the Sudan army, and the second was the attack on Lokirili post.

The Sudan army in Torit garrison heard of the first incursion of SPLA in the Equatoria area, so it sent forces to hunt and destroy the SPLA, so this force followed the SPLA to Owniy Ki bul area, where they came into contact, and they fought, making SPLA withdrew under pressure and marched to Lobone area.

Raid on Lokirili

When Zindia left Bor for Equatoria, forces were under overall command of Lt. Col Arok Thon and assisted by many officers; Maj Peter Panhom Thapiny, Captain Makuei Deng Majuch, Captain Dau Manyok, Captain John Akot (who was killed on raid on Lokirili),, Captain Aru Maan Chot, Captain Gatwic Duel, Captain Ater Machuor Kuluang, Lt Zaro Ajang Bior, Lt Malual Goc, Lt Mabil Deng Thon, Lt Aleer Awan. SPLA forces wandered from Lokirili through Owniny Ki Bul up to Lobone, where they had already recruited 2000 men from around Torit; Acholi, Lalupo, Lutuho, Pari, Langu. etc. In Lobone, the Sudan army came and assaulted them, although they fought back, they had to withdraw under pressure in to the mountains. At that time, the bullets had finished. Comrade Arok Thon reported this to the SPLA GHQ in Bilpam. Chairman Garang ordered a helicopter to bring ammunitions, but unfortunately jettisoning them to the Uganda side of the border, whereby the Uganda Army confiscated them and refused to hand over them to Zindia. Comrade Arok went to border and tried to plead to them but the Uganda military sent lance Corporal, the lowest rank in the army to come and talk to Cdr Arok, Uganda snubbed Arok, this was time when the relationship between President Nimieri of Sudan and President Tito Okello, were at their best.

Great Thirst

Zindia was now faced by two problems: (1) lack of ammunitions (2) pressure from the enemy. Cdr Arok decided to return to Bor. Another problem arisen up. It was dry season and there was no water in Tingli desert and in the nearby forest of east Mangalla and the enemy had deployed forces in all villages of Lirya, Ngala Ngala and Lokirili, where SPLA had passed before. By the time, Zindia walked to Lofon village, Cdr Arok communicated earlier to SPLA GHQs in Ethiopia and Baidit Zonal HQs in Bor respectively. Bilpam GHQs said, they would send water by helicopter from Ethiopia to Tingli. This idea of bringing water from Ethiopia was rejected by Major Benjamin Nyakot Biar, the commander of Cobra Battalion, who was in Baidit, he said why should the water be brought from Ethiopia what was his job in Baidit, he said, he would send two water tanks to Tingli.

SPLM/SPLA: History of Liberation (1983-2005)

When the two options were weighed against each other, to see which is feasible and possible urgently by leadership, it was agreed that Comrade Nyakot's option was the best, and he should send the water tanks and bringing water from Ethiopia by helicopter was cancelled.

Two water tanks left Baidit for Malual Agorbaar, where Total Company abandoned petrol station because of war with fuel in it. The drivers were told to put fuel into water tank at Malual Agorbaar, and fetched the water and rushed to Tingli Desert. By the time they were leaving Baidit, a message was sent to Cdr Arok informing him that water is on the way, therefore, Zindia should move to Tingli from, where they were staying, it would take soldiers 8 hour to reach Tingli, while it would take water tanks 10 to 12 hours to reach too because there was no road, water tanks were moving in forest.

Zindia moved to Tingli with 2000 recruits. The drivers of the water tanks were also advised not to drive on the main road, they were told to drive in forest. The drivers ignored this advice; they drove on the main road. Unfortunately, the first water tank was blown up by the land mine, and second tank it was pulling behind caught fire and all of two water tanks burned, killing 20 soldiers, who were escorting the water. It took 24 hours for the news of the disastrous accident to reach Comrade Nyakot in Baidit. Nyakot thought water reached safely.

When Zindia arrived at Tingli, where they would get water, there was no water, they had to walk for 10 hours from Tingli to River Nile at Mangalla without water. During the walk from Tingli to River Nile, about 500 recruits and 100 soldiers died of thirst. Some drank their urine; some were dehydrated and could not urinate. This confusion and worst incident led to the detention of Comrade Benjamin Nyakot Biar by leadership, where he allegedly later died .

Comrade Benjamin Bol Akok

Comrade Benjamin Akok was the SPLA/SPLM representative in London. By 1984, the SPLA had taken many foreigners captives, among them, French citizens including a woman, who was pregnant by the time of her capture. The French government contacted the SPLA offices in Addis Abba about citizens. The SPLA wrote to French government saying it would release their citizens on conditions that French government assisted the SPLA. The French government agreed to give any assistance to the SPLA except the weapons. That process of negotiation between the SPLA and French government was coordinated by Benjamin Bol in London. Since the French government agreed the assistance apart from weapons. Questions had arisen from the SPLA leadership, 'what kind of assistance shall the SPLA seek?' Some said money, others said communication equipment, and others said medicines. John Garang himself said communication equipment were right thing we should ask, because, he argued, if we ask for medicine, who might know, they give us medicine that would come and poison us. When the SPLA delegation went, and met the French embassy officials, the issue of money came up again. This prompted John Garang to go himself and told the French officials that, he wanted communication equipment only. The French government brought the communication equipment as it were requested, and their citizens were released.

After the swap of captives with radio calls equipment, a rumour allegedly emerged that some money was given by French embassy to SPLM Office in London. Based on that accusation, John Garang changed Benjamin Bol as representative of SPLA in London and ordered him to report himself to Bilpam, where he would go and attend the military training because he was not yet trained. This angered Comrade Bol and he refused to go to Bilpam, and he called for a meeting of Bahr el Ghazal people in Addis Abba. SPLA leadership heard of that meeting. A spy was sent into the meeting, who was a member of Bahr el Ghazal community. It was allegedly said Benjamin Bol said, 'recruits from Bahr el Ghazal region will not be coming to Ethiopia again for training, Ethiopia is very far, recruits from Bahr el Ghazal will be going to Central Africa Republic (CAR), I am going to London and there I will bring guns to CAR '. This information was given to the SPLA leadership, so when Benjamin Bol was leaving for London, he was stopped at airport by Ethiopian security men. It was allegedly said he was handed over to SPLA intelligent cadres who were in training in Addis Abba and who later on killed him. The SPLA was keen to avoid the Anya Nya I recurrent of factions and camps; this was why Benjamin Bol was killed. "(T)he organized group acts upon itself in order to make everyone better able to carry out his share of the common task"[3] ... "(P)urge are intended to reestablish an internal homogeneity'[4] "Through a purge - of whatever sort seclusion or execution, the purger constitutes himself a suspect."[5]

Cobra Battalion

Cobra Battalion was led by Major Benjamin Nyankot Biar. It has six companies. The first, the second, the third, the fourth, the fifth and sixth company, commanding the companies and platoons were; Lt. Jok Reng Magot, Lt. Manyiel Kueth Makuei, Lt. Machar Akau Machar, Lt. Akol Alith Akuei, and Lt Sadiq Ubuony. Lt Akur Aruai, Lt. Juach Nathan Garang Awer, Lt. Mathiang Aluong, Lt. Majier Deng Kur, Lt Achol Deng Achol Aka Achol-Malual, Lt. Garang Ngang Abui. Cobra crossed the border from Ethiopia to Sudan. As the guerrilla army, Cobra was faced with four major hard problems: (1) attacks by Anya-Nya; (2) carrying of ammunition on the head; (3) walking for long distance; (4) lack of food. Cobra had fallen into many ambushes, laid by Anya Nya II, inflicting many casualties on it. However, Cobra broke up these ambushes, repulsing the attacks and penetrating through the mire of perils of AN II, and making the splendid breakthrough the enemy till reaching Bor area. At Dhiam Dhiam, Cobra attacked two barges in the River Nile, resulting into the death of many civilians. The barges were not actually military one but SPLA attacked to pressure the government

Muor Muor Division: the centre of gravity

Whereas Koryom II graduated, and left for frontline, Muor Muor Division, the second largest division of recruits moved into Bonga training centre. Having parade of 8000 recruits, it was divided into seven Battalions – Tuek Tuek, Eagle (Kuei), Neiran, Bee, Shark, Wolf, and Nile. They began training in January 1985. These recruits joined the movement as the results of two Jamus companies, who went to Bahr el Ghazal under Comrade Kawac Makuei. It was through Kwac's effort and his team's effort that Muor Muor soldiers, the cattle camp youth were mobilized, to join the rank and file of SPLA/SPLA. The reasons why Dinka Bahr el Gazal (Aweil, Rek, Twic,) joined the SPLA/M were similar to those of Koryom of Dinka Bor, they were told to come and take guns to protect themselves and their cattle from hostile Baggera Arab known as Mauralin militia, who were armed by the central government in Khartoum. Kawac Makuei successfully accomplished his mission.

As Jamus Wau was returning from Bar el Ghazal, they met Major Ajok Malong's car, some 25 kilometre south of Bor town, the soldiers tried to stop the car, and the car did not stop, they fired RPG 7 rocket upon it, the car caught the fire, killing Major Ajok on spot. It was later discovered that Major Ajok was going to Bor in order to go to defect and join the SPLA. That was unfortunate incident.

Koryom II

On 2 January 1984, the second Brigade of Koryom forces were graduated, comprising of seven Battalions; Hadid, Bilpam, Agreb, Elephant, Lion, Hippo-Mazala and Aquila. Aquila Battalion was named after Anya Nya I martyr Commander Aquila Manyuon who was killed in 1969 by the Sudan government forces. These Battalions were dispatched into frontlines in the Sudan in three columns. Hadid went to Southern Blue Nile, Agreb travelled to Boma Plateau area. Bilpam, Elephant, Lion and Hippo-Mazala marched to Jekou area, deploying Bukteng, Thiajok and Mangok bases.

Hadid Battalion

It was led by Lt. Col Francis Ngor Maciec . It has six companies, the first, the second, the third, the fourth, the fifth and sixth company, commanding and controlling the companies and platoons at low echelon were; Captain Michael Miakol Deng Anyang, Captain Paul Malong Awan, Captain Alier - Machut, Lt. James Kalei Tang, Lt. George Bilim, Lt. Chol Gai Arou, Lt Gai Manyang Dot, Lt. Morris Agany Wek, Lt. Ayuel Bul Koc and Lt. Philip Chol Majak among others.

Hadid went to Blue Nile to destroy the Ethiopian rebels' bases on the behest of President Mengistu Haile Mariam Ethiopia, the mentor of SPLA. This expedition became the first SPLA/SPLM incursion to war zone II, the Northern Sudan. The aim of the expedition was destruction of the Ethiopian rebel's camps, based at the Ethiopian-Sudan border, and used as the springboard by the Eritrean separatist rebel, in attacking the Ethiopian army. It successfully destroyed them and capturing some rebels as prisoners of war including one of the rebel senior commanders, who were handed over to the Ethiopian government.

SPLM/SPLA: History of Liberation (1983-2005)

After the destruction of the Ethiopian rebel's camps, Hadid attacked the nearby Maban garrison, overrunning it, and tactically withdrawing back to bush, since it was guerrilla warfare of hit and run tactic. In the attack of Maban, Hadid lost 40 men in battle including Lt. Nyirou Deng Majuch, and then Hadid returned to Jekou area

Agreb Battalion

It was led by Lt. Col Ngacigak Ngaciluk, who was the alternate members of Political Military High Command (PMHC) and deputised by Major Anthony Bol Madut. It has six companies, commanding the companies and platoons were; Captain Chol Muorwel, Captain Gordon Gom, Lt. Dhieu Warabeck Ayuel, Lt. Dut Achuek Lual, Lt. Babur Mazi. The structural organization of SPLA was that a platoon is made up of 51 soldiers and company has 4 platoons, making the total parade 204 men. A battalion has 6 companies, making total parade of 1224 soldiers. It attacked Boma garrison, and liberating it in 1985 and becoming the first Sudan army's garrison captured and maintained by the SPLA. It was liberated at loss of 89 men including Captain Chol Muorwel.

Boma was the first liberated town, where the SPLA/SPLM flag was hoisted for the first time on Sudan's soil. The ceremony was attended by John Garang de Mabior, Chairman and Commander In Chief, Commander Kerubino Kuanyin Bol, Deputy Chairman and Deputy Commander In Chief, Commander William Nyoun Bany, Chief of Staff, Commander Salva Kiir Mayardit Deputy Chief of Staff for Security and Operation, and Commander Arok Thon Arok, Deputy Chief of Staff for Administration and Logistic. It was joyous celebration of the SPLA/SPLM ever.

Battle of Jekou I: The Catastrophe

Koryom II forces spent nine months in Bonga training centre and were passed out on 2 January 1985. They went to Sudan in three columns, the first column made up of four battalions of Bilpam, Lion, Elephant and Hippo marched to Jekou area, where they joined remnants of Battalion 105 and 104, Jamus, Tiger and Timsah Battalions in the battle fronts. The six battalions had the manpower of 5,296 troops. These larger fighting forces were led by brave, first-rate officers; Major Wilson Kur

Chol, Major Kuol Mayang Juuk, Major Francis Jago, Major Alfred Akuoch, Major Isaac Gatluk, Major Chol Deng Alak, Captain Maker Thong Maal, Captain Akol Gier Thiik, Captain Paulino Deng Ajuong, Lt Kenedy Khot, Dor Deng Dor, Moses Maal Duot, Lt John Maal Duot, Lt Alith Akuei, Lt Mayom Alier, Lt Duany Herjok, Lt Madul Kang Jang, Lt Manyok Chan, and among others. The overall commander was Lt. Col Kerubino Kuanyin Bol, the then deputy Chairman and Commander in Chief of SPLA/SPLM.

On February 2, 1985, the Battle of Jekou fallen, rumbling like thunderstorm, the six SPLA Battalions, each on its turn, willedly fished Jekou with half a millions rounds of ammos for three months, from February to April. During that the SPLA had aggressively tried to destroy the Sudan army in Jekou; but it had fatally been repulsed. Commander Kerubino Kuanyin was hysterically determined, at the time, to capture Jekou at all cost, and so, he had enthusiastically been sending every Battalion, beaten off by the enemy back to fire. He was bulldozing forces in the battle in unfavourable terrain and topography, because Jekou is grassless and treeless land, where SPLA had no way of attrition over the one mechanized enemy Battalion that dug itself up in the foxholes. When SPLA assaulted them at night, two things were happening; the SPLA was losing control in the battle, and the enemy was firing up the tracing bullets.

As the SPLA was fighting the Sudan army inside Jekou, the Anya Nya II, who were allied to government's forces were battling it at vanguard. At the peak of dying a reinforcement led by Col Mohammed Balla was sent from Malakal through Nasir to circumvent ambushes, unfortunately, it was interrupted and destroyed by Hippo Battalion at Majok area, killing Colonel Balla, who became the first Sudan army senior to be killed by the SPLA. Also, Hadid Battalion like Hippo Mazala, after returning from Blue Nile under the command of Cdr Francis Ngor Maciec, was tasked to ward off any reinforcement either from Malakal or Nasir.

As each Battalion was being sent back to battle and the enemy kept on destroying them it happened that Bilpam was most destroyed Battalion; the enemy killed and wounded most of its soldiers, reducing the manpower from 1224 to 400 soldiers. Also because of fatigue and great losses many soldiers deserted from Jekou.

SPLM/SPLA: History of Liberation (1983-2005)

On 29 April 1985, large, strong reinforcement under Lt. Col. Gatluak Deng Garang, a Southerner on the side of government in excellent camouflage arrived Jekou, hammering the SPLA, leading to subsequent withdrew in definitively or defeated according to the Sudan's army historians.

After the withdrawal from Jekou, and moving to distance areas of Mangok, Thiajok and Bukteng, Sudan army sent its rear-guard, the AN II to pinch the SPLA. Indeed, they came and scorpion-stung the SPLA, and bed-bugging in the villages. In those skirmishes AN II killed Cdr Francis Ngor-Maciec, the first SPLA senior commander to die in the war. The circumstances surrounding his death were unclear, some sources allegedly claimed, he was intentionally sent into a danger as a way of elimination him by some elements in the movement leadership.

In summary, Jekou was a military disaster. The failure to capture Jekou, brought up many school of talks, debates and analysis of what has happened, resulting into crisis of blame-games, scapegoatism and scuffles. And why actually the battle failed? The failure was attributed to different reasons (1) inexperience's of the SPLA Commanders, for example, most the commanders have no war experiences and never command largest forces as it was in Jekou, especially Commander Kerubino Kuanyin, who was, in May 1983, commanding company of 200 soldiers in Pochalla and by sudden and meteorite, he was commanding 5000 soldiers in April 1985 (2) application of the Mao Tse-Tung's Theory of the Battle, the SPLA officers were applying the Chinese philosopher Mao Tse –Tung's theory of battle:

In every battle, concentrate an absolutely superior forces (two, three, four and sometimes even five or sixth times the enemy's strength..., strive to avoid battles of attrition in which we lose more than we gain or even break.[6]

Absolutely, this Mao's theory was the one applied and indeed it became inconsistent, incoherent and incompatible with the SPLA battle of Jekou. The Sudan army had one mechanized Battalion with manpower of 840 soldiers, had four Saladin tanks and other Russian-made weapons like Gronov heavy machines gun, while the SPLA had AK 47, AK 46 and RPG 7 only. Here there was imbalance in term of armament between the SPLA and SPDF. Some soldiers said, Cdr Kerubino was telling the forces that the hollow of the barrel of a gun is filled, meaning more soldiers should attack so that more could be killed and the rest captured Jekou.

Through lack of experience and incompatible theory of battle, Comrade Kerubino allowed more than 5000 soldiers to fight 800 soldiers for three months, in unfavourable terrain. In addition, the tactics used in the battle were against the SPLA doctrine of guerrilla harassment, semi-conventional warfare in Manifesto. There was also a hostile environment; the local population was not supporting the SPLA. In this, they were not providing food or information to SPLA command, to help them in the decision making. The Battle of Jekou is incorporated in the Sudan's Military College's curriculum under topic entitled 'Bad Tactics and Bad Command'.

The Arrest of Officers

At the end of the battle of Jekou, all forces had arrived Thiajok, where hunger struck them. They stayed for six days without food. Some soldiers shot birds down to eat them. Some went to swamp, pulled out and chewed the roots of apai grass. At this time, the rumours were reaching Bilpam that Koryom forces intentionally refused to capture Jekou and deserted because of what Martin Majier said that the war was going to finish Bor people. An Ethiopian pilot called Michael was sent by Helicopter to Thiajok on fact finding mission, he was sent not to land, but to hover in air, and see whether the soldiers are there or they have escaped. When he came, he saw many soldiers down, he landed and loaded off 20 bags of maize and 5 bags of bean. As the forces were in Thiajok, another rumour emerged, security officers wrote to SPLA HQs in Bilpam that some officers were staging a coup against John Garang, and installing Martin Majier as new leader of movement.

A decision was taken by SPLM/A leadership to arrest coup plotters. Commander Kerubino Kuanyin was ordered to return to Thiajok and arrested the coup plotters, but he refused, saying Bor people were the one, who fought with him in Malual Chaat on May 16, and secondly, they fought whole heartedly in Jekou. He was left as defying the order, and William Nyuon was now sent to arrest them, he went to Thiajok. He called a meeting of all officers, in the meeting all pistols were collected, and he said: "There are some military officers here in this tukul, who are working with politicians. These people, when they are not in the leadership or in power, they sabotage. I am going to read their names out now; Lt. Maker Thong Maal, Lt. Jok Aring, Lt. Chol Gai Arou, Lt Majok Chol Nei, Lt. Ateny Mayen Deng, Lt Achiek Anot Deng, Lt Mach Guguei Kucha, Lt. Tuor Alier among others. All Bor South officers were arrested. A Platoon, to escort them was already prepared and came, put them in truck, taking them to Bilpam.

It is allegedly said, it was John Garang, who ordered their arrest, after confirming their arrest, he cunningly left for Cuba as he was not aware of the arrest, where he spent one month. Behind in Bilpam, General intelligence and security (GIS) charged them with: (1) mutiny (2) desertion (3) of staging a coup. In detention two officers Majok Chol Nei and Ateny Mayen Deng were tortured to death. According to officers, they denied all the three charges of desertion, mutiny and staging the coup or rebelling, they said, this was just a concocted plan by, GIS, who had personal vendetta or the prejudices for nothing, 'If we desert, why were arrested in Thiajok? The SPLA base. If we deserted, we would have been arrested somewhere not, Thiajok. If we stage a coup, why wouldn't we shoot people?'

When John Garang returned from Cuba, he ordered the release of all the officers. And later he himself came to Thiajok, where conceitedly apologised for what had happened, he said, the arrest was mistake, and he released all Koryom forces to Bor, he said you had been staying away from your wife and children for long time. So go home.

After that all Battalions. Lion, Hippo, Bilpam, Elephant and 104/105 were reorganized to tribes and sections. The four battalions, were only from Dinka Bor and Dinka Panaru, All Bor became Lion and Hippo and were released to Bor area while all Dinka Ngok became Bilpam and were released to Panaru

The First Arrest of Justice Martin Majier Gai

Molana Majier was one of the seven founding members of the SPLA/SPLM, sent to Libya as representative in 1984. Getting the news of death of two officers, he came back to Ethiopia, went to Garang, and asked what happened. Garang based on what GIS officers told him, ignored Majier's complaint. Majier kept asking Garang, 'Yego mith nok', what killed the children", according to him, he considered himself a senior politician and elder, this is why he was referring to soldiers as children. Garang became furious and concern about Majier, referring to soldiers as children. According to Garang, he said Majier was undermining him. Garang and Majier quarrelled over the death of, two officers. After their quarrels the two were now on open opposition to one another, beginning to make cynical remarks about each other. One time, Garang was allegedly quoted addressing euphemistically recruits in Bonga: 'There are people, who are used to hijacking leadership of others, here in the SPLM/A, what happened in Anya Nya I and after Addis Abba agreement, will never happen again. Some people acquire themselves nyogora asaya (simple stick) and call themselves politicians and they keep asking 'how many of our sons are in training centre now?' They will wait until they die'. Although Garang did not mention Majier by name, he was actually referring to him, because (1) Majier refused to go to military training, on the condition that, he is politician (2) Abel Alier became the President of Southern Sudan, instead of Joseph Lagu who was in the bush, while Abel Alier was not (3) There was a belief and fear, if peace come Majier will replace Garang as Alier replaced Lagu. Also Majier was quoted in his own forum, making his own cynical remarks about Garang, in that forum, it is allegedly said, Majier said, 'let Garang liberate the country first and I will contest against him in an election and we shall see, who will win? Garang is nothing to me in politics'. It is alleged, there was undeclared power struggle between Majier and Garang.

It is allegedly claimed that Majier and Garang quarrelled over many issues and many times before he (Garang) arrested Majier. The five quarrels came about like this (1) in 1984, Benjamin Bol Akok died in Addis Abba and he was put in coffin, Majier asked for the coffin to be opened, this was denied by Garang and they quarrelled over this. (2) When Koryom Division was graduated, Majier said, they should not be sent to frontline, because they were from one ethic group and they quarrelled over this (3) Majier called for separation of the role of the SPLA from the SPLM, they quarrelled over this (4) Majier called for the detention of the GIS officers, who tortured to death the two officers, Garang rejected and they quarrelled. (5) Garang claimed Majier wrote to Mengistu, explaining local issue that, an international figure like Mengistu could not understand. They quarrelled over that

At last, Garang arrested Majier, charging him of reactionary views in the movement according to his all Unit message of 1985, he said Majier has demonstrated clear attempt to overthrow him in a coup, In Garang's narrative, he said, Majier was forming his government in Itang refugee camp.

Muor Muor Division's Graduation

Muor Muor Division, the SPLA centre gravity, was the second largest division to Koryom, Muor Muor means 'small red biting ant that move in thousand' in Dinka language. Comprising of eight Battalions; Abushok, Nile, Neiran, Wolf, Bee, Tuek Tuek, Shark and Eagle. It has manpower of 9782 soldiers, who were 90% Dinka from Bahr el-Gazal that is Aweil, Gogrial and Tonj districts. They were dispatched into Sudan in four Expeditionary columns.

Kuei (Eagle) Battalion

Eagle Battalion, also known as Kuei in Dinka language, was the first expeditionary column of Muor Muor. It was led by Major Wilson Kur Chol and deputised by Captain Elijah Malok Aleng and under all over supervision of Lt. Col Kerubino Kuanyin Bol. It has six companies, the first, the second, the third, the fourth, the fifth and sixth company, commanding and controlling the companies and platoons were ; Captain Paul Malong Awan, Captain Macham Atem, Lt Magog Magog, Lt Garang Mabil Deng...etc.

As Eagle was sneaking to North, they established base called 'Longkuei' meaning 'the resting place of Eagle' in Dinka. Longkuei becoming big SPLA base and refugee camp. It was in Assosa region of Ethiopia-Sudan border. In Southern Blue Nile, Eagle conducted successful guerrilla warfare, capturing many military bases and out-posts at the peripheries of the Damazin town. It captured Jam, Soda the rear-guard of the Sudan army, defeating the enemy and capturing Colonel Mohammed Abulela Adam at Soda outpost, keeping him prisoner of war (PoW). They annihilated a battalion in that base, capturing many guns that included two piece of Howitzer, 16 piece of

60 mm mortar, 20 piece of 42 light machine and many G-3 rifles. They also seized ammunitions of difference calibre, different shells of mortars and cannons, mines and mine detectors. Eagle Battalion penetrated deep into the enemy territory in wandering guerrilla war force, in which they left Kurmuk and Gissan behind them, and returned to Longkuei, where the established a frontline at Kafaruka near the goldmine. Here they launched raids on surrounding garrison of Juret, Gazin, Mayak, Khor Amr and Khor Yabus.

Nile and Wolf Battalions

Nile and Wolf were the second expeditionary column of Muor Muor that went to Western Upper Nile of Bentiu area. From there Nile proceeded to Bahr el Ghazal.

Nile Battalion was led by Major Paulino Deng Ajuong and deputized by Captain Bangat Aguek. The companies were commanded by officers who included Lt Santino Deng Wol, Lt Charles Dut Akol, Lt Dau Aturjong Nyuol, Lt Akuei Adhal Akuei, Lt Peter Mangok, Lt Osman Akol Deng, Lt Tong Akok aka Menth Nhialic, Lt Clement Majok Wol Akok. In Bahr el Ghazal, Nile attacked Gogrial, capturing and tactically withdrawing to rural area.

Wolf was led by Lt. Col Dr Riek Machar Teny, alternate Member of Politico-Military High Command of SPLA/SPLM. Wolf invaded Nuba Mountain areas of Southern Kordofan, this was second incursion to the North Sudan, the first was in Southern Blue Nile. Wolf attacked Telusi garrison at the eve of Christmas of 1985 and returned to Bentiu area, where it kept raiding, attacking Bentiu, Mayom, and Leer Garrisons in Guerrilla warfare of hit and run from 1986 onward.

Bee and Neiran Battalions

Bee and Neiran Battalions was third expeditionary column that wound to Equatoria in a departing and intersecting movement, it was the second incursion into Equatoria after Zindia Battalion in 1984. Bee was led by Lieutenant Colonel Martin Manyiel Ayuel, alternate Member of PMHC. Its companies were commanded by a number of officers who included Captain Scopas Kenyi, Lt Johnson Juma Okot. Neiran Battalion was led by Major

Tahir Bior Ajak and deputized by Captain Anthony Bol Madut, who were assisted by many officer those included Lt. Anthony Sabayom, Lt Mirchael Ngor Mabior, Lt John Akot Garang, Lt Garang Mayuol Geng, Lt Anei Wol Achien, Lt Kon Micah, Lt Abraham Jongroor Deng, Lt Awuol Deng Awuol, Lt Awur Mawel. Neiran and Bee attacked Kapoata and failed to capture it, then laid siege to it.

Neiran and Bee were faced by several challenges: (1) they were not welcomed whole heartedly by the civil population of Toposa and Dingdinga (2) All of them were Dinka therefore, they treated as alien and invader, this made the chiefs not to collect food for them, they had to use force to get food, (3) they were attacked by the cattle camp youth who want to take guns from them, (4 the Equatorian politicians were inciting civilians not to corporate with forces, by calling the SPLA war as reaction to Korkora of 1983. Neiran and Bee had really faced hardest time in Eastern Equatoira. This made SPLA leadership to release them home, to Bahr el Ghazal in 1987, when Tingli and Kalany Battalions who were made up of 90% Equatorian arrived in the area. The achievements of Neiran and Bee were; (1) reactivating the presence of the SPLA in Equatoria after both withdrawals of Agreb around Kapoata in 1986 and Zindia around Torit in 1985, (2) opening of Nairus as the first SPLA base in Equatoria

Tuek Tuek Battalion

Tuek Tuek and Shark was the fourth expeditionary column of Muor Muor. Tuek Tuek means "wood pecker "in Dinka language. Tuek Tuek was first Battalion of Muor Muor division. It was led by Lt. Col Daniel Awet Akot, alternate member of PMHC, deputized by Peter Wal Athiu. Other officers in the command were; Captain Beda Machar, Captain Molana Deng Arok, Lt Paul Alier Nyok, Lt Mading Kuol Yak. Tuek Tuek wound from Ethiopia to Bahr el-Ghazal through Bor area, Tuek Tuek crossed to Sudan at Tiergol. On July 2, 1985, Tuek Tuek repulsed three consecutive attacks by the AN II at Kacuin area; they also attacked Akoba Garrison, particularly capturing it and tactically withdraw in to the bush. After they arrived in Bor. Tuek Tuek attacked many enemy positions in Bor of Langbar, Pakaw and Cuei Atem Beny, which were at round defence position. On 19 September 1985, they moved to Malek, here they crossed the river Nile to Bahr el Ghazal.

In Bahr el Ghazal, Tuek Tuek made fabulous military offensive in guerrilla warfare. It attacked Rumbek, Tonj and destroyed the enemy convoy on its way to Rumbek in the famous ambush and Battles of Ajak-Agau. While Shark led by Bona Bak Dhol reinforced other Koryom, who were in Acara Alif or Battle of Ten Thousand.

Subur Zaida: The Juba-Bor Road Front, 1985

Subur Zaida, commonly called Acara Alif by SPLA, was the series of ambushes, laid by Koryom forces, and their subsequent battles fought against them, by the Sudan's army on Juba-Bor road from 10th June to 24th November 1985. It had been the first major front in the 21 year civil war. At end of 1984, the SPLA had completely blockaded Bor-Juba road, no vehicles, barges or people were travelling between either on the road, on the water or in the air. Koryom had been ambushing the vehicles, destroying the barges and shooting down planes.

To open Juba – Bor road, the Sudan's army nominated out ten thousand soldiers from Northern Command, giving them refresher training in Shambat, a suburb of Khartoum. At their graduation, they named themselves "Lika Shambat" meaning " Shambat Encountering" in Arabic. The forces were air-lifted to Juba by planes, where they were prepared for the campaign to open up Juba- Bor road, After all their combat readiness were sealed, President Nimieri, in republican decree appointed retired Major General Ali Ali Saleh as the commander of forces and in similar decree, he named the the campaign 'Subur Zaida', meaning 'Extreme Patience or Resilient' in Arabic. In his state of union address to the Sudanese people, Mr Nimieri said, he had been patient enough with John Garang and that he had been trying to resolve the conflict peacefully and Garang was abusing his good intention by showing his muscles to him, therefore, he had run out of patient and, he launched Subur Zaida. He said the campaign has six objective: (1) to reopen Juba-Bor road, blocked by SPLA forces (2) reinforce Bor forces, who were under besiege by SPLA (3) delivering food and ammunitions to Bor garrison (4) to uproot and crush the SPLA around Bor and the whole of Jonglei (5) to end rebellion and closing the borders, and arrest any escaping SPLA soldiers, and lastly (6) to capture the Radio SPLA, and bring its studio's equipment to Khartoum, where they will be destroyed in public ceremony, celebrating the victory

SPLM/SPLA: History of Liberation (1983-2005)

over SPLA.

In early June, the great expeditionary forces started, marching to Bor. SPLA interrupted their coming. Thus, Hadid, Raad, Cobra and Lion Battalions were sent, to deflect them Koryom forces ushered into contact with Lika Shambat forces on June 10 in Doma Jana, South of Gemeza, and fiercest battle took place. Liika Shambat was pushed back. From June to November 24, 1985, the SPLA fought seven major battles against Sudan army at Jananuke, Gemmeza, Diaar, Panyang, Pan Modi, Goi and Panpadiar, Malual Agorbarn, and finally Subur Zaida entered triumphantly to Bor at 3 pm on November 24, 1985, firing up the tracing bullet in celebrating their victory. However, the victory was at highest in human casualties, loss in materials and time. It took them six months from Gemmeza to reach Bor, which is 45 kilometres from each, "it is easy to go to Tel Aviv than Bor" a soldier from Subar Zaida said after entering Bor. After the entry, the SPLA force withdrew to Kolyang area, the SPLA had lost 600 men and 1500 wounded.

Shark Battalion, which reinforced Koryom were released, to go to their home area in Bahr el-Ghazal. Shark went and attacked Rumbek, in the battle of Rumbek, Sergeant Garang Ayor, one of air defence sharp shooters, shot down helicopter over Rumbek.

The Martyrdom of Ngacigak Ngaciluk

After the liberation of Boma garrison in April 1985 by Agreb forces under the command of Lt. Col Ngacigak, Agreb also proceeded to Equatoria, invading the Kapoeta area, whereby the enemy inside Kapoeta garrison, came out encountered them outside. The heavy fighting took place in Rwoto area of Toposa. As the SPLA was engaging the Sudan army at rear-guard, they were attacked at vanguard by Toposa tribal militia, who were allied to the government, in that confused fighting, where one did not know, real direction of enemy led to killing of Lt. Col Ngacigak Ngachuluk, the second most senior officer to be killed in the war after Lt. Col Francis Ngor Maciek. It was in the same scenario like the one Lt Francis Ngor was killed, involving the AN II and Sudan army

Lt. Col Kuol Manyang replaced Lt. Col Arok Thon,

In December 1985, Lt Col Kuol Manyang Juuk, an alternate member of PMHC replaced Lt. Col Arok Thon Arok, one of five permanent members of PMHC of SPLA/SPLM as overall commander of Koryom forces in Bor. Lt. Col Kuol Manyang, who was wounded in Battle of Jekou, returned to Ethiopia in March 1985, where he was reorganized again with Aquila Manyuon Battalion. Cdr Kuol took the command of Koryom force at a ceremony at Pabek near Duk, Lt. Col Arok was called back to Ethiopia, after he had successfully conducted many battles, and ambushes, which took him up to Owiny-Kibul, when returning, he almost died of thirst. He also commanded operation of Subur Zaida or the battles of Ten thousand between Juba-Bor roads, the first longest battles, fought by the SPLA.

Notes
1. SPLM Manifesto, 31 July 1983
2. Sartre p. 595
3. Ibid p.593
4. Ibid p.596
5. Mao Tse – Tung, People's War, Peter A French, Exploring Philosophy, Schenkmam Publishing Company Inc, Cambridge Massachustle pp.226-227

CHAPTER 4

ZONAL COMMAND AND AXIS COMMAND, 1986-1989

Two First Zonal Commands

After dispatching Koryom and Muor Muor Divisions to different parts of Southern Sudan to conduct a guerrilla warfare of hit and run tactics, mobilizing the recruits and politicizing the masses about the ideology of the SPLA/SPLM as grandest strategies of destroying the Old Sudan and reconstituting in its ashes the democratic, secular, socialist, united, New Sudan, and forces subsequently returning to their home areas after facing several challenges. Those going-backs to home areas by the soldiers had made the largest number of soldiers' presence in two areas, that is, Koryom forces in Bor and Muor Muor forces in Bahr el Ghazal. This prompted the SPLA/SPLM leadership to create permanent presence in these two areas by establishing two zones, namely; Central Southern Sudan Zonal Command (CSSZC), which was commanded by Lt. Col Kuol Manyang Juuk with its headquarters at Baidit in Bor and Northern Bare el Ghazal Zonal Command (NBZC) commanded by L.t Col Daniel Awet Akot with its headquarters in Gomchok. It was worth mentioning that, before these forces returned to their own homes, they achieved almost 80 % of the objectives, they were sent for, that is conducting guerrilla warfare of hit and run tactics, those small hit and run attacks were amplified by the Radio SPLA as its ultimate goals of the war of propaganda. They mobilized the recruits, who went to training centres in Ethiopia. They persuaded the masses until they supported the national liberation movement by feeding the soldiers with food and supplying new recruits into its rank and files.

Central Southern Sudan Zonal commands (CSSZC)

Baidit GHQs of CSSZC lies 35 kilometres North of Bor Garrison, where the Sudan army is stationed with aggressive posture toward the SPLA. Bor has three main roads leading to it. On each road the SPLA set up a frontline across, blockading all of the roads and these were on; Bor-Kongor-Malakal road, Bor – Pibor, Bor- Juba. The CSSZC put up a frontline at Duk, on far north of Bor, to block the enemy coming from Malakal, Wat or Ayod garrison. Another frontline was at Panwel, far south of Bor, this was to repulse the enemy coming from Juba. Bor was constantly raided, shelled from four directions, from toch (swamp) west bank of the Nile, from east, south and north. By July 1986, there was no man or woman leaving or going to Bor. There were no barges leaving or going to Bor on the River Nile. There was no plane landing too. It was at time that the sharp shooter Sergeant Majier Mayom had shot down a plane that was bringing food. As the result of blockade, the Sudan army soldiers were starving, they had to eat dogs, cats, rats and leaves of trees and old hides on the beds. When the plane would drop the food from air, sometime, food could fall outside the town where the SPLA could take it.

False Socialism

SPLA/M was prototype of Soviet socialism or communism. They called themselves comrades, meaning sameness in the status, but this not the case. One day Sergeant was on duty and a bull was slaughtered and the culture was, when the bull is slaughtered, stomach's thing like liver, kidneys were called 'mahimat 'meaning 'most important' in Arabic, which were always first brought out and cooked quickly and given to officers as their snack before the main meat is served. The sergeant on duty that day did not give the mahima to officers, but mixed them in main meat.
When mahimat delayed, he was called by the officer on duty and asked:

'Where are the mahimat?'
'I distributed them to all soldiers and are mixed in the meat all"
'Why?'
'We are all comrades and we are the same and we must eat the same thing'.
'Who told you? We are same'
'It is John Garang'
'What is your rank?'
'I am sergeant'
'What about Garang? What is his rank?'
'He is Colonel'
'Then, why are you Sergeant and not a Colonel like Garang, take him to prison, he is stupid!' barked the officer.

The sergeant was jailed because, he said a hard fact.

CSSZC became one of the first SPLA well-organized and well-established zone under Kuol Manyang, creating the first good Civil-Military Administration (CMA), which collected food from the civil population to the SPLA in form of sorghum, maize, simsim, aliop and bulls, unlike before that, the SPLA was using force to get food from civil population. The food and bulls were collected from civilians through the chiefs of the villages. Here, the SPLA/SPLM Disciplinary and Penal Code of 1984 was first justly or unjustly applied inside Sudan in deciding civil, criminal and military cases by Revolutionary Tribunal set up by Cdr Kuol Manyang.

Rioting of Lion Battalion

After the CSSZC abolished, outlawed the grabbing of food by force from civil population and introduced the Nyin Anya-Anya policy, which means 'a turn of donating food to Anya-Nya', In that policy, the chiefs were ordered to collect every types of food, goats, sorghum or cows. As the result of the colleting cattle as food of SPLA, there were a good number of cows available in the SPLA bases now. Among these cows, some officers from Lion Battalion picked out some beautiful, young and milking cows, and took them to their own homes. This form of corruption in forces inflamed some soldiers and they rioted. The soldiers rioted and arrested five officers. The soldiers tortured the officers whom they accused of stealing the cows.

In torturous method, they poured the pebble of sand into their eyes, and they mocked and challenged them to see through anus. When the news of rioting and detention in Lion Battalion at Poktap reached Cdr Kuol Manyang. Kuol went to Poktap, and ordered the soldiers to put down their guns and released the officers. The soldiers refused to lay down their guns. One of the soldiers snatched the Radio Call from Kuol's guard.

Cdr Kuol returned to Baidit, he upgraded the riot to coup level and ordering for more forces, and sending them to arrest the soldiers with orders, 'if they refuse, shoot them'. The forces moved in and disarmed the Lion forces, during their disarming two soldiers were shot and killed on spot. And other soldiers were peacefully disarmed. The whole force was sent into disciplinary training course in Panyagor. As the period of training course was about to end, Cdr Kuol went to Panyagor and called out one soldier called Panchol, who was accused as a ringleader of the riot (since the riot was upgrade to level coup). As simple as joke, it was allegedly said Cdr Kuol ordered Panchol's hands to be tied backward and in front of the soldiers, he ordered them to fire squad him, he was fired squad, dead . When Kuol called another soldier called Amel, Amel collapsed. 'You did thing badly, and you just collapsed when you are not touched even', Cdr Kuol said and he spared Amel. Panchol became the second soldier to be executed after another soldier called Jok Gai, who was executed by firing squad after he accidently killed four civilians in dance ground.

Execution of Three Women

In 1986 CSSZC had banned the travel between Bor town and villages. No one was coming from Bor and no one going to it. However, the people in villages were in need of salt. So, some women had been sneaking into Bor and came out with salt. Unfortunately, two women were caught by the SPLA reconnaissance, detained within few days; sadly, executed by firing squad at Paluer base to set example. This shocked the civil population, from there, no one ever attempted to go to Bor anymore.

SPLA- Mundari conflict: where did the buck stop?

In 1984, Raad Battalion went to Mangalla through Mundari areas, attacking Mangalla, capturing it and tactically withdrawing. At time, there was no problem between Mundari tribe and SPLA. The Mundari chiefs were collecting bulls, goats, and groundnuts to SPLA as their food. The SPLA established two bases in Mundari area, one in west of Nile in Tombek and the other in east of Nile at Gemmeza, which the SPLA abandoned and returned to Bor area, their stronghold.

In May 1986, the CSSZC sent three companies to Mundari area again under the command of Major Thon Ayiei Jok. The objectives of the mission were (1) to mobilize Mundari youth to go to training centre in Bilpam and (2) to conduct raid at the west of Juba City. When the SPLA soldiers arrived at the area, they found Mundari militia men already recruited by the government to act as the rear guard of the Sudan Army. This militia man began ambushing SPLA and fighting them. As result of ambushes and skirmishes between the SPLA and the militia men, fighting spilled over, and the major conflict broke out between the SPLA and Mundari youth. The Mundari youth claimed that, they were humbled by the SPLA behaviours in their community, and joined government soldiers, and fought the SPLA. This prompted the SPLA forces under Major Thon Ayiei, to conduct a limited military operation against the both militiamen and local youth. In that fighting, about 2,000 cattle were raided from Mundari cattle camps. Some elements of Dinka Bor cattle camp youth also joined in conducting their own parallel operations against Mundari cattle camps, raiding their cows. In Mundari land, there were fighting, in those fighting's, SPLA and Bor youth were on one side, and Sudan Army and Mundari youth were on other side. The war took place in Terekaka area, about 100 kilometres from Baidit, the HQs of CSSZC, where Cdr Kuol Manyang Juuk was staying.

As the fighting intensified, one Mundari chief called Lagoya, of Gabuta area with one Bor man, Awan Ajak, who settled with his cows and family in Mundariland went to Kuol Manyang in Baidit, reporting and narrating, what was happening in Terekaka. Cdr Kuol ordered the ceasefire and stopped the mobilization together. After the fighting was stopped, three soldiers stole about 20 cows and rushed them to their village in Bor. These soldiers were arrested and charged with two count of crimes (1) Desertion (2) Stealing of cows. The two soldiers, who hailed from the Kolnyang area of Bor, were allegedly tried, sentenced to death and executed by firing squad.

Major Thon Ayiei's Case: The Justice Overweighed the Crime
In relation to the operation in Mundari area, Major Thon Ayiei was arrested allegedly charged with; (1) ordering of firing squad of two soldiers, (2) failed the mission, he was a sent for, (3) he allowed the soldiers to raid Mundari cows, and took some cows himself, (4) disobeying his superiors in military. He was tried several times, in his first trial, he was stripped off his rank, and dismissed from the SPLA. That verdict of the first trial was not approved by the SPLA leadership, arguing that, if he was released in community, he would defect to government and form his own movement. In second trial, he was sentenced to death by firing squad. This second verdict was approved by SPLAM/A leadership and Major Thon was taken from Baidit HQs to Panyagor in Twic area, where he was executed by the firing squad, making him the first senior SPLA to die by fire squad. Major Thon was taken to his death place, with about ten other officers, who were accused of different crimes, some who sold guns, others stolen cows, and disobedience. These officers included comrade Major Andrew Anhiem Aliet, who was transferred from Northern Bahr el Gazal Zonal Command (NBZC), where he was facing death row to Bor, Captain Garang Ngang Abui and many others who were later cut out off from the rope of death.

Major Thon Ayii Jok's execution was politically motivated or prompted by undeclared power struggle in CSSZC. He was unfairly tried and executed because of self-explanatory. The crime claimed to have been committed by Major Thon, which was politicized as tainting the image of SPLA leadership, was first committed by SPLA in 1983/4.

First, it was claimed that Major Thon ordered execution of the two soldiers, who stole cows and deserted. This was not true because the SPLA Penal Code of 1984, punish desertion with death. Second, it was claimed that Major Thon raided the Mundari tribe cows. This was not, in fact, raiding of cows was not crime because SPLA raided 1,000 cows in Bilpam from Anya Nya II in September 1983. And in the subsequent war of the SPLA against Anya Nya II, about 3,000 cows of Nuer were taken by SPLA, these cattle were kept in Itang as cattle camp of the movement. These cows were stolen by senior commanders, and given in their marrying woman in Itang. They claimed Major Thon ordered the attack of Mundari villages,

Thon's forces were fighting Mundari militia men. SPLA was attacking Nuer civilians when the SPLA was fighting the AN II. No one was held accountable for the death of Nuer civilians.

Lastly, there was one true charge against Major Thon that is disobeying of his superiors; this was the true charge against him. Major Thon disobeyed Garang's order in 1984, when he was ordered to go to Bentiu with Timsah and Tiger Battalions. Major Thon refused and Paul Dor Lumpur was instead sent to Bentiu. This disobedience of the orders could not warrant his death, but, some good number of years in prison. However, the SPLA leadership had the dilemma of the other mind problem, because it was said, if his rank were stripped off and set free, he might go and form his own parallel movement.

Rainbow Operation

In 1986, CSSZC chief Kuol Manyang planned the Rainbow Operation, first SPLA operation codenamed; it was the extension of Koryom operations around Bor to Equatoria. The operation started in the both west and east of Juba. At the east of Juba, SPLA attacked Radio Juba station at Gumbo, destroying all the equipment; this led to the shifting of the Radio station from there. In the west, SPLA attacked Juba international airport, destroying some planes on the ground at night. From there, the forces moved westwards. These forces were commanded by many officers who included; Captain Achol Deng Achol aka Achol Malual, Captain Kur Deng Kur-keny, Captain Garang Ngang Abui, Captain Mathiang Aluong. The forces attacked Wuduroba, Lainya, Terekaka and Kagwada in guerrilla warfare of hit and run tactic. This was the first in incursion of SPLA into western Equatoria.

The Koka Dam Declaration, 1986

After the overthrow of President Nimeri as a result of combine effect of escalation of the war and political pressure from masses, two parties' alliance under the National Alliance for National Salvation (NANS) contacted the SPLA/SPLM to work for the possible way of bringing the war to an end. The NANS delegation was led by Dr. Khalid Haji who came and met with Dr. John Garang at Koka Dam Town in Ethiopia. The two sides agreed on the Principles of the Declaration (DoP) as the framework for the agreement, which includes; (1) the problem in Sudan is not 'Southern Problem' but 'National Problem', (2) lifting of the state of emergency, (3) repeal of the September laws or the Sharia laws, (4) adoption of the 1956 constitution etc. In May, 1986, elections were organized in the Sudan by Transitional Military Council (TMC) and Sadig al-Mahdi won the election and became the Prime Minister Replacing Field Marshall Sowar al-Dohad. Prime Minister al-Mahdi rejected, what was agreed upon in Koka Dam Declaration between the SPLA/SPLM and NANS. In his meeting with John Garang in Addis Abba, at the side-lines of Organization for Africa unity (OAU). He rejected the DoP.

The Axis Fronts-1986

After the failure of Koka Dam peace talks and its rubbishing of the principles of declaration (PoD) and the subsequence declaration of all-out war in dry season offensive by Sadiq al – Mahdi. In its response, Chairman John Garang called the five permanent members of SPLA/M Politico-Military High Command (PMHC) for a meeting in Zinc near Gambella. In that meeting, the strategic operational and structural organization were introduced. The three structures of command and operation were decided upon; (a) Axis command was created and to be headed by the member of PMHC, (b) Zonal command was expanded to zones and to be headed by the alternate members of PMHC (c) Battalion formation was abolished and replaced with Task Force formation. Following resolution of the Zinc Meeting, John Garang formed five axes, each was to be headed by one of five member of PMHC.

> The enemy is desperate and has launched and will continue to launch fierce and massive offensives during this dry season in their futile attempt to crush the SPLA. This is wishful thinking as the enemy plan cannot succeed. However, we must take the challenge very seriously and avoid the same mistakes of wishful thinking that the enemy will fail while we do not take appropriate required action. The enemy offensive must be contained and repulse and our own major offensive launched by the beginning of rain. This military situation demands that all members of SPLA/M High Command be physically present in the field during the

whole of the dry season to direct the operation[1].
The axes were as follows: Axis One – Pochalla-Pibor- Bor- commands by John Garang or the Thunder, Axis Two is Dajo - Maban –Malut commanded by Kerubino Bol or Dragon, Axis Three is Jekou- Nasir-Ulang commanded by William Nyuon Bany, Axis Four is Raad- Boma-Kapoeta-Torit command by Salva Kiir, Axis Five is Akobo –Wat- Ayod was commanded by Arok Thon or giraffe. The overall objective was to liberate the whole east Nile of southern Sudan from Nimule to Renk by 31 December 1987 while intensifying guerilla and semi-conventional warfare on the west Nile, southern Kordofan and southern Blue Nile. Success of this plan will shift our logistic stating point on the Nile by the end of 1987.[2]

Kazuk Division, 1986

As Muor Muor graduated from training in 1985, Kazuk Division moved in to training centre in Bonga. Kazuk means "problem" in Arabic. In 1986, it graduated with more 3500 soldiers ; which were organized into Kalany, Zalan, Rajaf, Tahrir, Namus, Mut, Tingli, Joseph Okuen, Boma and Mazulum task forces . Mazulum Task Force was led by Major Daniel Deng Alony and deputised by Captain Moses Dhiieu Chol. Kalany Task Force led by Captain Akol Kuol and other like Lt Gai Chol, Lt Marol Mangok. Zalan Task Force was led by Captain Andrew Anhiim Aliet and assisted by; Lt Philip Ayuen, Lt Peter Maduok, and Lt Maliech Mangar.

Tingli Task Force

Tingli, from Kazuk Division, was the first SPLA force comprised entirely of Equatoria's sons. It was named after Tingli desert, where these gentle; strong young thirsted, about hundreds of them died of thirst in March 1985. It was commanded by Glario Modi Hurinyang, one of the Alternate members of PMHC and deputised Captain Obote Mamur. It carried out guerrilla warfare by raiding Kapoeta, Torit and Lofon in 1987. In the battle of Torit, many soldiers were killed including Captain James Jada.

Fall of Pochalla: The Effect of Military Demonstration

Three task forces of Kazuk Division went to Axis one. Joseph Okuen TF, named after Commander Joseph Okuen, who was killed in the first civil war of Anya Nya I in 1960s, Okuen hailed from Anuak tribe. The force was named Okuen because most of the soldiers were from Anuak tribe. Boma TF was named after Boma Mountain Plateau, because most of the soldiers were Kacipo and Murle tribes in Boma. The three forces stage biggest spectacular, and threatening military demonstration outside Pochala garrison. The three task forces marched to the nearest enemy fox-holes at nine o'clock in the morning, without firing at enemy, but moving with hugest and harassing posture. They went and camped two kilometres from the enemy fox-holes, cooking their food. At night, the enemy in Pochalla withdrew without single bullet shot. The withdrawal marked the beginning of success and victories of SPLA from 1989 to 1990

The Fall of Pibor

Col. Dr. John Garang de Mabior, the commander of Axis One, addressed the combined forces of Koryom, Kazuk, Zalzal in Pochalla, boosting their morale by explaining the external situation of the enemy and their internal situation. He also explained the objectives of the SPLA/M of waging protracted war. On February 15th, 1987, the sand model of liberating Pibor was designed and it was attacked. Forces were led by officers of Koryom; Captain Madul Kang Jang, Captain Kennedy Gayain, Captain Malong Akau, Captain Jurkuch Barach and Captain Pitia. The first attack was on Febrary 27 1987 that assault failed to capture it. Several attacks were carried out till Pibor fell down to SPLA forces on March 3rd, 1987. The Murle pro-government militia almost disrupted the battle when they attacked the SPLA behind, but fortunately SPLA forces drove away all militiamen

Zalzal Division, 1987

As Kazuk Division graduated from training, the new group of recruits called Zalzal Division entered Bonga training centre in January 1986 and graduating in March 1987. It was made up of Zalzal I and II. Zalzal mean "earth quake" in Arabic. It was comprised of many Task Forces- Mujunu TF, Lazim TF, Tagkayany TF, Shakush TF, Kasha TF, Shoki TF, Bunia TF, Dem TF, Kokap TF, Mushasha TF etc. The Task Forces were commanded by; Captain Maciek Akucpiir, Captain Solomon Adier Deng,

SPLM/SPLA: History of Liberation (1983-2005)

Captain Agustsio Akol Tong, Captain Riny Lual Riny and Captain Alfred Lado Gore. The combines' forces of Kazuk, Zalzal and Commando forces captured Jekou at last in 1987. Majunu TF spearheaded the battle, this was second battle of Jekou, the first battle of Jekou occurred in 1985 which became military disaster for SPLA.

Longkuei-Addis Abba Crisis, 1987

Longkuei-Addis Abba crisis was the second crisis, rocking and shaking the SPLA/SPLM after Itang-Jekou crisis that culminated in the detention of Martin Majier Gai and Joseph Oduho, since inception, the movement in 1983. The SPLA launched its counteroffensive to defeat Sadig al-Mahdi's dry season offensive in 1987. The Axis Commands were created to encounter, repulse and contain enemy in as many fronts as possible, therefore, Deputy Chairman and Deputy Commander in Chief of SPLM/A Kerubino Kuanyin Bol was assigned to Axis II Command, that is the War Zone II, the North Sudan.

In Zinc meeting, where Fronts were created and each member assigned accordingly, Comrade Kerubino accepted the assignment with all his heart without any reservation, and he went to Southern Blue Nile front. In Southern Blue Nile, the problem arisen, Comrade Kerubino Kuanyin was accused of rebellion. There were different unconfirmed versions and allegations of what exactly happened in Longkuei? There were also different reasons given of why it happens too?

The first and official version of SPLA/M leadership, claimed that when Cdr Kerubino arrived at Longkuei, he did not begin the war first, he camped, encircled himself in round defence in Longkuei refugee camp at Sudan- Ethiopian border, and began eating the boat, the cat-rat story as narrated by John Garang. In this version, he rebelled and declared himself the leader of the movement from there; he began to write radio massages back to SPLA GHQs putting forward some conditions after condition as a prerequisite for his successful military operation in his Axis. In fact, this communication between Cdr Kerubino at Longkuei in Southern Blue Nile and SPLA/M office in Addis Abba escalated into biggest problem that became known as Longkuei-Addis Abba Crisis.

The second version claimed, some officers from Kerubino's home-area came from Addis Abba to Longkuei and persuaded him to rebel and he rebelled, he staged a coup. It is allegedly claimed, these officers, knowingly or unknowingly provoked Kerubino to rebel.

It is claimed also some politicians told him, that Garang has hijacked his leadership in the first place. That he was the one who spearheaded the Bor Mutiny, but Garang was not respecting him. Look! They said, when people from your home area arrived, they were not promoted and given higher the rank they have, however, when people from Garang's home area arrived, they were promoted.

In those days when Kerubino had imbibed, he would exclaim, "My Revolution with Bor Boys', in reference to Bor Mutiny, because, the company of Battalion 105, which resisted the transfer to the North, and that was attacked from Juba, and finally leading to formation of SPLA, was manned by soldiers from Bor only. It is claimed that, another officer from Kerubino's home area, brought from Addis Abba, what he claimed to be, "Garang's Note on D-Day", and copy of a newspaper, where John Garang said, he came to Bor, to bail out Kerubino after he embezzled the money. The officer told Kerubino, 'You always brag and loud-mouth about May 16 as the revolutionary day, look, this is, what Garang is saying about May 16. Garang says, May 16 is not Honour Day, the honour day is the August 18th, May 16th is the just a day of those who embezzled the money, whom I came and bailed out'. This inflamed Comrade Kerubino and he insulted John Garang, it is allegedly said, he said, 'what is Garang? Garang said he is Colonel but in 1983, he came without single soldier, he will see, I throw his head '.

The third version claimed that the problem between Garang and Kerubino was administrative issue not political one, it is claimed that. Some money was brought from Cuba, Kerubino was given his share, he finished, and he asked more money. This resulted in the quarrel between John Garang and himself. In that quarrels, they exchanged bad words, Garang declared that Kerubino has rebelled and he had to be purged.

The fourth version claimed, at Longkuei, Kerubino began to write radio massages as the prerequisite to start the war fighting in War Zone II, one after another. The first condition was that he needed the big weapons. The second condition was that Baggara Arab militia, the Muhraleen were finishing his people in Bahr el Ghazel, and he wanted to go to Bahr el Ghazal, Garang denied that request, he argued that issue of one going and fight in his home area would bring division in the movement and it would divide the people like what happened during Anya Nya I war, when every region had its own camp different from camps of other region.

The fifth version claimed some soldiers escaped and tried to go to Bahr el Ghazal, and were arrested in Bor and executed by fire squad. Kerubino complained to Garang about this but Garang did not take it seriously.

In Longkuei, Kerubimo was fond of insulting Garang as a weak man, who in 1983, came without soldiers. Garang responded by insulting Kerubino as mad man, and mentally sick. Garang went further after he had detained Kerubino that he had his underground movement before the May 16 Revolution as claimed by Kerubino, this was how the underground movement narrative was talked in existence by Garang. After Kerubino was detained the Radio SPLA staffs were instructed not to mention Kerubino on yearly May 16 celebration.

There was also a problem between Kerubino Kuanyin and Elijah Malok Aleng. Kerubino criticised Malok as man who was '' bitterly opposed to Bor Revolution in 1983" in his letter President Mengistu and like Elijah Malok also criticised Kerubino, in his book 22 years later as a man who stole money and a fugitive from justice.

At the time, there were groups of people, who were moving between Longkuei and Addis Abba, bringing what Garang is saying to Kerubino and what Kerubino is saying to Garang. Garang as philosopher, who knows how to manage people, and finding solutions to any problems, he set up Kerubino, he contacted President Mengistu of Ethiopia, Fidel Castro of Cuba and he told them, what was happening between him and his deputy. Both Presidents Fidel Castro and Mengistu approved the arrest of Kerubino.

Garang came to Kapoeta area to divert attention from Kerubino's issue, and returning secretly to Addis Abba. From there in Addis Abba, President Mengistu contacted Kerubino and asked him, where he had been for some time. Kerubino replied that, he was in frontline in Southern Blue Nile. President Mengistu jokingly warned him 'if you are fighting the war in Blue Nile, don't attack the Roseris Dam, that will bring Egypt into the war and when Egypt come into war, Ethiopia will go into war too. Don't pitted two countries against each other '. Kerubino laughed and replied 'I know Comrade Mengistu ', and he added 'Comrade Mengistu, I have got some serious problems with the Chairman Garang'. Mengistu pretentiously asked 'what is the problem? ' . When Kerubino began narrating to him over the Radio Call, Mengistu interrupted and told him come to Addis Abba to tell him, what the problem between him and Garang was. When he asked of how he would travel to Addis Abba, Mengistu said, he would send a plane. A plane was sent to Assosa. And from, Kerubino was flown to Addis Abba to meet Mengistu. Since it was a set up, he was detained and transferred to Read Detention Centre in Boa Plateau, where two founding members of the SPLA /M, Martin Majier and Joseph Oudh were already being detained indefinitely without charges.

By taking two versions, for example, the first and second versions, that talk of rebellion or coup plot, which are the official SPLA/SPLM versions are implausible because of two reasons (1) Kerubino never attack anyone or arrest anyone as always the case with the coup staging or rebellion making (2) Kerubino did not announce in any media that he overthrow John Garang, therefore, there is no any evidence to prove the rebellion or coup as claim by the SPLA/SPLM leadership, against Kerubino .

The second version of the administrative problem, not a political one, is probable as it has self-evidences that could substantiate it. This version is confirmed by many sources, in *Jungle Chronicles* by Atem Yak Atem, he wrote:

We could hear some angry words being exchange between Kerubino and Martin Manyiel. Kerubino and Gerang locked up in a quarrel and Menyiel had intervened openly chiding Kerubino for doing something wrong he might have done ... Later we learned the quarrel had nothing to do with how the movement was run by Garang, for example, but that the issue was related to unmet and excessive and endless financial demands. In 1987, Kerubino Kuanyin Bol was arrested and detained for allegedly (since he was not tried to prove his innocent or guilty, this is an appropriate way of putting it) plotting to overthrow the leadership of SPLA/M.'[3]

Kerubino's innocence is perhaps proven by many sources, a letter he wrote to president Mengistu, raising ten problems in the movement, substantiated that too. In memo, Kerubino though emotional, still addressed Garang honourable as the comrade Chairman which analytically clarified there was no rebellion or coup but administrative problem, which President Mengistu would have resolved and the movement move forward, however, Kerubino was purged to avoid future occurrence of the same problem of insubordination, rebellion or coup. Kerubino was actually emotional and overreacting in his letter to president Mengistu.

TOP SECRET

Comrade Mengistu Haile Mariam
Chairman of the Provisional Military & Administrative Council
Commander –in-chief of the Revolutionary Army of Ethiopia & Secretary General of the Workers
Party of Ethiopia
Subject: memo on SPLM/SPLA Current Problems.

At the very inception of the movement, we unanimously agreed that comrade Col. Rd. John Gerang be the chairman of SPLM and commander in chief of SPLA. We all bowed to follow the socialist path of development (see the SPLM manifesto). We also agreed to exercise the concept of collective leadership. As trusted friends and comrades, I have to painstakingly tell you that these days. I am in serious conflict with Comrade Col. Rd. John Gerang of how the affairs of the movement are being single handily runs by him. Comrade Col. Dr. John Garang has seriously deviated from the most basic and important principles which we initially agreed upon at the formation of the SPLM/SPLA. Our point of conflict is hereby summarized below as follows.

a.   Absence of collective leadership
b.   Absence of structures
c.   Lack of ideology and revolutionary directions

EXPLANATIONS
1.   Lack of Ideology and Revolutionary Directions
From daily practices of our Chairman it is apparently clear that there is serious deviation in the chosen socialist path of development. This

is reflected by the penetration of the SPLM by imperialist intelligence agent, opportunism in the diplomatic field, promoting reactionary tendency with SPLM/SPLA in command structure and appointment, selling of movement secrets to foreign agencies disregard of the manifesto, hostility to scientific ideology, etc.

2. Decision Making

Collective decision making of the members of the high command is our basic principle. But unfortunately Comrade Col. Dr. John Garang has thrown these in waste basket. He is single-handedly doing almost everything in the movement e.g. selection of cadres for political, military and other technical course, foreign affairs, promotions, formation of committees, dictatorial practices, mostly erroneous decisions and actions.

3. Internal Rules and Regulations

I have been consistently requesting our chairman of the establishment of internal rules and regulations to regulate the functions, responsibilities and accountabilities of the members of high command. This was and is purposely suppressed by the chairman to give himself free hand to do things as he likes without accountabilities.

4. Quarterly Meeting of the High Command

Since the formation of the SPLM/SPLA the five members of the high command rarely meet. They only meet when it pleases the Chairman. As a revolutionary movement there is no need for self-regression of the movement. Our Chairman, knowing that he had deviated, does not want to meet the five members of the high command, leave alone alternate members. Most of all he always practices the policy of pitting one member of the high command against the other i.e. the policy of divide and rule.

5. Appointment to High Command

Chairman appoints the members of high command without consultations or agreement of the rest of members of the high command. Central issue is that he is building a personality cult, by appointing people who can support him to push through his own ideas/interest, a fact rejected by the principles of socialism.

6. Committees

There are no committees with prescribed powers and functions and if any they were only formed by the Chairman. Definitely such committees will only serve the interest of the people who forms them. Good example, is the trade and economic commission which his relative Lt. Col. Elijah Malok [who] was bitterly opposed to the uprising of this very revolution which fruits he is enjoying at this early stage. In a revolutionary like ours, we are supposed to have committees like financial, security committee, foreign affairs committee, education committee, technical committee for the selection of the cadres to various courses etc.

7. Distribution of Military Equipment/ Deployment

It has been practice of the Chairman to distribution ammos, shells, and other military equipment's to his interest. Also the recent one-man no system organization creating Axis of command has reflected perfectly the intention of Chairman. His Axis has been most favoured in terms of military equipment, armament and deployment of forces. Other axis despite of the size and the prevalent dangers, were poorly equipped and with limited forces. The intention is to reflect that other members of high command have failed to achieve success and his were the only successful ones. This selfishness does not serve the purpose this revolution was founded for.

8. Equality

Despite the fact that we are fighting to establish a democratic system in the Sudan whereby equality and justice are the right of every individual, it is absurd that Comrade Chairman still displays the act of favouritism, nepotism and tribalism. Most of the people whom he chooses to go for course are hand-picked base either on blood relation or association. Another example is that recently one of his close relative, Lt. Col. Elijah Malok, committed a crime and disobeyed my orders. Consequently,

I ordered his arrest. Without same the chairman intervened and turned down my order. This is a stranger to a revolutionary spirit. A revolutionary is supposed to fight against all evils of favouritism, nepotism and tribalism.

9. Finance

It is only comrade Chairman who knows the funds of the movement. He is the only signatory to the accounts of SPLM/SPLA. He disposes these funds and no financial report for the consumption of the five members at least, and nobody is held accountable for the misuse of funds. He is not even disclosing the sources of the funds to five members of the high command.

10. Relationship with Socialist Ethiopia

Without any doubt all the SPLM members have great allegiance to the people of Ethiopia. Our policy towards our Ethiopian friends is not to interfere in internal affairs and vice versa and our adherence to the policy of mutual respect. The Ethiopian people have done so much for us and we should therefore be grateful rather than making malicious policies geared to destroy their system and the revolutionary spirit [they] had exerted to make the SPLM a success.[4]

London-Addis Abba crisis

London-Addis Abba Crisis was the fourth crisis that shaken the SPLA/SPLM as a national liberation movement, involving Cdr Arok Thon Arok with the leadership of the movement, almost dividing it, but, fortunately ended peacefully, "he was pre-empted and arrested on 8 January 1988 and without any bloodshed "as it was communicated by John Garang in message to 20 SPLA senior officer. There were unconfirmed information and allegations surrounding how Cdr Arok Thon was arrested. The wife of Commander Arok Thon got sick and died in Ethiopia. She survived some children. John Garang told Arok that his children would be taken to Cuba, Arok refused this suggestion, instead he said, he would take his children to one of his relatives who resided in London.

SPLM/SPLA: History of Liberation (1983-2005)

As he was about to leave for London, John Garang instructed him to go and meet the officials of embassy of Sudan and UN agencies in London to agree on how to distribute relief food to the SPLA and government soldiers in Southern Sudan as confirmed by John Garang in his order of arrest

> "Whereas the C-in-C specifically instructed Cdr Arok Thon that his visit to London was a private one and that he was not to make any contact with Sudan government, army and /or political parties or foreign organizations, but that should a situation arise, he must first get approval from the C-in-C before holding such meetings.[5]

When Arok arrived to London, those in embassy reported Cdr Arok presence in London to Khartoum, a delegation led by Major General Fadlalla Burma Nasir, the Minister of state for defense, was sent to London. This delegation arrived in London to meet Cdr Arok. Cdr Arok wrote back to Addis Abba to get approval from John Garang. At the time Garang was in frontline inside Sudan, so there was no response to Arok's request. When Arok found, there was no reply, he formed a committee headed by himself, and they went ahead with the meeting. When Arok returned from London, this meeting turned out to have been unauthorized meeting. Indeed, the meeting was not approved by the C-in-C. In addition, some other disagreements, tension and conflict of interact in movement. Garang tricked Arok to Boma as if they were going for hunting, he arrested him in Boma, Arok was taken to Raad Detention Centre where other detainees like Majier Gai, Kerubino Kuanyin, Joseph Oduho were in, charged with holding unauthorized meeting, planning assassination of John Garang, maintaining contacts with enemy for a long time, planning to defect to enemy and insubordinate behaviours.

Objectively all these charges against Arok Thon were false except one, because Arok was given first orders, if there is no second orders given, then the first orders are working in Arok's line of reasoning. Actually, there is no evidence available of Arok's attempt to assassinate Garang, therefore assassination attempt was just Garang's opinion to build his case against Arok in order to purge Arok as he did. What was true and has sufficient evidence is Arok's insubordination behaviour and could be the reason, why he was arrested, towards Cdr William Nyuon and Cdr Salva Kiir, whom he claimed he was senior to them in the old Sudan army's rank. Arok's crime is insubordination behaviours. Assassination and coup were just Garang's claims to justify his action.

Five Functional Zonal Commands, 1988

After the two crises - Kerubino's and Arok's, Axis Command was lessened and Zonal Command was strengthened in administering civil and military justices and conducting war. As the result of that operational and administrative restructuring, five functional zonal commands (ZC) and five adjacent Independent Areas Command (IAC) were established, and administering, controlling and commanding those zones and areas were : (1) Central Southern Sudan Zonal Command (CSSZC), Cdr Kuol Manyang as Zonal Commander (2) Northern Bahr el Ghazal Zonal Command (NBZC), Cdr. Daniel Awet Akot as Zonal Commander (3) Western Upper Nile Zonal Command (WUNZC), Cdr. Dr Riak Machar Teny as Zonal Commander (4) Northern Upper Nile Zonal Command (NUNZC), Cdr. Dr. Lam Akol Ajawin as Zonal Commander, (5) Southern Kordufan Zonal Command(SKZC), Cdr. Yusif Kawa Mekki as Zonal Commander (6) Southern Blue Nile Zonal Command(SBNZC), Cdr. Malik Agar as Zonal Commander (7) Central Western Equatoria Zonal Command (CWEZC), Cdr James Wani Igga as Zonal Commander, Maban Independent Area Command (MIAC),A/Cdr. Makuei Deng Majuch as Area Commnder, and Eastern Equatoria Independent Area Command (EEIAC), Cdr. Glario Modi Hurnyang as Area Commander

Central South Sudan Zonal Command (CSSZC)

As the war intensified and the number of soldiers begun to dwindle there, and there was less fervour to join the rank and file of the SPLA, because of high and ultimate price paid by Koryom and other divisons. The CSSZC came up with a quota system of recruitment strategy, locally known as Buluk ke Diak, 'every sub chief contributing three recruits', in Dinka Bor language. That policy was introduced by Kuol Manyang. The chiefs of the Dinka Bor were ordered to mobilized and contributed by selecting 3 men as recruits to join the SPLA from his section of the community.

The recruits mobilized through 'Buluk Ke Diak "went to Ethiopia, trained with other recruits from other parts of Southern Sudan and becoming the

Intifada Division. The second quota of recruits known as Buluk ke Rou" or "two recruits per a sub- chief", went to Ethiopia, trained with other recruits from other parts of Southern Sudan becoming Intisar Division 1990.

The Buluk ke Diak or Ke Rou recruitment policy caused bitter resentment among the masses. Because the different families, who contributed their sons to join the SPLA have not the same number of the sons. Some families had one son and other families have five sons or three sons. If it is the turn of the family, who has one son, the son had to go to SPLA, and the family had to remain with no one to support it, in case the family members are old people e.g father or mother.

If happened that, there was a family, having a son, whose father was killed in first civil war of Anya-Nya I (1955-1972). That son was the only one in his family with his mother. They were only two, him and his mother. Besides that, he was not married, but, their turn came for their family to contribute a recruit. That young man refused to go to Bilpam. He raised his complains to the SPLA authorities, but the SPLA refused to listen to him. He lamented in songs that became classic song of the war time:

> Please tell Kuol Manyang Juuk,
> My father
> Leave me to day
> And come and take me tomorrow;

> Sometimes I heard from some soldiers;
> All men in the villages will join SPLA
> It's only lame and blind
> Who will remain in villages

> All able men will go to Bilpam
> The way of Bonga is the way that
> Took my father's life
> If it needs my life also
> I will go

Tell my mother, the daughter of Ayuen
Do not weaken and deteriorate yourself
The way of Bonga is what took my father's life
And it needs my life too
I will go

Am not like other men who pitifully say
Oh God, why can't you give me one eye?
So I refuse to go to Bilpam

SPLA Ate 150,000 Bulls, Goats and Sheep in Bor Areas

In 1984, when Koryom forces arrived Bor, there was hooliganism, indiscipline and destruction of the civilian property, be sorghum, simsim, groundnuts, beans, maize, sheep, goats, bulls and heifers by the SPLA rogue elements. At time the soldiers were taking food by force. Two soldiers could go to the village, grabbed a bull and slaughtered it and in real sense, the two men could not finish eating the bull. The SPLA soldiers started first by eating all goats and sheep. When they had finished goats and sheep, they switched on to the bulls. When they had finished the bulls, they tried to move on to the heifers.

At that time, some soldiers were more eager to finish the cattle. One chief warned them about the dangers of finishing:

'Why do you like finishing?

'And why do you worry cattle finish? Let us the cattle finish', uttered one soldier.

'Finishing of thing is not good. When your water finish in Tingli desert, how did end with you?', answered the chief.

The soldier ran wild, flogging the chief's buttock with 50 lashes, because he reminded in sarcastic way the sad story, because Zindia finished water in Tingli in 1984, many soldiers died of thirst.

This attempt to eat heifers and cows was stopped by Cdr Kuol Manyang in 1986 through Nyin Anya Nya Policy or Mior Anya Nya. He gave orders to chiefs to collect the bulls for SPLA. He also gave the order, 'if a soldier grab or kill a bull without permission, six heifers will be taken from his father or his own cows in his home or from his wife or any relative.

SPLM/SPLA: HISTORY OF LIBERATION (1983-2005)

The policy of 100 bulls per a Payam was introduced in Greater Bor areas. Greater Bor areas has twelve payams or centres which are; Kolnyang, Anyidi, Makuac, Baidit, Jalle, Maar, Paliau, Pawel, Warnyol, Wangulei, Duk Padiet, Duk Payuel. These 12 payams or centres have contributed 57,600 bulls to SPLA as food for four years, from 1984-1989. This number of bulls eaten by SPLA/M was calculated like this, there were 12 payams, and each payam contribute 100 bulls per a month. Therefore, each payam has 1, 200 bulls per a year. 12 payams have 14, 400 bulls per year. 12 payams have contributed 72, 000 bulls for a period of five years from December 1984 to April 1989. In 1984, bulls, sheep and goats were being eaten randomly through abuortem, and mior mum if you add, what had been eaten from 1984 to 1989, SPLA/A had eaten 150,000 bulls, sheep and goats in Greater Bor until the time SPLA captured Bor garrison and relief food was brought by UN agencies.

Infijar Division, 1988

As Zalzal graduated, Infijar Division, the fifth largest SPLA Division entered the training centre in January 1988 and graduated in July 1988, it included Malek TF commanded by Cdr Akech Aciek Dor, Deng Nhial TF I and II commanded by Cdr Dominic Dim Deng, Bar el Nam TF commanded by Cdr Dut Domkoch, Shambe TF commanded by Cdr Daniel Deng Monydit and Ali Gbatala TF commanded by Rusum Ali Mustafa, the only Arab in the SPLA who ever went to frontline.

Liwa Radar Retrogrades

The SPLA had completely, effectively besieged Bor garrison, and soldiers were starving. When the Sudan army tried to reinforce or supplies Bor from Juba, the SPLA deflected and destroying that. In 1988, the military planners, organized a Convoy known as Liwa Radar of 100 vehicles, tanks and other mounted vehicles, carrying food and ammunitions. This convoy moved out from Malakal secretly to Canal Mouth. From there, they moved out secretly again in the forest between Akoba and Ayod, until they entered the savannah grassland between Pibor and Duk area. This movement was to circumvent the SPLA position in Duk and other Nuer areas. The Sudan army moved in forest without being notified or detected by the SPLA, till they appeared at 20 miles from Baidit, where they were seen by women from Mathiang village, who went to collect fire wood. The women saw vehicles and threw away the firewood and ran. Within ten minutes, they entered Mathiang and started burning grass-thatched houses.

At Baidit, the SPLA didn't bother to fight, but evacuated its headquarter. Sudan army slept in Mathiang, in morning, came to Baidit, burning it and then went to Bor. When the SPLA was returning to Baidit, a car carrying Major Geu Athar-Kuei was blown up by the land mines, planted by the Sudan army. When a car left Baidit. The enemy saw the wheel mark of the vehicle between two big trees; they knew that if it returned, it would pass through the same place. So they planted a mine. Exactly, when it returned. It passed through it, and it was blown

Kuol Manyang's Escape narrowly in Palur

In 1988, Kuol Manyang moved to front around Juba with almost all Koryom forces, setting up a frontline at Magure, where they blocked Juba-Bor road. Cdr Kuol established his headquarters at Paluer. 30 miles from Magure deep in the forest between parallel roads that departing near Juba at Gumbo. One road winds up to Torit through Ngala-Ngala and other to Bor through Magure. Based on its intelligent, the enemy discovered that the famous SPLA Cdr. Kuol Manyang was in Palur. Sudan army organize an expedition from Juba, and they followed the roads as if they were going to Torit and in the forest, they changed direction with the help of local people, attacking Palur, Cdr Kuol ran and many of his body guards and other soldiers were killed including renowned Captain Alier Biar Akol.

SPLA's war was important than Blood Relation

Orders came in 1988, all forces around Juba, should move to Kapoeta area. When the forces of Koryom left for Kapoeta, it was allegedly claimed that a Sergeants, who was a direct cousin to Cdr Kuol Manyang Juuk, escaped and returned to Bor with some soldiers. On their way, they were arrested at Panwel. In kangaroo courts, they were tried, Sergeant was sentenced to death, because, he violated the law of the desertion. His sentence was carried out, and he was executed by firing squad. This shocked many people, because, he was direct cousin Cdr Kuol Manyang Juuk, who would have spared his life. He would have kept him in prison for six months and later on he would release him. However, for worse or better, he executed him, on assumption they were fighting a nationalist and patriotic war, which was more important than the blood relation, what would the SPLA do to Cdr Kuol which his cousin could not do to him?

Two Soldiers Executed in Kapoeta

Among the Koryom soldiers who moved from Juba to Kapoeta area. One soldier was arrested and charged with inciting other soldiers to desert. Another soldier was accused of robbing a Toposa woman with 100 Sudanese pound, that soldier was also arrested. The two soldiers were executed by firing squad in front of other soldiers in order to set example.

South Kordufan Zonal Command (SKZC)

Volcano forces, led by Cdr. Yusuf Kawa Mekki and deputized by Niconora Magar Aciek, comprised of many task forces went to Nuba Mountain. This was the first SPLA contingent to invade the area. The task forces were commanded by; Captain Elijah Hon Tap, Captain Akech Aciek Dor, Captain Gut Paka, Lt Deng Awol, Lt Yunis Bushera, Lt. Yunis Kaunda, Lt. Kuol Monyror Bior and Lt Machar Thiong Ayuel. Volcano carried guerrilla warfare in Southern Kordufan establishing the zone command, which mobilized thousands of recruits and sent them for training in Ethiopia

Western Equatoria Zonal Command (WEZC)

Shakush forces led by Cdr. James Wani Igga deputised by Major Makor Lual. The Task Forces were commanded by Captain John Koang Nyuon, Captain Dau Manyok, Lt Deng Ajang Duot, Lt Scopos Kenyi, Lt Chol Ajak, and Lt Garang Monykuer. Shakush under James Wani, established SPLA zonal command in Western Equatoria. They carried guerrilla warfare in the many areas; attacking Laso, Morobo, Nyori, Amodi, and Kaji Kajj. Tore, destroying many police stations in the area. In these operations, some white men were captured as the PoWs as well as the retired Sudan army Colonel Martin Kenyiboro, who was assassinated by SPLA.

The Fall of Kurmuk I, 1987

Although, there was Southern Blue Nile Zonal Command (SBNZC) in Igessinna Hill area, commanded by Cdr. Malik Agar. The military operations were either intentionally taken over by one of the five permanent member of PMHC or it was overlapped by himself present in the zone voluntarily. All the major battles were commanded by one of three members of PMHC at a different time. The first was the Cdr Keubino Kuanyin Bol, the second was William Nyuon Bany, and last was Salva Kiir in 1990. Eagle was reinforced by Numus and Kasha Battalions. They captured Kurmuk in 1987, under the supervision of Cdr. Salva Kiir Mayardit, but the Sudan army retook it again. In that battle, T-55 tank model was captured in good conditions. This tank used later in battle of Kapoeta in 1988.

Progressive Officers

In Itang Refugee Camp, a group of SPLM/A officers, called for meeting. The agenda of the meeting were to discuss the general state of affairs in the SPLM/A. The group accused some of senior members of SPLA/M not being progressive, because, they were not educated in the movement. That group calling itself Progessive officers were charged of conducting unauthorized gathering, Prominent among was Dr Amon Wantok.

Notes
1. Akol p.331
2. Ibid p.331
3. Atem Yaak Atem, Jungle Chronicles
4. Igga, 2008, Kampala pp. 241-242
5. Akol pp. 350-351

CHAPTER 5

SPLA/M CAMPAIGNS: THE LIBERATION AT ITS PEAK, 1989-1990

JEKOU DECLARATION: THE RESOULTION OF INTERNAL CONFLICT OF SPLA AND ANYA NYA II

In 1988, after five years of infighting among Southerners themselves, the SPLA struck a peace deal with the archenemy, the Anya-Nya II Movement. This first infighting started in 1983 as result of disagreement over the approach of liberation and the objectives of the movement. Anya Nya II then wanted the independence Southern Sudan, which is fighting for separation while SPLA wanted united Sudan on new basis that was the fighting for unity of the Sudan. That contradiction in approach and objectives brought conflict between the SPLA and AN II that was solved in Jekou, at the aftermath of the top leadership of AN II; Akuot Atem de Mayen, Samuel Gai Tut and Abdhalla Chuol Deng; were killed by SPLA or by themselves for some cases, AN II abandoned its call for separation and joined the SPLA in fighting for a united, New Sudan .The agreement unifying the SPLA/SPLM and AN II, was signed by Commander In

SPLA/M CAMPAIGNS: THE LIBERATION AT ITS PEAK, 1989-1990

Chief of Anya Nya II Gordon Koang Chol and SPLA/SPLM leadership at Ketbek near Jekou and it became known as Jekou Declaration or the Ketbek Agreement . Indeed, Gordon Koang was the oldest AN II leader before being joined by Akuot Atem and Samuel Gai in 1983.

Unity Campaign

The unified forces of SPLA and AN II attacked Nasir garrison on January 26, 1989, in military operation code-named Unity Campaign, in honouring and celebrating the new unity between the SPLA and AN II. The forces who attacked and captured Nasir were commanded by Cdr William Nyuon Bany and assisted by many officers like Captain Gabriel Jok Riak. Nasir was captured with casualties from both sides of SPLA and the Sudan army. The Commander of Nasir, Colonel Majud was captured with more 100 other PoWs.

Col Majub died under unclear circumstances, when SPLA was fleeing Ethiopia.

Bright Star Campaign (BSC)

By 1988, Zonal Command (ZC), which was the military operational and administrative structures of the movement, had finally achieved its objectives, which were the establishment of the permanent presence of the SPLA/SPLM in different zones as well as independent areas commands. At the time, Zonal Commanders had been conducting the war, and administering justices through junior officers, who were controlling and overseeing the Battalions, Task Forces and the Civil Military Administration (CMA), who were in charge of the civil affairs in the Zone.

Having established the permanent presence in zones, the National Mobile Forces (NMF) were created at the zonal headquarters. These NMF were organized and transferred from one zone to another one, and from one area to another area as reinforcement. CSSZC in Bor organized Koryom forces into NMF and sent them to Eastern Equatoria Zone in 1988 as it was requested by the movement leadership. NBZC in rural Bahr el Ghazal, organized Muor Muor forces in to NMF and sent them, too, to Eastern Equatoria. Koryom, Muor Muor forces and other freshest forces from training centres in Ethiopia, were amalgamated in Kapoeta, retrained for one month. At the end of refresher training course, the SPLA/ SPLM changed its strategy of fighting the war, from guerrilla warfare to conventional one, because before that, SPLA had been waging a guerrilla warfare and semi-conventional warfare for six years from 1983 to 1989. The conventional warfare was adopted, and a campaign code-named Bright Star Campaign (BSC) was launched. BSC was the biggest of its kind since the war broke out in 1983 in Southern Sudan. It was indeed the revamp of objectives of the Axis Command operation of 1986, which was meant to liberate East bank of Nile, from Nimule in Eastern Equatoria to Renk in Northern Upper Nile. That operation was never executed and leading to the failure of Axis Front and its objective all together in 1986 to 1988. BSC became big, brilliant and tremendous success for the SPLA since 1983, liberating triangle areas of Sudan army garrisons, beginning at the right angle at Kiyala, to the height at Nimule in Eastern Equatoria, to where the base and hypotenuse meet at Renk in Northern Upper Nile. In mathematical speaking, it is pure triangle; however, it is a triangle with gerrymandering line crossing over the different regional maps.

Intifada Division, 1989

When Infijar Division was graduated, Intifada Division, the sixth SPLA largest Division entered training in June 1988 and graduated in March 1989. It was comprised of many Task Forces (TF) that included; Mandela I and II TF (this Task Forces was named after President Nelson Mandela of South Africa, Samora I and II TF (this task forces were named after President Samora Michel of the first of Mozambique, Kurmuk I and II, Ngacigak I and II, Kapoeta TF, Gerder TF, Nkrumah I and II (named after President Kwame Nkrumah of Ghana, which were commanded by the following officers; Cdr Dominic Dim, Cdr Bol Agany.

BSC Phase I

BSC had manpower of 6,000 troops, who were organized into eleven task forces of Neto I and II (named after President Augustine Neto of Angola, Deng Nhial 1 and II, Lomumba I and II (named after President Patrick Lumumba of Democratic Republic of Congo (DRC), National Mobile Force I, II, III, IV and V. other forces included Gerger TF, Fass TF, Boma

SPLA/M CAMPAIGNS: THE LIBERATION AT ITS PEAK, 1989-1990

TF, Mergel TF, Kokap TF. BSC was entirely commanded by Commander in Chief John Garang de Mabior, and he was assisted by many officers who included ; Cdr Kuol Manyang Juuk, Cdr Oyai Deng Ajak, A/Cdr Tito Achuil Madut, A/Cdr Anthony Bol Madut, Captain Kon Anyieth Mabil, Captain Jok Duom Mayen, Captain Kuol Mayen Mading, Captain Majok Anyieth Akou-beny, Captain Akuei Deng Akuei, Captain Aru Maan Chut, Captain Paul Tiopic Liet, Captain Ajith-Manyangdit, Captain Arok Isaiah, Captain Taban Deng Gai, Captain Johnson Luk Jok. Captain Wilson Deng Kuoirot aka Deng-wek

The Battle of Kiyala

As the first SPLA conventional warfare campaign, since its inception in 1983, BSC was well-organized and well-armed military campaign. It was launched at time when the first SPLA batch of Tanks Unit, who went for training in Awasha in Ethiopia, returned with 12 tanks, plus one tank that was captured in Kurmuk garrison, bringing total number of tanks in SPLA to 13 tanks and many other support weapons. At lagurony 25-mile south of Kiyala, the sand model of BSC was set out and the operational chart was laid out. BSC was divided into phases, Phase I was meant to liberate east bank of Nile from Kiyala and sweeping along the Nile up to Canal Mouth in Jonglei province. The Battle of Kiyala was the onset of the campaign. The fresh forces of Gerger TF, Fass TF, Mergel TF, attacked Kiyala but they were repelled by the enemy several times. When it became hardest for the new forces to capture it, the old experienced forces of Koryom and Kazuk were called in and took over the fighting. Addressing forces, John Garang, the Commander of BSC, told Koryom forces that they were the only soldiers, who would teach Col. Mohammed Self al- Dolla, a lesson, he would never forget in his life. At the time, Col. Seif al- Dolla, the commander of Kiyala garrison, was being lionized by state Radio Omudurman, after he had been repulsing the SPLA attacks several time. 400 soldiers of Koryom and Kazuk were given hand grenades each soldier with one. At dawn the forces went crawling until they were 50 metres from the foxholes, and they threw grenades at once into the trenches, there was powerful explosion, followed by heaviest firing from all calibre of guns until the enemy ran out of fox-holes in panic and disarray. Within 10 minutes Kiyala had fallen into the hand of the SPLA, with 600 soldiers killed including the martyrs of the several attacks that were repulsed. The battle of Kiyala became second worst catastrophe for SPLA after Battle of Jekou I in 1985. On the side of enemy, there was highest unknown number of soldiers killed, including Col Mohammed Self al- Dolla, the commander of Kiyala garrison.

Yarmuk Brigade

After the fall of Kiyala to SPLA, this was the vanguard of Torit garrison. Torit became under eminent pressures from attack. As the result of this, reinforcement, code-names Yarmuk, under a Southern Sudanese commander Colonel Kamilla Odongi was sent from Juba to rescue Torit. This convoy was ambushed and destroyed by the SPLA forces of Abur Matung TF near Ngala Ngala. After Yarmuk sustaining the greatest losses in manpower and materials, the force returned to Juba for reorganization. While it was reorganized in Juba and recode-named as Seif al Batar, and as it was preparing itself to go to Torit, Torit fallen to the SPLA.

The Battle of Torit

From February 24th to 26th, 1989, six SPLA task forces had been fighting the Sudan army in Torit garrison. The battle was led by bravest officers like; Captain Wilson Deng Kuoirot, Captain Abednego Ajak Anyieth, Captain Jok Duom Mayen and many others. The forces that were battling enemy were Neto I and II, NMF 4, and 2. Torit fallen to the SPLA forces after two days of fighting on February 26. The commander of Torit Garrison fled to Uganda.

When the Radio SPLA announced the fall of Torit. The editorial teams praised the officers who commanded the soldiers in the battle. A row broke out among the officers, especially the Captain, who claimed his forces were, actually, the one who captured the town, but the victory was announced in the name of another captain, whose forces did not capture the main garrison. He argued that he had been stripped off of his honour and attributing his glory to another captain. This irritated Captain against C-in-C John Garang, who he accused of giving erroneous information to the Radio SPLA. When John Garang arrived Torit for victory celebration, the said Captain raised him complain to John Garang, he pulled out of his pocket a flag of Sudan he said was the proof that he was the one who captured the main Barrack, this is why he had the flag. John Garang was annoyed by way the Captain presented his case and he responded by not promoting him later, when he was promoting all officers of BSC. After Torit, SPLA overran five Garrisons in one month; Parajok, Lirya, Nimule, Mangalla and Gemmeza.

The Battle of Bor

The sand model for the battle of Bor was designed at Baidit, while the forces were stationed at Gakyom base. The assault on Bor garrison was led Captain Ajak Yen Ajak. Bor was captured after fighting that result into capturing of Colonel Farah Adam Farah, who was later summarily executed after he exchanged insult after insult with SPLA Commanders. It was alleged that Col Farah Adam told the SPLA, "from skeleton to high command, what a nonsense! When the commander of SPLA arrived, all prisoners of war were told to stand up as signs of respect. Col Adam Farrah refused to stand up. When he was asked, why he not standing, he asked, who was coming, they told him High Commander was coming. He replied, "I know that man, he was a mechanic in garage five years ago, when did he become army officer. From there Col Adam was finished in summary execution.

Waat Debate

BSC phase I ended with Waat debate, The Sudan army forces in Waat garrison ran into confusion after the Radio SPLA had reported that the forces in Akoba had defied order to reinforce them. The Radio SPLA also reported that Akoba forces were leaving because their ammunition and food had finished and the rainy season was coming and there would be no mean to get food and bullets through the year. There was a confused communication between Waat and Akoba garrisons. This became known as Waat Debate as broadcasted by Radio SPLA. This disinformation and misinformation as part of SPLA psychological warfare led to the withdrawal and evacuation of Akoba and Waat garrison respectively

SPLM/SPLA: History of Liberation (1983-2005)

THE THREE FRONTS AND THE THREE CAMPAIGNS

At the end of the liberation of Kapoeta-Nimule - Canal Mouth Triangle in BSC Phase I. The SPLA introduced the concept of front into the organizational and operational structures and strategic planning. Three fronts were created; each front was headed by one of the three remaining permanent members of PMHC (because the other two members; Cdr Kerubino and Cdr Arok were now political prisoners at the Raad Detention Centre in Boma Plateau). Thus the first front was commanded by C-in-C John Garang, second front by Cdr. William Nyuon, and the third front by Cdr Salva Kiir. In the three fronts, three campaigns were launched; Bright Star Campaign (BSC) as continuation, New Funj Campaign (NFC) and Kon Anok Campaign (KAC). In May 1989, three campaigns were now planned. KAC commanded by CDR Salva Kiir, was to liberate Lake Provinces to Warap that is starting from Rumbek, Tonj, Gogrial, Aweil up to Raja, North of Wau. BSC commanded by John Garang, was to liberate Western Equatoria upto Bussere, South of Wau. NFC was to liberate Southern Blue Nile up to Ignessena Hills.

Bright Star Campaign (BSC)

It was now in the first front, has two phases, Phase I, which was covering areas east of the Nile and south of the Sobat River, which borders Ethiopia, Kenya and Uganda and these were commanded by Cdr Kuol Manyang Juuk., alternate member of PMHC. Phase II, which was covering Northern Upper Nile that is Kodok, Renk, Bailit, Maiwut, and Maban, were commanded by Cdr. Gordon Kong Chol, alternate member of PMHC. The overall operation commander was John Garang. Eventually, there was no military action or campaign took place in BSC Phase II of Cdr Gordon Koang, as it was planned from July 1989 to January 1990.

New Funj Campaign (NFC)

The second front was covering the whole Southern Blue Nile. The military operation herein was code-named New Funj Campaign. Funj is the name of oldest black kingdom in Sudan before the coming of the Arabs into Sudan. That second front was commanded by Cdr. William Nyuon Bany and assisted by Cdr. Galero Modi Huriyang. NFC captured Kurmuk town in July 1989, and liberating all out posts around Kurmuk that included Yabus and others. However, the victories were short-lived, because, the enemy retook Kurmuk town after two months, driving SPLA forces back to Ethiopia border.

Kon Anok Campaign (KAC)

KAC was one of the three largest military campaigns of the SPLA/M grand strategy. It was an amalgamation of twelve (12) task forces, having manpower of 6,000 troops; each was composing of 500 soldiers. It was led by Cdr Salva Kiir, one of the three Permanent members of SPLA/M PMHC. He was assisted by; Captain Dominic Dim Deng, Captain Gerang Mabil Deng, Captain Aleu Ayieny, Captain Riing Chol, Captain Bol Agany, and Captain Jurkuch Barach, Captain Ayuen Mabior, Captain Abot Riak Abot, Captain Madin Duor . The forces moved from Ethiopia to Malek beach on River Nile, 15 kilometres south of Bor town, where Cdr. Kuol Manyang came from Torit to see them off. At Malek, KAC was face by River Nile as an obstacle. How to transport vehicles amounted with artilleries across the River was a problem. A barge was brought, crossing the soldiers.

After reaching Yirol, Payii River was another big obstacle. However, an old ferry boat that sank before the war in 1983 was dug out. The digging out of boat known as Fulaka took two weeks involving 2000 troops, each company digging by its turns. After it was dug out, wielder called Ali Abdhalla Ramadan who came from Ethiopia wielded it. The engine was flew in from Kenya by Twin Otto Caravan plane to Yirol. After fixing the engine the ferry carried the vehicles and three tanks crossed over Payii River.

In July 1989, Rumbek was attacked by KAC simultaneously with Kurmuk in Southern Blue Nile by NFC forces. It was a last hour's attack at 5pm. The main barrack was overrun. One tank APC was captured. All the crew including a captain were killed. It became dark and battle was halted, that was the first day.

On the second day, another last hour attack was launched, the enemy resisted rigidly. One SPLA tank fell in tank ditch, and never got out, another tank was surrendered to the enemy by its crews. In the action, there was no artillery fire support, therefore, the forces withdrew back. SPLA two captains were martyred, that is Captain Bol Agany, Captain Juruc and SPLA suffered 200 casualties.

On the third day, the enemy moved to the House of Commission and Rumbek Senior School respective and using evacuators, it dug and built round defence from those two positions. From there, it resisted the SPLA attack till the reinforcement arrived from Wau. Reinforcement entered Rumbek without being noticed by SPLA, because, it circumvented the SPLA ambush on main road with the help of local people. The active attacks on Rumbek were halted, but, tactically sieged.

The SPLA freed the siege of Rumbek, when the forces were divided into three. Some forces left with Cdr Salva Kiir to encounter Junti Watan al wahid Brigade, which was coming out of Malakal to reinforce Western Equatoria. Some forces went to Gogrial with Captain Dominic Dim Deng, and some forces went to Maridi area with Captain Gerang Mabil Deng. That is the end of Kon Anok Campaign in summary, KAC failed to achieve the SPLA objectives at last.

BSC THREE PHASES

After the failing of both NFC and KAC operations to achieve their ultimate objectives of liberating Southern Blue Nile and Lakes and Warrap provinces, they were scrapped off. And all military operations in whole of Southern Sudan and Southern Blue Nile were brought under the BSC, which was divided into three phases, with each phase divided into different sectors.

BSC Phase I

It was divided into two sectors; Northern and Southern sectors. This Phase I mission was defensive one. The mission of the Northern Sector was to repulse and destroy the enemy convoys that attempt to move South of Sobat River and to capture Canal Mouth and Pam Zeref garrison. It was also to be on standby to participate in the capture of Malakal. The Southern Sector was to repulse any enemy convoy that attempt to move out of Juba, and to capture all enemy outposts of Juba on east bank, to close down Juba international airport, and to be on standby to participate in capturing of Juba in the Operation Final Lapse (OFL). OFL was ringing at back head of John Garang.

BSC Phase II

It was divided into two sectors; Northern and Southern one. Northern Sector comprised of towns and outposts around Renk, Kodok on the Nile. Their mission was offensive one (1) to capture Renk, Melut, Johlak, Kodok, (2) to be on standby to participate in the capture of Malakal (3) to repulse the enemy convoys coming from Kosti, (4) to take and launch guerrilla warfare in to Kennan and beyond. Eastern Sector was comprised of Maban, Ulu, Kurmuk and all out posts. The mission was (1) to capture Maban, Yabus, Ulu, Kurmuk 2) to proceed to occupy the Igessinna Hills (3) to take guerrilla warfare to Damazin (4) To threaten the Roseiries Dam.

Intisar Division 1990

Intisar Division was seventh and last SPLA/M largest Division to be trained in Ethiopia. Graduated in 1990, comprising of six task forces of; Konyo Konnyo TF led by Angelo Juckuch Jol, Atabalara TF led by Captain Lochodok, Jebel Lado TF led by Captain Manguardit who was killed in action in Kagwada, Jebel Kujur TF led by Captain Malek Ruben Riak, Kator TF led by Captain Garang Bul Pageer, Danga TF led by Captain Aruei.

BSC Phase III

It started in January 1990 to March 1991 from Kaji Kaji in Western Equatoria to Bussere near Wau in Western Bare el Ghazal. The Intisar Division forces captured Kaji Kaji, Kaya, Morobo, but got greatest resistance from Yei garrison. Yei was attacked but the enemy repulsed the SPLA. Yei was under attack and Juba was besieged and was shelled at the time by SPLA.

Junti Watan el Wahiid Brigade Retrograding

Yei was under maximum military pressure from the SPLA. Juba was also now embattled city from artillery shelling and total besiege, Juba international airport was closed, there was no plane landing. A Brigade known as Junti Watan al Wahid; of 4,000 troops was organized in Khartoum and transported to Malakal. It was a well-equipped convoy of 200 vehicles, 30 tanks, one bore-hole digging truck and one mobile bridge. At Malakal, it moved out secretly avoiding the SPLA position, by circumventing through forest. It was second large force to circumvent the SPLA positions, after Liwa Radar Brigades in 1988. Its mission was to reinforce Juba and Yei respectively. It avoided the roads, moving in savannah grassland between Bor and Pibor.

The SPLA discovered it at last when it was already approaching Juba. SPLA Forces under Cdr Salva Kiir and Cdr Jok Reng Magot, were sent to ambush and encounter them and destroy them, but, with the help of their radars' equipment moving with them, they by-passed three ambushes, until they fell in last ambush at Khor Makuac between Mangalla and Juba. They broke up that ambush, which was laid by Koryom and Muor Muor forces, in that ambush the best morale song composers of Muor Muor; Magiir Deng and Mangok Kuc were killed. The Junti el Watan al Wahid triumphantly marched to Juba. In Juba, it was renamed Watan Jiduk, and sent to reinforced Yei garrison. These forces flashed SPLA forces out at around Yei.

The Fall of Maridi

After the failing to capture Yei, the BSC Phase III of 5,000 troops organized into ten Task Forces, commanded by C-In-C John Garang himself and assisted by Cdr Oyai Deng. And Task Forces commanded by; Captain Nhial Jongkuch Nhial, Captain Machok Atem, Captain Marial Chanuong Yol, Captain Deng Kuot Nyang, Captain Yaak Deu Yaak, Captain Wangchok Koryom, Captain James Koang Chol and Captain Garang Mading Agok. The forces left Yei and moved westward, attacking and capturing Maridi. The battle of Maridi was biggest one, because, the forces under Southern Colonel Henry Akoon Agiu put up stiff resistance. After the fall of Maridi to SPLA. With the help of Radio SPLA propaganda effect, other towns garrisons withdrew before an attack or falling to SPLA with little resistance; Mundri, Yimbe, Eba, Bar el Nam nose of Maridi, Tombura, Tertisobo. etc, The SPLA liberated Western Equatoria up to Bussere near Wau in 1990.

While KAC forces were under Garang Mabil were containing reinforcement to Maridi from Rumbek. These forces were blocking all routs leading to Maridi. After the fall of Maridi and Mundri garrisons and their forces subsequent withdrawal to Rokon. Forces under Cdr Oyai captured Rokon. The reinforcement came from Juba and dislodged the SPLA force from Rokon.

Unlaunched Operation Final Lapse (OFL)

In April 1991, there were four main Sudan army garrisons in Greater Equatoria; Juba, Yei, Rokon and Terekaka. The SPLA massed 20,000 troops, besieging Juba and awaiting final orders to launch the OFL. The deployment in preparation of OFL was as follows: South North Juba, Jebel Lodo, Luri, Khor Mine, Kaji Kaji road and Terekaka road. In East Juba, SPLA forces were in Magure, Mabau, Bilnyang under Cdr Oyai and Cdr Mamur. All forces were on standby to attack Juba. They were waiting for logistics. Unfortunately, it was disrupted by the split of SPLA/M into SPLA/M Mainstream and SPLA/M Nasir Faction.

The Incursion to Darfur

In 1991, Ariath Makuei TF led by Cdr Abdel Aziz Adam al Hillu invaded Darfur. That was the first SPLA column to enter there. Those forces attacked six out posts and garrison in guerrilla warfare of hit and run campaign. Unfortunately, the deputy of Cdr Abdel Aziz surrendered himself, because, he was from Darfur. From there the SAF came dislodged SPLA from Darfur. The forces were dispersed in disarray. Some went to Chad and CAR, others were captured. The incursion to Darfur became fifth military disaster for the SPLA.

Ferjeer el Sadiq Convoy

In 1991, after the SPLA flashed out enemy forces in Western Equatoria that was after the fall of last garrison Ezo, a brigade in a convoy known as Ferjerer el Sadiq under the command of Brigadier General (PSC), Molana Abdhal Jalil Mohammad, was sent to retake Western Equatoria. SPLA encountered this convoy at Bo Bridge, 100 miles from Tombura and 67 miles from Wau. A worst battles took place at Bo jungles, in one of battles, Commander of Abdhal Jalil was killed, the missions of this convoy failed and ended there.

CHAPTER 6

SPLA/M'S BLACK CHAPTER: THE STRUGGLE AT ITS LOWEST LEVEL (1991-1995)

In the 21-year civil war, 1991 to 1995 had been the blackest chapter of the blackest history of SPLA/SPLM. This painful part of history, originated from both the external and internal situations. The external situation could be traced to the fall of Berlin Wall, marking of the end of history or precisely the end of cold war between the United States of America (USA) and the Union of Soviet Socialist Republics (USSR). The cold war was just the political war of blackmail and sabotage between the West and the East fought through capitalist and communist ideals. This cold war ended with the fall of Berlin Wall in 1989 or subsequent collapsing of USSR in 1991. The domino effect of the fall of Berlin Wall made other falls around the world that were link to it. The Derge government of President Mengistu that was supporting SPLA/SPLM through money from USSR collapsed as a result, too.

The Fall of Mengistu's Government

The war had been raging between Ethiopian government of President Mengistu Haile Mariam and Rebel of EPRF of Meles Zenawi for many years. In May 1991, the Mengistu's government was collapsing, in solidarity with their mentor, the SPLA/M sent forces of the Red Army (division of youngest soldiers), who were fresh from Bongo training centre to salvage the government. This force was graced by Cdr. Salva Kiir to the Ethiopian frontline. The SPLA forces were deployed alongside the Ethiopian friendly forces in Dembidolo and Gore frontlines. At the onset of the battle for Dembidolo, the Ethiopian government forces switched sides to the rebels, turning their fire against the SPLA. The Ethiopian army that defected to rebel EPDRF killed 400 SPLA soldiers, dispersing them in disarray into the mountainous forest. As the result of running to forest and loss of direction, another 600 SPLA Red Army soldiers got lost, as they were coming, falling into ambushes on the way to Gambella region at Ethiopia-Sudan border. At last the Red Army arrived at Gambela in hundreds, fifty's, tens, 5, and 2.

In May, President Mengistu fled from Addis Abba. The Wuyane or EPRF rushed and captured Gambella. The refugees in both Itang and Pugnidu had to flee to the Sudan border. Those in Itang fled to Jekou, and those in Pugnidu to Pochalla. In May, the famous Radio SPLA went off air in Addis Abba, closed by the new government. The SPLA/M was finally expelled from Ethiopia.

The Drowning in Gilo River:
The Sad Ending of Ethiopia's Hospitality

Ethiopia had been accommodating the SPLM/A and its refugees from 1983 to 1991. For eight years, President Mengistu Haile Mariam was generously hosting refugees and soldiers, giving them all they needed. That helps ended sadly, when the Mengistu government collapsed, and the SPLA tried to salvage it, by sending soldiers to defend Dembidola. As Derg regime collapsed, and the Southern Sudanese ran back to Sudan. The last of group of Southern Sudanese was caught up at Gilo River by rebels. Reaching them at Gilo, the Ehtiopian rebels attacked them mercilessly, killing them, and chasing them into river. When Gilo was attacked, Commander Salva Kiir was present, he had to run and walked to Pochalla, it was the first time, Salva Kiir walked on foot since 1983, when he walked to Ethiopia.

Nasir Declaration/Coup

Prior to August 28, 1991, there were rumours from the SPLA top leadership that Cdr Dr. Riek Machar and Cdr Dr. Lam Akol were planning a coup. This was encountered by Cdr Riek and Cdr Lam that there was a conspiracy to arrest them being cooked by Dr John Garang, Cdr William Nyuon and Cdr Salva Kiir. This prompted Riek and Lam to move with huge forces between Nasir, Itang and Pugnidu from 1990 to 1991. At the time, Dr. Lam has secretly written his infamous hypothesis of 'Why Garang Must Go?' According to the rule and regulation of the SPLA, this document itself was coup de 'tat and treacherous altogether.

In 1991, the SPLA/SPLM GHQs was transferred from Bilpam in Ethiopia to Torit in Sudan. After the SPLA/SPLM left Ethiopia, John Garang as the Chairman and Commander in Chief of the movement, called for extraordinary meeting of PMHC in Torit, to discuss the fall of Mengistu government and new strategy of the movement. He sent out all Unit Message to all members of PMHC. Three members of PMHC; Dr Riek Machar, Dr Lam Akol and Cdr John Koang Chol, who were in Nasir, based on the fear of being arrested in Torit, instead, of coming to attend the meeting in Torit, they declared that they had overthrown the SPLA/SPLM leader Col. Dr John Garang de Mabior in what is called Nasir Declaration. The statement on the BBC Focus in Africa at 6 PM on August 28, 1991 claimed that the three members of PMHC namely; John Garang, William Nyuon and Salva Kiir were overthrown, the rest of the SPLA/SPLM senior commanders should remain in their position, and they had to declare their allegiance to the new leadership of the SPLA/SPLM in Nasir within 24 hours.

The Response from Torit SPLM/A Headquarters

In response to Nasir Declaration, SPLA/SPLM leadership called Torit Conference in September 1991, the conference was attended by Cdr

William Nyuon Bany, Cdr Salva Kiir Mayardit, Cdr Yusif Kawa Mekki (in Radio message because he was in Nuba Mountain), Cdr James Wani Igga, Cdr Daniel Awet Akot, Cdr Kuol Manyang Juuk, Cdr Martin Manyiel Ayuel, Cdr Lual Diing Wol, and Cdr Glario Modi Huriyang and many other junior commanders. The conference seriously deliberated on the Nasir Declaration. The movement leadership was divided, on how to respond to Nasir incident. Some members talk of military action to pre-empt attack on Nasir group in order to subdue it. Other members talk of dialogue to solve it amicably. The meeting went on in Torit for many days. John Garang was insisting on, attacking Juba and capturing it since, the plan had been underway and since it had already been besieged. After the conference, SPLA/SPLM released the communique of Torit Conference with 18 Resolutions on 12 September 1991, the first resolution reads:

> Resolution no 1: The Riek/Lam theoretical coup of 18/8/1991, in its first session held on 6 /9/1991, the PMHC resolved that, the Riak / Lam theoretical is denounced and condemned in the strongest terms as divisive and destructive, only the enemy can benefit from it. The Nasir coup situation will be approached peacefully and an amicable solution sought and reached, in order to maintain the cohesiveness and unity of our people1

Despite the SPLM/SPLA Torit calling for amicable solution, realities were different on the ground. Within a week of the Nasir declaration, there was great confusion and escaping from one place to another in rank and file of the SPLA officers and men. The officers and men, who supported Riek, began moving to Nasir direction. Likewise, officers and men, who supported Garang and who happened to be in Nasir attempted to move to Torit areas.

In this process of one finding out his own side of allegiance, hundreds of officers and men were executed. By September 5, SPLA/SPLM in the whole of Equatoria, Bare el Ghazal, Bor, Pochalla and Khor Fulus and Pariang resisted the Nasir coup, and stood with John Garang and declared their allegiances to him. But SPLA/SPLM in the whole Upper Nile declared their allegiance to Cdr Riek. Sadly, some officers in Nasir were executed for not supporting the declaration or trying to escape among them; Captain Hakim Aluong. However, in the SPLA Garang's faction, there was no major incident execution of officers of Nuer origin, although, there is a claim that many Nuer officers and soldiers were killed. In fact, there was one incident, some Nuer soldiers led A/Cdr James Kailei Tang deserted their position in Laso in near Yei. These soldiers were ambushed by SPLA and James Kalei lost his life in the ambush. After the spree of killing of so and so and of they who supported Garang or them who supported Riek for that matter, the real infighting started.

Internecine Fighting

By October 1991, it became clear, the SPLA/SPLM had divided itself into the SPLA/SPLM Torit faction and SPLA/SPLM Nasir faction. The SPLA/M Nasir mushroomed and began to attack Bor on its way to capture Torit, the headquarters of the SPLA/SPLM Mainstream. Serious infighting took place at Bor areas. The SPLA Torit faction forces were defeated and Bor fallen to SPLA Nasir forces. From Bor, they were moving quickly to Mangalla., John Garang had to call off the attack and capturing of Juba, and all forces around it, were sent to encounter the advance of Nasir forces.

In place called Gut Makur, 25 kilometres from Mangalla, fighting took place. Combination of regular SPLA Nasir soldiers and civilians of Lou-Nuer White Army were defeated by the SPLA/M Torit. As these Riek's forces were coming to Torit, they attacked Bor civilians, killing them and looting properties. The Nasir forces attacked Bor people for two reasons (1) revenging for what Konyom forces did to Nuer civilians during the SPLA war against AN II of Samuel Gai Tut (2) to destroy Bor to weaken Garang's power base. In the invasion of Bor, all cattle were raided and about 1000 people were killed and about 100 girls and women were taken captives or wives. When Riek's forces were defeated at Gut Makur, they returned to Nasir, Cdr Riek made a round defence in Nasir, Akoba, Leer etc, he was not fighting the SPLA or the Sudan Army until he later signed Khartoum Peace Agreement (KPA).

Seif al Ubuur: The Eschatological War

The war in the Sudan had largely been defined as a civil war, from 1983 to 1989. When National Islamic Front (NIF) of ideologues and fundamentalists led Dr Hassan al Turabi, took power in military coup in 1989, the junta leader, President Omer Hassan el Beshir declared Jihad or the holy. The NIF changed the definition of war from civil to eschatological war, as ploy and stratagem to defeat the SPLA. The change of narrative of the war into eschatology, was to give its a divine character, in order to drum up support from the Arab world. President Beshir and NIF fraternity portrayed the war as a struggle between good and evil, between Muslims and Christians in South of the country, who were being aided by Zionist Americans.

After the declaration of jihad, President Bashir had, for three years, been preaching eschatological meaning of the war as preparation for a military campaign. At last, in January 1992, Seif al Ubuur, meaning 'unstoppable sword 'in Arabic was launched. It was largest military campaign, a counteroffensive against the SPLA Bright Star Campaign (BSC) of 1989 to 1991 that liberated the whole of Equatoria except four military garrisons; Juba, Yei and Terekaka and Rokon, and also liberating whole of Upper Nile except Malakal, Maluth and Renk.

Having the manpower of 35, 000 troops,Seif el Ubuur was organized into seven Brigades, namely; Liwa Kel Kabar el-Yain (Kel Kabar el Yain Brigade), Liwa Abdhal Jalil (Abdhal Jalil Brigade, this brigade was named after Brigadier General Abdhal Jalil Ibrahim, who was killed by the SPLA forces in 1991 at Bo Bridge in Western Equatoria), Liwa al Feshe (Al Feshe Brigade), Liwa Seif al Dolla (Seif al Dolla Brigade, this brigade was named after martyr Mohammed Self al Dolla, who was killed by SPLA forces in the battle of Kiyala in 1989 near Torit), Liwa Ismael (Ismael Brigade), Liwa Duress (Duress Brigade) Liwa Muktar (Muktar Brigade). These seven Brigades making up Seif al Ubuur were sent to south by air, on land and on river in five columns.

The first column was airlifted from Khartoum to Juba. The second column marched from Khartoum-Kosti-Renk-Malakal. The third column sailed on river from Khartoum to Malakal. The fourth column flanked the SPLA through Ethiopia. The fifth column was airlifted from Khartoum to Wau.

SPLM/SPLA: History of Liberation (1983-2005)

Silvano Alor Deng Makuei

Kuol Manyang 1989. Copyright SBBC.

Garang and Nyuon

Nyuon and Salva Kiir 1980s

John Garang 1980s

Deng Banan

SPLA/M'S BLACK CHAPTER: THE STRUGGLE AT ITS LOWEST LEVEL (1991–1995)

Gutarist from Nuba

John Garang poem

John Garang, Ethiopia

John Garang reciting in Pinyudu

John Garang inspecting forces

Koryom forces Bor in 1989

SPLM/SPLA: History of Liberation (1983-2005)

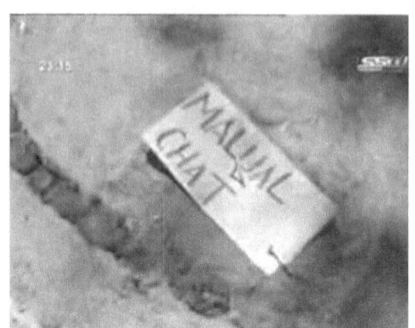

Malaul Chat. Copyright SSBC

SPLA Southern Blue Nile

SPLA attack Nasir 1989

Ululation during John Garang speech

School children Pinyudu

SPLA flag red star before 1991. Copyright SSBC

Wounded heroes Pinyudu

SPLA/M'S BLACK CHAPTER: THE STRUGGLE AT ITS LOWEST LEVEL (1991–1995)

ABOVE: Riak
INSET: Dr Samson Kwaje

Tacking Forces

Table 1

SPLA OJS Parades in Eastern Bank of the River Nile as it stood on 24 August 1996

S/N	Unit Line of Defense space	Parade
1.	Agoro	519
2.	Kit	419
3.	Omu	315
4.	Emoruk	338
5.	Magwi	221
6.	Moli	072
7.	Pageri	105
8.	Reserve	-
		1989

Source: Cdr Gabriel Jok Riak's war time files

Table 2 : SPLA Armaments in 2nd Front on 25 February 2000

S/N	Calibre		Tindilo Front	Jambo Front	Mile-40 Front
1.	BM-21 (122 MM)		1		
2.	D-30(122 MM)		1		
3.	M-38(122 MM)		1		2
4.	107 MM		1	1	2
5.	105 MM		1		
6.	105 MM A/TANK		1	1	
7.	120 MM		4	4	3
8.	GRADE –II		1		
9.	82 MM		6	4	2
10.	82 MM A/ TANK		6	2	2
11.	SPG-9		2		
12.	B-10		1		3
13.	14.5 MM (4B)		2	1	1
14.	14.5 MM (2B)				2
15.	14.5 MM (1B)			1	
16.	12.7 MM		10	4	6
17.	BROWNING		1		
18.	RPG-7		18	22	2
19.	60 MM		22	14	11
20.	PKM		16	8	8
21.	ZSU-37 (2B)		1	1	1
22.	ZSU-37 (1B)				
23.	ZSU-23 MM		1		
24.	RPD-44		10	11	3
25.	106 MM				
26.	KGK		1		
27.	TANKS		6	3	3
	Total		113	77	51

Source: Cdr Elias Waya's war time files

SPLA Parade in 2nd Front as per 25 February 2000

S/N	LOCATION	PRESENT		MISSION		TOTAL	REMARKS
		OFFICERS	NCOS+MEN	OFFICERS	NCOS+MEN		
1.	TINDILO FRONT	056	0691	004	062	0813	
2.	JAMBO FRONT	056	0890	NIL	NILE	0946	
3.	MILE-40 FRONT				123	0725	
4.	TOTAL	142	2140	017	158	2484	

Source: Cdr Elias Waya's war time files

Parade of 1st Brigade of 2nd Front

	PRESENT	MISSION	MEDICAL REFER	PERMISSION	ABSENTEES	TOTAL
OFFICERS	56	4	2	2		64
NCOs & Men	691	62	7	19	22	801
TOTAL	747	66	9	21	22	865

Source : Cdr Garang Bul Pager

Table 5

Parade of Martyrs, Wounded Heroes and Missing or Captured of SPLA Tank Unit in 1997

S/N	Space	KIA	WIA	MIA or CIA	Time	
1	Yei –Alero	1	-	-	13/3/1997	
2	Gigumini	-	13	-	13/3/1997	
3	Mile 40	4	-	-	28/3/1997	
4	Jambo	-	1	-	03/4/1997	
5	Amadi	-	1	-	5/4/1997	
6	Rokon	2	6	-	07/4/1997	
7	Mbolo	6	-	2	25/4/1997	
8	Rumbek	-	-	-	28/4/1997	
9	Tonj	-	-	-	15/5/1997	
10	Yirol	2	7	2	14/6/1997	
11	Tali	2	3	-	28/6/1997	
12	Mundari Boro	3	17	-	3/7/1997	
13	Situ	1	2	-	26/7/1997	
14	Tafari	-	-	-		
15	OJS East Bank of Nile	9	-	-		
	Total	30	50	4		

Source: Cdr Gabriel Jok Riak's war diary

Table 6

The parades of SPLA Forces that captured Tonj Garrison on 18 May 1997

S/N	Number of Column	Name of the officer leading the column in the battle	Number of officers in each column	Number of men in each column
1	1st Column	Captain Mamuor	8	74
2	2nd Column	Captain Magok	2	46
3	3rd Column	Captain Makuer	30	475
4	4th Column	Captain Mangar	7	108
5	5th Column	Division	27	330
	Total		73	1006
		Grand Total		1079

Source: SPLA Tank Unit

Table 7

Operation Thunderbolt (OTB) Armaments as it was ready for combat orders on 7 March 1997

S/N	Types of Calibre	Number of pieces available	
1	130-mm	4 pcs	
2	D-30 mm	4 pcs	
3	ZSU -23 mm	4 pcs	
4	ZSU-37 mm	4 pcs	
5	14.5 –mm four barrels	3 pcs	
6	SAM-7	4 pcs	
7	120 mm	7 pcs	
8	BM-21 mm 40 barrels	2 pcs	
9	BM-107 mm 12 barrels	8 pcs	
10	Tanks	20 pcs	
11	Red Arrow	3 pcs	
12	Milan Anti- Tank recoilless	6 pcs	
	G/Total	69	

Source: SPLA Tank Unit's war time files

Table 8

Details of the Sudan army 10 tanks captured by SPLA OTB in 1997

Tanks captured in good conditions

S/N	Type of Tank	Place	Pieces	Date
1	T-55	Yei	2	12/3/1997
2	,,	Jambo	1	3/4/1997
3	T-62	Yei	1	12/3/1997

Tanks captured with defects

S/N	Type of Tank	Defect	Pieces	Place	Date
1	T-55	Barrel	1	Yei	12/3/1997
2	,,	Fuel tanker	1	,,	,, ,, ,,
3	T-62	Fault is not yet traced	1	,,	,, ,, ,,
4	T-55	Main Gun	1	Kaya	9/3/1997
5	,,	Engine	1	,,	,, ,, ,,
6	,,	Head Cylinder Gasket	1	Jambo	3/4/1997
		G/Total			10 pcs

Source : SPLA Tank Unit

Table 9

The first class SPLA tank gunners who fired 12 shells in Battle of Tali on 28 June 1997

S/N	Name of Gunner	Number of shells he used	
1	Yel Deng	7 shells	
2	Matoc Dut	2 shells	
3	Peter Panhom	3 shells	
	Total	12 shells	

NB: In an ambush on 26 July 1997, 34 shells were used, the biggest number of shells ever in OTB in 1997.

Source: SPLA Tank Unit's files

Table 10

Details of SPLA 4 Tanks lost in Mile-40 on 28 March 1997

S/N	Type	Pieces	Condition
1	T-55	3	Destroyed
2	T-62	1	Got a problem in sprocket
	Total	4	

Source : Cdr Gabriel Jok Riak 's war diary

Table 11

Number of SPLA Tanks as war was declared over 2005

S/N	Location	Functioning tanks				Nonfunctioning tanks				
	Location	T-55	T-62	APC	Saladin	T-55	T-62	APC	Saladin	
1	Tindilo	3	-	-	-	-	-	-	-	
2	Mile-40	3	-	-	-	-	-	-	-	
3	Yei	-	-	-	-	1	2	-	-	
4	Aruu	2	-	-	-	4	-	-	-	
5	Moli	-	-	-	-	1	-	-	-	
6	Nimule	-	-	-	-	1	-	-	-	G/Total
7	Magwi	-	-	-	-	2	-	-	-	
8	Parajok	-	-	-	-	1	-	-	-	
9	Tsertenya	-	-	-	-	1	-	-	-	
10	Kiyala	8	-	-	-	4	-	-		
11	Khor Glario	-	-	-	-	-	-	-	1	
12	Production Camp	-	-	-	-	1	-	-	-	
13	Buna	-	-	-	-	-	1	-	-	
	Total	16				15	4	2	1	
	G/Total									37

Source: SPLA Tank Unit files

Table 12

Trucks available in SPLA 1ST Brigade of 2nd Front

S/N	Types of Trucks	Number of Trucks available	Mounted with which type of weapon	
1.	Tata Lorry	4	Mounted with 14.5 mm, ZUU 23 each	
2	Jeep	1	Mounted with 107 MM BM 12 Barrels	
3	Raul Truck	3	Mounted with Howizter 122 mm each	
Total		7		

Source: Cdr Garang Bul Pageer' war time files

Table 13

Communication Equipment in SPLA 1ST Brigade of 2nd Front

S/N	Types	Number available	
1	Long Range Radio Call	2	
2	Short Radio Call	6	
3	Thuraya	-	
4	Total	8	

Source : Cdr Garang Bul Pageer's war time files

Table 14

Parade of Koryom Division 1984

S/N	Name of Battalion	Parade	Remark
1	Zindia	1224	
2	Raad	1224	
3	Rhino	1224	
4	Cobra	1224	
5	Hadid	1224	
6	Agreb	1224	
7	Bilpam	1224	
8	Elephant	1224	
9	Hippo	600	
10	Aquilo	500	
11	She-Company(Katiba Banat)	150	
12	Lion	1224	
	G/Total	12,266	

Table 15

Parades of Muor Muor Division 1985

S/N	Name of Battalion	Parade	
1	Tuek Tuek	1224	
2	Shark	1224	
3	Nile	1224	
4	Wolf	1224	
5	Eagle	1224	
6	Neiran	1224	
7	Bee	1224	
8	Abushok	1224	
	G/Total	9, 792	

NB: Zalan and Becer Battalions remained in training until 1986

SPLM/SPLA: History of Liberation (1983-2005)

After all the forces were in vicinity of their target, President Omer Bashir flew to Malakal town in January 1992, in colourful and belligerent ceremony, he graced and rejuvenated their appetite for war, by delivering a religious and political speech to 8,000 troops. After the flagging off ceremony, he handed over the command and the overall conduct of the war to a retired Major General Mohammed al Zain.

The Fall of Pochala from SPLA

The fourth column of Seif al Ubuur flanked the SPLA, by entering Ethiopia and travelling inside Ethiopian territory till it attacked Pocholla by surprise in Eastern Jonglei province. It was actually astonishing to SPLA because it was unexpected. On 8 March 1992, Pochallla fell to SAF with many losses from SPLA both soldiers and civilians. When Seif Ubuur attacked, it was first thought, as though, it was Anyuak militiamen of Ethiopia, who were constantly attacking, because earlier in August 1991, the Anyuak miltia men attacked Pochalla. So soldiers ran out of town, when they heard sounds of gun, knowing they were Anyuak militia. At first, they were firing light machine guns, however, at 5pm; the tanks appeared on Pocholla stream firing into civilian population, killing tens of hundreds. And there, Pocholla was captured. The civilians, who ran from Pocholla were divided into two. Some went to Kapoeta through Boma and other to Bor through Pibor. Pochalla was the first SPLA liberated area captured by Seif al Ubuur Campaign.

The Fall of Bor from SPLA

The third column of Seif al Ubuur moved from Malakal on land through Ayod, which was controlled by SPLA splinter group, Nasir Faction. This column circumvented the SPLA position at Duk and appeared at Warkok, 15 kilometres from Bor town, SPLA tried to attack, but, it was of too little effect, and they marched into Bor easily on April 10, 1992. They entered in military procession on loud speakers. The state owned Radio Omdurman announced the capturing of Bor by Seif al Ubuur, in the broadcast, it said, "Dosa Brigade entered Bor 10 April 1992, the birth place of John Garang, and they found no people, but, the bones of those who died of hunger, and dying children and their mothers, who were held hostage against their will in so-called SPLA liberated areas of hunger and starvation, and Government is now sending food to save their lives".

Abdhal Jalil Brigade Retrograde

Without wasting anytime in Bor, Abdhal Jalil Brigade left immediately. Named Abdhal Jalil in honour of Brigadier General, Justice Abdhal Jalil Ibrahim, former director of military justice, who was killed by SPLA in 1990 in Bo Bridge. The forces left Bor as if they were going to Pibor, but in savannah treeless land between Bor and Pibor, they changed direction southward, to Equatoria. After two weeks of moving in forest, they appeared in Rwoto areas near Kapoeta. When the SPLA tried to stop them by ambushing, it was impossible to defend Kapoeta. The SPLA tried to fight for two days in forest; however, aided by some Toposa elements, they entered Kapoeta by circumvention in another direction. SPLA forces and civilian left Kapoeta at night in confusion after heavy shelling from the distance by Abdhal Jalil forces. As the SPLA was leaving the town, they were attacked by some Toposa militia men, who just switched sides and declared allegiance to coming SAF. Announcing the Fall of Kapoeta from SPLA to Seif el Ubuur at Juba Stadium, the Minister of Religious Affairs standing next to Col Ibrahim Chamisidin, the deputy minister of defence and Presidential Adviser for Security said '', our forces, the holy forces of Prophet Mohammad entered Kapoeta. This year, there is no place that our forces shall never put their feet on. The foolish infidels used to say, we don't fight in forest, that is why they are killing people and run to the bushes, we are fighting them now in the forest. We shall not leave John Garang until he either changes his name to Mohammad or he is killed ''

Hakim al Gaba

The second column of Seif Ubuur went Wau. In Wau they sent expedition to west Equatoria under the operation codenamed Hakim al Gaba to reinforce its forces in Bo Bridge and proceed to Tombura, fortunately this force, despite, it was well equipped, it was destroyed by SPLA on February 17, 1992. Many of the weapons captured and the advances of Hakim al Gaba were paralyzed. They returned to Wau.

The First Column of Seif al Ubuur

In February 1992, the first column of Seif al Ubuur moved out of Juba toward Torit, the General Headquarters of SPLA/M, destroying the SPLA defence position at Molbok, 20 kilometres from the city, triggering the SPLA to free the siege of Juba. The SPLA forces that were in the North of Juba, on Juba- Terekaka roads and those in west of Juba, on Juba - Yei road, withdrew all, moving to Torit road. However, the tempo, in which SAF was rushing was powerful and agilely. It overran the SPLA at Khor Hangreb. It also flank-attacked SPLA forces by moving the forces in forest and capturing Ngala Ngala just two, days after their first battle when they moved of Juba. SPLA moved to Liriya. It came and dislodged SPLA in Liria. After the fall of Liria. SPLA laid another ambush at Khor Iglish, 60 kilometres from Torit, halting the SAF from April to first week of June.

Operation Jungle Storm (OJS)

By May, the SPLA was on verge of defeat. Seif al Ubuur, was like shaving the devil hair in one of fables. In that fable a woman was shaving a head of man, who was actually man eater or devil, when he shaved the hair, it continued to grow immediately, as if it was never shaved at all. Seif al Ubuur was driving SPLA to Piny Gut or the end of the earth. It was attacking on air, on river Nile and on land. In words of John Garang, when somebody is boxing and pushing you to the end of the earth, you dived and appeared on his belly. The SPLA dived by attacking Juba, the belly and the centre of gravity of Seif al Ubuur in order to disrupt its momentum on the war in Operation Jungle Storm (OJS) . OJS was devised by C-in-C John Garang, Cdr Lual Diing Wol, Cdr Alfred Lado Gore, Cdr John Baibai, Cdr Oyai Deng, Cdr Bior Ajang Duot, Cdr James Hoth Mai, Cdr Pieng Deng Kuol, Cdr Gier Chuang Aluong, Cdr Thomas Chirilo Swaka, Cdr Agustino Jadhala Wani, Cdr Elias Waya, A/Cdr Majok Mach Aluong, A/Cdr James Koang Chol, A/Cdr Edward Lino Wuor, A/Cdr Wangchok Koryom, A/Cdr Anyar Apiu, A/Cdr Chol Thon Bolok, A/Cdr Garang Mabil Deng, A/Cdr Ajoung Malou Goc, A/Cdr Garang Mading Agook, A/Cdr Abuoc Arok Deng, A/Cdr Malual Majok Chiengkuach, A/Cdr Kuai Kuei Kuai, A/Cdr Deng Kuot Nyang, A/Cdr Machar Thiong Ayuel, A/Cdr Majok Deng Biar, A/Cdr Majur Aleer, A/Cdr

SPLA/M'S BLACK CHAPTER: THE STRUGGLE AT ITS LOWEST LEVEL (1991-1995)

Battles of Juba I and II

In the operation codenamed Operation Jungle Storm (OJS), on June 6 the SPLA attacked Juba the capital city of Southern Sudan for the first time in its ten years' period of waging war. When designing and laying the sand model of the battle of Juba I, there were ten enemy defences targeted in Juba city, these were; Juba International Airport, Seif al Ubuur headquarters on the way to airport, Buluk, Kuer (barges) on the river Nile, Radio Juba, Mess 40, Mess 80, Rajaf and Juba Bridge. At 3 pm, the SPLA attacked eight targets inside Juba, Juba International Airport was the main target of forces, who were commanded Cdr Garang Mabil Deng. These forces did not take action on the airport as planned, because, they were repelled by enemy at New site, the rear-guard of the airport. New Site became the major obstacle for the forces under Garang, making them not to progress, to capture the airport despite heroic, whole-hearted attempt by Cdr Garang to capture airport. Cdr John Koang Nyuon overran Rajaf and withdrawing later. Cdr Pieng Deng partially destroyed Juba Brigade and withdrew back, too. At 10.00 am, the SPLA withdrew from Juba at great loss of many soldiers including; Captain Majok Deng Biar, Captain Kunka Gat Tuak, Captain Awou, Captain Deng Ageny

On July 7, 1992 the second battle of Juba started. The SPLA forces tried their best to capture, but and still they were repelled. In this battle, brave soldiers like Cdr Kuai Kuei Kuai, and Prophet Bith, the SPLA first ever prophet were killed. In addition, Captain Arok Manyang was captured on the top of the mountain Kujur and with some soldiers, where he was directing the SPLA artillery fire with communication equipment.

The Fall of Torit from SPLA

In August, Marum Brigade marched to Torit and capturing it. The SPLA set out a front at Jebel Labalwa on Torit-Kapoeta road and another at Torit-Magwi road. From August up to December 1992, there was no fighting between the SPLA and SAF. It was rainy season, SAF was so lethargic as well as the SPLA.

SPLM/SPLA: History of Liberation (1983-2005)

The Escape of Political Prisoners, 1992

As the SPLA/SPLM had been waging the war, there had been internal disagreement for one reason or another. From 1985 up to 1992, there were 30 political detainees in prison, including Martin Majier Gai, one of seven cofounders of SPLA/M, two permanent members of PMHC, Cdr Kerubino Kuanyin Bol (who was the de facto leader of movement from May 16 up to July 1983, when Dr John Garang was elected the Chairman and the Commander in Chief) and Cdr Arok Thon Arok, who was number 5 in the movement hierarchy. Other detainees were; Lt. Col (PSC) Martin Makur Aleiyou (who was accused of contempt to others, emanating from his great military training and seniority in old Sudan army), Cdr Kawac Makuei Kawac (after he complained of, why he was sent for mobilization in Bahr el Ghazal, and behind was left out from Political Military High Command (PMHC) in February 1984, Cdr Faustino Atem Gualdit, Cdr Perer Bol Maguak, Joseph Malath Lueth ... etc. By 1992, these political prisoners were detained by the movement leadership without charges, prompting many people to sympathize with them in their detention. Because of that sympathy, some elements in the SPLA organized them to escape. In 1992, it was allegedly said, all political detainees escaped in prison near Kaya except Martin Majier and Martin Makur, who refused to escape for the reasons well known to themselves. Cdr Kerubino Kuanyin, Cdr Arok Thon, Cdr Joseph Malath Lueth (unconfirmed reports said, he was killed on the way to Uganda) ...among others escaped and ran to Koboko at Uganda border, then to Kampala where they released a statement after first escaping from prison. After the escape of other political detainees, Martin Majier, Martin Makur, Kawac Makuei Kawac.... among others were released by John Garang, ordering them to go for political asylum abroad or wherever they wanted.

William Nyuon's Mutiny in Pageri

There were many unconfirmed information and allegations surrounding the defection of William Nyuon in Pageri. In 1992, peace talks were called between the Sudan Government and the SPLA/M in Abuja, Nigeria, mediated by the Nigerian President Ibrahim Babangida. Cdr William Nyuon, who was CI2 of John Garang, was sent as head of the delegation.

When he returned to Pageri, there was high tension between him and Cdr Kuol Manyang Juuk. There were about three to four incidents of shooting out between their bodyguards in Pageri market. According to Nyuon, he allegedly said, he heard that Cdr Kuol was given orders to arrest him. According to the SPLA/M, it was allegedly said Cdr William was bribed by Sudan governmnt in Abuja and he was planning to defect from the SPLA. Cdr William Nyuon was also accused of capitation by signing the unification document between SPLM/A Mainstream and Nasir faction before consulting the whole leadership. Attempt to reconcile Cdr Nyuon and Cdr Kuol failed. And finally, Cdr William Nyuon left Pageri and he was ambushed in Panyagwar and fighting broke out there. An Aid worker was killed, first aid worker to be in liberated areas, after Cdr William left. He fought the SPLA until he surrendered himself to Sudan army in Magure.

Second Arrest of Martin Majier Gai

As soon as Martin Majier was released, there was allegedly smear mongering or praising about him by his political opponent or allies, he was derogatory or honourably called Mandela, because, he was released by the time Nelson Mandela of South Africa was released after 27 years in prison at Robin Island. Based on some rumours that Martin Majier and Martin Makur would announce their government/ movement in January 1993, Majier and many other officers were arrested in December 1992, some in west bank of Nile in Kaya while some other in east bank of Nile in Pageri. Two officers; A/Cdr. Majok Nyieth and Captain Akuak Kudum were tortured to death in Pageri. After one month, there was a report on BBC Focus on Africa news summary, which said a group of political prisoners had escaped from prison and were running toward Juba. It was not known, who were these political prisoners who escaped and ran toward Juba.

Demise of Uncle Jospeh Oduho,

By 1993, the SPLA/M Nasir of Dr Riek and Dr Lam called for a meeting of all the factions, and other members of SPLA/M, who disagreed with Dr John Garang. A meeting was convened in Panyagor, Twic East. SPLA/M Mainstream heard of this gathering through its intelligence. As they were preparing for the meeting, SPLA was preparing to attack them. Forces left

SPLM/SPLA: History of Liberation (1983-2005)

Equatoria hurriedly at the end of February 1993. In Panyagor, all defectors from SPLM/A had gathered; Dr. Riek Machar, Dr Lam Akol, Cdr Arok Thon, Cdr Kerubino Kuanyin, Uncle Joseph Oduho....and many other. As their meeting was in progress, by surprise, they were attacked by the SPLA, as they were running, Uncle Joseph Oduho died under unclear circumstances either of exhaustion from the run or by the SPLA bullet. The rests had to run through Duk to Yuai, where they were picked and airlifted to Nairobi. Joseph Oduho was the first member of seven cofounders of SPLM/SPLA to die. Despite he died out the SPLM/A, he contributed so much to the liberation of Southern Sudan, from Anya Nya I to SPLM/A.

Glerio Modi Hurnyang:
The largest group of Equatorians to leave SPLA/M

Glerio Modi Hurnyang, an alternate member of SPLM/A Political Military High Command (PMHC), rebelled against the movement in 1992, either simultaneously or after William Nyuon's rebellion. The reasons of his rebellion were not well spelt out, though; he accused some members of movement of tribalism. He was the last man to leave with last, largest Equatoria soldiers, after the Mundari group that left in 1991, joining militia leader Clement Wani. Commander Glerio died few years later in mountains in Equatoria, after he left the SPLM/A.

Two Fronts on both sides of River Nile

At the end of 1992 or precisely, at the end of Seif al Ubuur, the all-out dry season offensive of 1992 to 1993, there remained six military garrison taken from Sudan by SPLA BSC of 1989 to 1990. These nine garrisons were Nimule, Kajo Keji, Kaya, Maridi and Yambio and Parajok. At the end of 1993, two military expeditions were organized in Juba for the dry season of 1994. The two expeditions moved out of Juba, one to Kajo Keji and the other to Nimule. The one moving to Kajo Keji was code-named Usud al Gaba, 'Lions of jungle' in Arabic. These forces swept through Kaji Keji jungles, where they met stiff SPLA resistance at Rojo area. The SPLA forces at Rojo were commanded by Cdr Mach Paul Kuol. The SPLA was overwhelmed by the Usud-al-Gaba, captured Kajo Kaji and Kaya respectively. The SPLA moved to border villages of Bumeri that became Internal Displaced Camps.

West Nile front of Commander Juma Urus of Uganda

In 1992/3, the proxy wars intensified in regions, thus, President Beshir of Sudan in order to encounter President Museveni's of Uganda support to SPLM/A, he supported the rebel West Nile Front (WNF) of Commander Juma Urus. These rebels established the bases in Kaya areas, where they could attack Northern Uganda.

Jebel Awence Front

After falling of Torit to the hands of Sudan army in 1992 and evacuation of SPLA/M to Nimule Corridor at Uganda border, and the failure of the SPLA to capture Juba in 1992 and the subsequent pushing out of the SPLA from the vicinity of Juba to Jebel Awence Fronts. Nimule Corridor became the final epicentre of the war because all Triple A Displaced camps of Ame, Ashwa and Atepi moved to Nimule. In January 1993, SAF set out to capture Nimule, the last stronghold of SPLA. At Jebel Awence, the successful advances of the SAF were halted by SPLA with help of natural obstacle. A road passes between two precipices of the mountain. At these two precipices, SPLA laid ambush. The SAF advanced, but, the SPLA kept beating them back at Jebel Awence. There was no way the tanks of SAF could manoeuvre because of the precipice. SAF tried for the whole of 1993 to breakthrough this defences but it is impossible. The SAF kept deceptively small force at Awence, and biggest forces returned toward Juba and finding the alternative route that passed through Lobonok. It started moving from Rajaf to Lobonok. SPLA noticed that enemy advances, when it was already at Karpata, almost behind the SPLA defences at Awence, swiftly rushing to Nyarbang. The advances caused panic among the SPLA forces by fearing that the enemy would cut them off from Moli junction. Therefore, the SPLA had to withdraw from Jebel Awence front without a fight, coming and laying the ambush at Moli junction in May 1994; SAF came in and broke up. SPLA tactically withdrew to Ashwa river when the SAF was advancing toward Ashwa river, SPLA dismantled Ashwa Bridge using powerful explosive, the SAF tried to drive SPLA to Ashwa, but, it is difficult because of Ashwa River became another natural obstacle helping the SPLA. The SAF fought the SPLA for two months on Ashwa River in June to August 1994, but it was difficult, so SAF had to find an alternative route to Nimule through Pogee. SPLA discovered and rushed in halting the advances of SAF again at Pogee until 1995.

SPLM National Convention 1994

The SPLA/M held its first national convention in 1994 at Chukudum. The convention was at first planned to take place in 1993 at Borongole near Pageri, however, it was disrupted by mushrooming of enemy from Juba to capture Nimule. And then it was shifted to Chukudum in Eastern Equatoria.

The aims of convention were to evaluate the war fighting, success, failures, challenge and opportunities in the SPLA/M at the backdrop of the disintegrations of the USSR, the collapse of friendly Mengistu government in Ethiopia, the split of the SPLA/M into SPLA/M Mainstream and the SPLA/M Nasir faction. John Garang opened the meeting with the acknowledgements of the failures and success and mistakes made. Some commanders were gullible enough, when Garang cunningly said, he had stepped down as the Chairman and Commander in Chief of SPLA/M. Some commanders took that whole-heartedly, they proposed the replacement of John Garang as the Chairman. One Commander stood up and said, yes John Garang should be changed as the Chairman. The master of the ceremony asked the delegates to the second motion. There was no one, responding to second motion to replace Chairman. Another commander stood up and said, " Garang should not be replaced".

When the motion of the no change was put to delegates to second it. "Hundreds of hands were up' in seconding the no change motion". Therefore, the chairman of organizing committee say, your motion is defeated. Therefore, John Garang is now reaffirmed the Chairman and Commander in Chief of the SPLA/M. The new change Commander felt ashamed and after he fought in battle of Kapoeta, he left for London without permission from John Garang, the C-in-C of SPLM/SPLA in 1995.

SPLM/SPLA Fall Back: The Secessionist War

At the end of the convention, many changes were made in the objectives of war, the war was redefined and changed it, from a civil war to a secessionist war, as fall-back position from original position of the liberating whole Sudan. The SPLA/SPLM was rewritten as the SPLM/SPLA. Before, the military wing was senior to political one. The red star in the flag of the movement, symbolising socialism was changed to yellow. The movement manifesto was declared irrelevant, because, it has socialist or communist phraseology or leaning. The Politico-Military High Command (PMHC) of 1983 was dissolved and was divided into three organs, namely; National Liberation Council (NLC) that became the legislature or parliament, National Executive Council (NEC) that became executive or cabinet, and General Field Staff and Command Council (GFSCC), which was comprised of 40 red-collared commanders of SPLA. The Convention also established Civil Administration of the New Sudan (CANS), which appointed the Governors, Payam and Boma administrators. The payam and Boma were coined as the new political expression of SPLM/SPLA.

Battle of Kapoeta II

At the end of Convention, the political mobilisers went to Kakuma refugee camp in Kenya to mobilize the new recruits and old soldiers, who deserted. 2000 Red Army volunteered themselves to return from refuge and come back to the war front. These Red Army entered Latuke Training Centre near Chukudum. This red army were graduated and became known as Ingas or 'Salvation' in Arabic. They were commanded by officers who included Cdr Thomas Cirilo Swaka, Cdr Pieng Deng Kuol, Cdr Jame Hoth Mai, Cdr Aleu Ayieny Aleu, Cdr Dominc Dim Deng, Cdr Atem Garang de-Kuek and Cdr Majok Mach Aluong, Cdr Anyar Apiu, Captain Luol, Captain Akech Mach Akook. These forces attacked Kapoeta. The battle went on for three consecutive days, unfortunately, it ended with the SPLA tactically withdrawal from town with killing of many men and officers, like Cdr Mach Majok Aluong, Cdr Anyar Apiu, Captain Akech Mach Akook aka Akech Obang and Captain Luol, the composer of the famous revolutionary song "Chala abui adiu tanga". The SPLA moved out and mounted a front at Bunia between Kapoeta and Nairus to the Kenya border.

Hot Spring Conference

After the national convention's resolutions that separated military and political wings of the SPLM/A. Conference for the GFSCC only was

SPLM/SPLA: History of Liberation (1983-2005)

called. Although GFSCC, established in 1992 after the dissolution of PMHC, it was first time it convened to discuss the technical role of the army, which was not discussed in national convention in Chukudum. It had to discuss how the war be conducted. This question, however, was presented in form of six concept papers; (1) enemy situation (2) relation between the SPLA and other organized forces, police, wildlife and prison (3) relation between the SPLA and New Sudan in general (4) recruitment and mobilization (5) the structure of the SPLA (6) service and support (COMSCOM) artillery, Engineering, Signal. One of the resolutions of the conference was the diversional warfare. It was resolved that war should extend to Northern Sudan through New Sudan Brigade (NSB) in Blue Nile and Eastern Sudan. This was to take war to the defensive depth of enemy. The chief of Staff (COS) position was created and its deputies. Cdr Salva Kiir was appointed as COS, Cdr Oyai Deng as deputy for operation, Cdr Peter Wal Athui as deputy for Administration and Cdr Anthony Bol Madut for Logistics, etc.

Demise of Judge Martin Majier Gai, 1940-1994

Judge Martin Majier Gai passed on in 1994; he was one of the seven founding fathers of SPLM/SPLA. The other founding fathers were; John Garang de Mabior, Kerubino Kuanyin Bol, William Nyuon Bany, Salva Kiir Mayayrdit, Arok Thon Arok and Joseph Oduho Awero. His death was confirmed by John Garang in interview, and this is how Dr Achol Deng Achol described in tribute

One worst fear had now been confirmed. The death of Martin Majier Gai Ayuel, former student leader, judge, advocate, Member of Parliament for Bor South constituency, Regional minister who was under detention by Sudan People's Liberation Army SPLA since 1985, has been announced by John Garang, 14 months after event. Only fools will be gullible enough to believe the cynical version that he was shot while escaping from detention.

A man of high pedigree, penetrating intelligence, untainted integrity and immense popularity, Martin Majier Gai was envied, feared and consequently detained by a number of Sudanese administrations including the Mengistu-style Stalinist regime of John Garang who took his life and despicably dumped his body in the river, in a macabre manner of which the Rwandese thugs would have approved, John Garang like the scheming manipulator that he delayed the announcement of Martin Majier's assassination in the vain hope that he would break the news of his criminal act of his own choosing . But no time is good for announcing this premeditated murder.

Martin Majier Gai Ayuel Yuot was born to a well-known Dinka Bor family and thus did not need to affect nobility, unlike some so-called SPLA leaders who, through inferiority complex, use the commonplace of Dinka to delude outsiders, particularly Europeans, with a pedigree they do not actually have in Bor society. Martin Majier was a natural leader in his age group, whether in the cattle camp or at schools. His leadership qualities were to stand him in good stead in his later roles in judiciary, advocacy and politics.

Martin Majier attended Malek Elementary School, Atar Intermediate School and Rumbek Secondary School where he left brilliant academic records. A good all round student who could have studied at any faculty of his choice, he had a solid education at Faculty of Law, University of Khartoum where he graduated in 1967 with honours, unlike some so-called SPLA leaders who have been bragging about useless higher degrees from fourth rate Americans Universities. After an outstanding performance in the Sudanese Bar Examination, he started his legal career as judge becoming advocate when he responded to his people's call to be their representative in the Regional Assembly in Juba. A man of penetrating intellect, Martin Majier did not suffer fools, particularly academic upstarts and pseudo intellectuals, too gladly. Therein lay his difficulties with so-called SPLA leader.

Martin Majier was a man of unstained integrity. He stands out as the only Southern Sudanese politician who has ever resigned a ministerial post on an issue of principle. It was this trait that was responsible for his fundamental difference, with the opportunist John Garang, a Mengistu protégé who masqueraded as a socialist. Along with late veteran Southern politician, Uncle Joseph Oduho, another victim of John Garang, Martin Majier called for a separation of the roles between the political and military wings of the SPLA, a step which is allegedly being undertaken now. They also opposed the blatant communist manifesto that SPLA adopted at the behest of Mengistu. Above all, Martin Majier and Joseph Oduho refused to participate in the cover-up of Garang's cold-blooded murder in 1984 of Benjamin Bol Akok, the Makerere and Oxford educated Southern politician from Aweil. Martin Majier and Joseph Oduho expressed doubts about how an erstwhile healthy Benjamin Bol could have died of liver failure only few hours after the Mengistu security police, at the instigation of John Garang, made him disembark from a flight to London, at Addis Abba airport. Like the good lawyer that he was, Martin Majier had demanded that the coffin be opened to identify the corpse and that autopsy be done to determine the cause of Benjamin Bol death. This was anathema to Garang who flew into fury of rage. It is therefore understandable that Martin Majier and Joseph Oduho were, alas, not to be allowed to live to tell the tale.

Because he confronted the issues headlong, unlike the devious, insecure and obscure John Garang, Martin Majier was immensely popular in his home base Bor, a popularity that translated in the single honour of returning him unopposed as Member of Parliament. Indeed, his reputation as Mr Clean which he earned as a judge in the Blue Nile, Kordofan and Bahr el Ghazal provinces enhanced his stature beyond the confines of his constituency and staked out his claim as a genuine Southern Sudanese leader. Martin Majier was an obstacle to John Garang's ambition. To ensure that John Garang achieves popularity at his home base, where he hardly had any roots and to which he owned to allegiance, Martin Majier could be removed from the Bor scene. How foolish, short-sighted and risky, indeed a new Bor had to be constructed from ashes of the old to suit John Garang's ego. This explains John Garang's complacency, indeed sheepish and smug satisfaction, in the face of the unprecedented on slaughter on the innocent children, women and men of Bor by evil forces he had foolishly antagonized and who unleashed vengeance on Garang's people, little knowing that only a tenuous nexus existed between himself and Bor. In 1992 Garang showed how little he cared about Bor people when he failed to defend them on the ostensible ground that he wanted to capture Juba. He allowed Bor to be devastated. This skewed logic must have been music to the ears of his enemies.

Martin Majier joint the struggle to rectify legitimate grievances against the central government. But like Benjamin Bol, Joseph Oduho, Malath Joseph, Thon Ayii, Gai Tut, Hugo Lugi Aduok, Martin Kajiboro and Martin Makur Aleyou, to name few, he was to die in the hands of a wicked comrade-in-arms, who mistakenly believed he would benefit from his treachery. But Martin's family, friends, supporters and political allies across the country who have been denied the right to give him a DECENT BURRIAL, will not accept this treachery.

Martin Majier, through no choice of his, achieved the dubious distinction of being, until recently the longest serving detainee of John Garang. Not content with humiliating and torturing him, Garang ignominiously murdered him. If the assassination in cold blood of Martin Majier stirs the conscience of all the Sudanese and helps unmasks the treacherous, blood-thirsty buffoon and upstart that John Garang is, then Martin Majier will not die in vain. Let this assassination to be the last. Let this be the last straw that broke the Carmel's back. Let words go forth firmly, loud and clear. Enough of the eleven years of buffoonery and gratuitous fraternal blood-letting. It is time for a change. John Garang, who thrives in fostering disunity among Southern Sudanese, and whose hands are stained with blood, must go. Away with the dictator. John Garang must go.[2]

There were unconfirmed information and allegation about the issues and problems surrounding death of Martin Majier. The problem of Martin Majier with the SPLM/A leadership or in particularly John Garang started in 1984, according to Majier, he said, as a political adviser to John Garang, he advised John Garang not to send Koryom forces to the frontlines, but, he should let them wait for recruits from other tribes and they are mixed and sent to the frontlines together.

After the battles of Jekou failed, it was categorically reported that the two civilian Martin Majier and Joseph Oduho who were among seven men leadership committee, had started new opposition, intended to divide the movement, in case they can't take over it .

Finally, Martin Majier called for the separation between the political and military wings of the SPLM/A. Majier was always talking to John Garang to institute the political wing of the movement in order to administer the town capture by the SPLA. John Garang rejected this, and he accused Martin Majier of trying to bring the old Anya Nya I system, where there were cabinet ministers in bush

When Majier and Garang did not understand themselves, it was

SPLM/SPLA: History of Liberation (1983-2005)

claimed that Majier wrote to President Mengistu explaining his problem with Garang. Some sources close to Majier said he never wrote any letter, that the letter was concocted by John Garang's pretext to arrest him. Martin Majier was briefly released from detention in 1992. He went to his family in Yundu Internal Displaced Camps. There, there was new allegation that Martin Majier and Martin Makur, would declare their movement in January 1993. They were arrested in Kaya and they were allegedly killed in Lobojo on the River Nile by SPLM/A leadership. Martin Majier refused to leave the liberation struggle despite hearing of his imminent killing by SPLM/A leadership because he loved liberation more than his life and he loved to die in SPLM/A.

Norwegian People Aid (NPA)

As Southern Sudanese were fighting their war, the international community was with them through UN Operation Lifeline Sudan (OLS). Many international non-governmental organizations (NGOs) had been helping Southern Sudanese, both, in internally displaced persons (IDPs) camps in Southern Sudan as well as in the refugee camps in neighbouring countries; Ethiopia, Kenya, Uganda and other countries. World Food Programme (WFP) had provided millions of tonnes of USAID-marked bags of sorghum, lentils and salt through many partners like Catholic Relief Service (CRS).

UNICEF had entirely supported the education by providing books and writing materials through partners to liberated areas and refugee camps.

During the war, three international aid workers were killed in the cross-fire between SPLA and mutinying troops of Cdr William Nyuon in 1992. The killed aid workers were ; Myint Maung, from Burma, who was working for UNICEF, Vilma Gomez, a well known staff by SPLM/A fraternity through her open-handedness in giving out, from Philippines, who worked for Interlaid, and Helga Hummelyoll, a Norwegian journalist.[3]

Above all, when the SPLA was almost defeated and situation became fragile and most NGOs left, NPA remained and continued providing the humanitarian works to Southern Sudanese, especially Mr Dan Effie had, for a number of occasion, been seen, running into bunker amongst Southern Sudanese, during the aerial bombardment in Nimule in 1994. Other white were Brother Mike and Sister Veronica of JRS.

Notes
1. Mohammed al Amin Khalifa, 2003, Khartoum, Making Peace
2. Dr Achol Deng Achol, Press Release published 1 July 1994 from King's College, England
3. Associated Press (AP), October 1, 1992.

CHAPTER 7

THE SPLA OPERATIONS: THE WAR AT ITS RENAISSANCE, 1995-1999

By December 1995, the SPLA suddenly chased the Sudan army from Ashwa, after two years of fighting there and the four years of its small-eyedness in the all fronts, pushing them away from nine defensive positions in the bushes of Ashwa. The hurricane turned its tide against the government forces due to changes in the international geopolitics toward Sudan, because of their political and religious ideologies.

The SPLM/A succeeded in 1995, because, it was now backed militarily up by three African Countries; Uganda, Eritrea and Ethiopia. These countries were acting on the behalf of the World's superpower, the United States of America (USA), after it had fallen out with the Sudan in 1995 because of many reasons; (1) Sudan declared on eschatological war or jihad in the country (2) Sudan consecrate itself as the headquarters of the Muslim brotherhood. By this virtue, Sudan became the radical Islamic heartland, being advanced by Dr Hassan Al-Turabi.

As the centre of the Islamic fundamentalism, the most wanted men around the world convened in Khartoum as their safe haven (a) Osman bin Laden of Al-Qaeda network, who declared a jihad against the US, he first stayed in Khartoum before relocating to Afghanistan, after pressure from the Americans (b) Carlos the Jackal, who was wanted by the France Government on charges of terrorism, also was staying in Khartoum (c) the members of Hezbollah of Lebanon and Hamas of Palestine, who were considered terrorist organizations by the US were staying too in Khartoum (3) Sudan was accused and implicated in the three alleged international crimes (a) aiding of the Somali warlords like ; Muhammad Farah Aidaad and others (b) attempted assassination against Egyptian President Hosni Mubarak in Ethiopia's capital Addis Ababa (c) two Sudan's diplomats tried to blow United Nation General Assembly in New York .

Based on these Sudan's subversive, sabotaging activities around the world, which were threatening the US interests, the US decided to use the SPLA against the Sudan. Unlike, during Nimieri era, when the US was supporting Sudan's army against the SPLA, because of cold war politic of the time. Now for the US to achieve its objectives of toppling President Bashir from power, it had to work with SPLA. Therefore, US secretly worked with regional leaders in Horn of Africa; President Yoweri Museveni of Uganda, President Isaiah Afeweki of Eritrea, and Prime Minister Meles Zanawi of Ethiopia. The strategic plan of the US and its allies in the region played now in the hands of SPLM/A. It was found out the SPLA was only best implementer of this plan of overthrowing president Beshir. And in order to get rid of him; weapons, tanks and artillery, money and manpower (specialists in tanks and artillery from Ethiopia and Eritrea) were given to the SPLA. The Christians in Western World began to lobby for support to SPLA/M materially and morally. It became necessity for them to give pressure to US, Norway ...etc., that Christians in Southern Sudan were being massacred, mistreated, persecuted and marginalized by the Islamic fundamentalist government in Sudan. From that support given to the SPLM/A at the time, Christianity became only the reason, why the SPLA/M was supported in 1990s by the Western world, unlike before, it was supported by President Mengistu because of communist agenda to support the oppressed people around world to liberate themselves from capitalists' yoke.

SPLM/SPLA: History of Liberation (1983-2005)

Demise of William Nyuon Bany 1996

Cdr William Nyuon Bany was one of the seven cofounders of SPLAM/A in 1983. He rebelled against the SPLM/A in 1992 and seriously fought it until he later surrendered himself to Sudan army at Magure point near Juba. Cdr William Nyuon stayed briefly with the Sudan government before redefecting and returning to SPLM/A in 1995. In January 1996, he was sent for mobilization at his home area of Jonglei. Shortly after his arrival there he was killed by other Southern Sudanese pro-government militia group. The former second Deputy Chairman and Deputy Commander in Chief of SPLM/A, after detention of Kerubino Kuanyin, William Nyuon Bany was the third cofounder of SPLM/A to die. SPLM/A historians believed if William Nyuon remained loyal to SPLM/A until 2005, he would have been the first president of South Sudan, after the death of John Garang.

OJS Phase III

In 1995, the SPLM/A had acquired a Battalion of 24 tanks. In order to get crews to operate tanks, 300 soldiers were sent for a training course in Polataka, to be trained as drivers, gunners, loaders and commanders of the tanks. The 300 soldiers were the second batch of tanks' crews, because the first batch was trained in Awasha in Ethiopia. The training was in preparation for OJS Phase III. The OJS Phase I was the battles of Juba; the first Battle of Juba on 6/6/1992, and the second Battle of Juba on 7 /7/1992 respectively. The OJS Phase II was the ambushes laid by SPLA, in fighting against the advances of the Sudan army, from Juba to Nimule Corridor, the last SPLA stronghold in Eastern Equatoria that remained after Seif al Ubuur captured all the garrison towns liberated by the SPLA in its BSC of 1989. OJS Phase III was meant to push and chase away the Sudan army from Parajok at the Uganda border, east of Nimule to Jebellein Front, 45 kilometres south of Juba, main garrison of government forces in Southern Sudan.

In preparation of the OJS Phase III, the bodyguards of the 40 SPLA red collars members of GFSCC, who attended the Hot Spring Conference, were organized into one task force of 900 soldiers and Marshall Law mobilisation in the IDPs' camps of Lobone was organized into a Task

Force of 900 soldiers. There were also 1500 soldiers who were in ambush already, blocking the enemy from capturing Nimule. These forces in Pogee were organized into five fighting task forces with manpower of 3000 troops, supported by 11 tanks and a number of artillery which were operated by the Ethiopians, Eritreans and Uganda gunners, surprisingly attacked Parajok. At first, the foreign friendly forces shelled Parajok with a maximum artillery fire. When the assault troops moved in the enemy was already exhausted and on the flight. The SPLA captured Parajok with little resistance. With that momentum, the SPLA attacked seven round defences at Obwo, Owiny-ki- Bul, Amee, Magwi, Opari and Moli and overrunning them all in one month.

Brigadier Ugel Mohammed Ugel Hold out

As the SPLA was enjoying victories over Sudan army, capturing seven defence positions within one month with little resistance from enemy, However, Brigadier Ugel and two colonels dug themselves up, in around defence in Lou area between Ashwa and Pageri until, they were cut off from the rest of their forces. In his defence, Ugel vowed that he would not return to Juba, before, he would go to Nimule. Ugel, with 1,000 soldiers, resisted the SPLA assaults, raids and shelling for three months until he himself withdrew tactfully on his own accord later on, when he had no food and ammos. When the food and ammunitions were dropped from the air by Antonov, they were falling outside their defence, and were picked by the SPLA.

Operation Black Fox (OBF), 1996.

By 1996 the SPLM/A had re-established the oldest relation with the new Ethiopian Government of the Prime Minister Meles Zenawi. At time, the SPLA sent mobilizers to Kakuma Refugee Camp. There, they mobilized 2,000 Red Army boys (from the group who were later resettled in US and became known called Lost Boys). The 2,000 Red Army (or the so-called child soldiers in jargon of humanitarianism) were sent to Dima in Ethiopia for military training. After the training, they were combined with the old soldiers. In 1996 commanded by Cdr Kuol Manyang Juuk, Cdr Wilson Deng and supervised by John Garang, they attacked Pochalla in operation known as Operation Black Fox, capturing it. After the fall of Pochalla, these forces were sent to Southern Blue Nile under Cdr Majak D'Agot Atem. In Southern Blue Nile, they launched Operation Black Fox Part B, liberating Kurmuk garrison in 1996 for the fourth times since 1987, but, it was retaken from them after one month.

Demise of Arok Thon, 1996

Commander Arok Thon Arok was the fifth permanent member of Political Military High Command (PMHC) of SPLM/A from 1984 to 1988. He was shortly detained when Battalion 105 under Major Kerubino rebelled on May 16, 1983. He came to movement in 1984, after he was released from prison, when the movement leadership had already been established in 1983. Although, he was senior to Major Kerubino, Major William and Captain Salva, he got the theory of" first come, first serves" already applied. That new arrangement brought clash between him and those three men until, he was detained and he escaped from prison and went to Nairobi. In Nairobi, attempts were made to reconcile him, with John Garang, in hoping of joining ranks and file of the SPLM/A, those attempts failed and Commander Arok went to Khartoum. In 1997, he signed Khartoum Peace Agreement (KPA) with those of Dr Riek Machar, Kerubino Kuanyin Bol and he was appointed a minister in national goverment. Honourable Minister Arok Thon Arok died with Sudanese vice president Zubeir Mohammed Salah, the plane; they were travelling crashed into Nasir River in 1996. Arok Thon Arok was the second permanent member of PMHC to die after William Nyuon. Despite Arok Thon's disagreement with SPLAM/A leadership he will be remembered for destroying Subur Zaida, the largest compaign against SPLA by Sudan army.

Operation Thunderbolt (OTB), 1997

Operation Thunderbolt (OTB) was a highly planned, coordinated and executed military operation of SPLA in 1997. It was second successful campaign after BSC of 1989. The mission of OTB was to destroy the enemy in the outskirts of west of Juba, to liberate Kaya, Bazi, Morobo, Kaji Kaji, Alero, Mile 40, Jambo, Amadi, Mbolo upto Bongu area, 25 miles from Juba city. That was done in phases. The OTB started with mobilization of new recruits, from Lakes province areas of Yirol, Cueibet and Rumbek. The sons of Lake State' areas, who were commanders went to their home areas and mobilized 1500 young men in 1996. These 1500 recruits underwent training in Bumeri which was codenamed as Aribi

After training, John Garang came and named the forces Achondok Battalion, "Achondok" means a tree with strongest curved thorn' in Dinka languages. He graduated them. In Aribi, the sand model of OTB was designed and lay out. With coordination and participation of foreign allied forces of Uganda, Ethiopia and Eritrea, the OTB was launched in March 1997. Achondok and the other forces who were mobilized in Yambio and other areas of western Equatoria and older forces were organized into five brigades; namely; Brigade 2, 7, 8, 9 and 39, each has a parade of 1200 soldiers, bringing the total parade of these brigades to 6000 soldiers. It had the best armaments: 20 tanks and more than 100 artilleries of different calibres that include; 130mm, D-30MM, Zsu-37mm, 14.5mm, SAM-7, 120mm, Bm -21mm, Bm 107mm, Red Arrow, and Milan missile. The forces were commanded by; Cdr Marial Chanuong Yol, Cdr George Athor Deng, Cdr Gier Chuong Aluong, Cdr Augustino Jadhalla Wani. The operation group members were; Cdr Salva Kiir Mayardit, Cdr Oyai Deng Ajak, Cdr Garang Mabil Deng and Cdr Elias Waya Nyipuoc and under supervision of C-in-C John Garang and Cdr James Wani Igga. The Uganda People Defence Forces (UPDF) kicked off the operation by shelling Kaya with excessive volume of artillery fire. Kaya garrison was clouded with smoke and flames of burning huts. The shelling was followed by tanks and infantry assaults. Within 25 minutes, Kaya was captured. The main reason, why UPDF participated in the campaign was that, the OTB was engulfing areas of Uganda-Sudan border, which were used as springboard by West Nile Front (WLF), Uganda rebel group of Juma Oris, to attack Uganda, and was also a part of wider regional policy of removing Bashir from power.

West Nile front (WNF)

West Nile Front (WNF) of General Juma Orus, who was fighting, to topple President Museveni of Uganda, was operating in Bazi and Morobo inside Sudan. Thus, UPDF on pretext of fighting the WNF, captured Bazi and

Morobo respectively from Sudan Army. On the other hand, the SPLA and Ethiopian-Eritrea forces attacked six Sudan army round Defence simultaneously. The SPLM/A strategic headquarters where John Garang was in Pakula Mountain, some 40 miles from Yei town. At Pakula six columns of forces marched to the different battles.

The Battle of Yei

The first column of OTB attacked SAF in Yei. It was SPLA infantry forces, supported Ethiopia-Eritrea artillery fires. It was commanded by Cdr Augustino Jadhalla Wani. The tank unit was led by A/Cdr Gabriel Jok Riak. The second column attacked Aloro and Kargulu west of Yei, under Cdr Gier Chuong Aloung. The third column attacked Lainya and Kagwado commanded by Cdr George Athor Deng and assisted by A/Cdr Angelo Jongkuch Jol. The first column that attacked Yei garrison faced got resistance from the enemy. However, the volume of fire from tank shells forced them to succumb, and ran for their lives. At the fall of Yei, 150 soldiers were killed including 3 red collared officers or commanders; Commander Mayen Akuak Mayen, Commander Kut Maketh Duk, Commander Tito Tong Ajak.

The Battle of Mile 40

All the Sudan army units that were wiped out at Yei and its surrounding outposts came to Mile 40, building up the firmest defence on Yei-Juba road bridge, 40 Miles from Juba city. All artillery and tanks were dug down for the defence behind a small bridge along the small river. They had Milan Missile, new anti-tank missile, because the SPLA was attacking them with many tanks. The SPLA struck Mile 40. Thus, this battle became one of the sturdiest battles SPLA fought since 1989 after battle of Kiyala or Nasir. In this battle, SPLA was repulsed back and six tanks were destroyed by SAF Milan missiles.

After the failure to win the battle of mile 40, the SPLA abandoned its dream of capturing Juba through Yei road, but, it turned all the forces to attack and capture other Sudan army defensive position at Jumbo, Lui, Amadi, Mundri and Mbolo. In one of battles Garang Akok shot down an Antonio war plane.

Operation Deng Nhial (ODN)

After the SPLA liberated fourteen enemy spaces of Kaya, Bazi, Morobo, Kaji Kaji, Alero, Yei, Loka, Kagawda, Kargulu, Lainya, Jambo, Amadi, Mbolo, Lui, which were in the West of Juba, it turned the focus westward to Bahr el Ghazal and changing the operation from Operation Thunderbolt, to Operation Deng Nhial (ODN) in honour of Southern politician, assassinated in 1968 by the government of Prime Minister Sadiq al Mahdi. Honourable William Deng Nhial was killed as he leaving Rumbek during an election. ODN had 2000 soldiers with six tanks. The ODN began by capturing Rumbek on 28 April 1997 and destroying a convoy before proceeding to Tonj. On 15 May 1997, Tonj was struck by 1079 men and officers and taking it easily.

Operation Final Lapse (OFL)

At the end of ODN, the SPLA returned toward Juba, and changed the operation to Operation Final Lapse (OFL) that was meant to liberate Juba city. When SAF learned of it, they released a statement rubbishing it as Operation Final Looting, which will fail to start . OFL would have swept the SAF from west of Juba and should have met with OJS Phase IV, which was also by itself OFL of its own because it was aimed at Juba, which was the final, major SPLA target in Equatoria or in Southern Sudan in particular. OFL liberated Yirol, Tali, Mundari Borou, and Tindilo. OFL was halted by heavy defence of SAF at Situ Bridge, 55 miles from Juba. On the other hand, OJS Phase IV which was launched at the West of Torit and East of Juba intensified. This OJS Phase IV in Eastern Bank liberated Lirya and Nyolo and it also pushed out militia forces, which were at Khor Inglis. SAF dug itself in Lankabo and Jebelein, Jebelein was a precipice of two mountains, which was dangerous for the SPLA to attack or approach. In that precipice, three different group of forces of SAF, stationed themselves in strong defences, the three group were; Dabapin, Mujahedeen and Popular Defence Force (PDF), who were manning to the front. That front was commanded by Hassan al Bashir, the brother to President Omer el Bashir, who was the Emir of Mujahedeen. Hassan el Bashir was killed in last battles by the SPLA.

Demise of Kerubino Kuanyin Bol

Commander Kerubino Kaunyin Bol, the leader of Bor Uprising in 1983, deputy Chairman and deputy commander in Chief of SPLM/A from 1983 to 1987, was killed in Mankien area of Bentiu by the Southern militiamen. Kerubino was detained in 1987 and he escaped from prison in 1992. In 1997/8, he fought internecine war against the SPLM/A. In 1998 after he signed Khartoum Peace Agreement, he wrecked the SAF's boat in Wau and supported by SPLA/A infiltrators in town, he fought bloodiest fighting, but later he was flashed out by the government forces. Kerubino Kuanyin returned back to the SPLM/A in 1998. As he was now the full member of SPLM/A, he was looking to be reinstated to his position of the Deputy Chairman and Commander in Chief, that became difficult, as Garang kept dodging him. That angered Cdr Kerubino, returned to Bentiu, in hope to go to his home area but he was killed before he could reach. Despite his impulsive and unprincipled behaviours and his disagreement with SPLM/A leadership, his monumental contribution of sparking the war on May 16, 1983 will passionately illuminate until the end of time.

CHAPTER 8

THE PEACE PROCESS, 1985-2005

Since the outbreak of the civil war in 1983, there have been 15 proposals of peace initiative, starting in 1985, between the Sudan government and the rebel SPLM/A. Out of the 15 initiatives, only one initiative brokered by IGAD brought last peace to Sudan, but 14 initiatives failed either at the negotiation stages or never started in the first place.

The first peace initiative was SPLM/SPLA 1985 call for a constitutional Conference but it was stillborn as President Nimieri was soon overthrown. The second peace initiative was Koka Dam Declaration, it was the second peace initiative and the first contact made between the warring parties, which is the SPLM/SPLA and the Sudanese political forces. It was the first contact between those in the bush and those in Khartoum since the civil outbreak of war in 1983.

A group, calling itself the National Alliance for the National Salvation (NANS) that took power after the popular uprising that toppled President Nimieri in 1985, initiated this peace talk. The talk took place at Koka town, near Addis Ababa, Ethiopia in March 1986. The NANS delegation was led by Dr. Khalil Yaji and the SPLM/A was led by Dr. John Garang. The talks were moderated by Ethiopian Ministry of foreign affairs. It was

SPLM/SPLA: History of Liberation (1983-2005)

in that meeting, where Dr John Garang, for the first, unveiled his political philosophy of democratic, socialist, united New Sudan in a face to face talks with other Sudanese although, he had frequently been talking about in the radio interview or on the Radio SPLA. The third peace initiative and third contact was one of Prime Minister Sadiq al-Mahdi, who after he won elections in 1986, met with John Garang at the side-lines of OAU meeting in Addis Abba.

Prime Minister Sadiq rubbished what was agreed upon at Koka and called for fresh talk between his government and SPLM/A, because, he argued that Koka Declaration was not negotiated at official level but on individual party levels and positions and he was not a signatory either. In his fresh talk stance, he instead called for John Garang to declare ceasefire before any talk could begin. In his response, John Garang also called for Prime Minister al Mahdi to abolish Sharia Law as its reciprocity. The fourth peace initiative was between Democratic Unionist Party (DUP) and the SPLM/A in 1988. John Garang and Mohammad el Merghani signed an agreement, on how the internal conflict of the Sudan be resolved. This was also repudiated by President Beshir as private, unofficial agreement, when he came into power in military coup in 1989. The fifth peace initiative was Carter Initiative, which took place between the Sudan government and SPLM/A in Nairobi, ending without breakthrough. The sixth Peace Initiative was president Daniel Arap Moi's of Kenya that never begin at all. The seventh peace initiative was proposed by the Libyan Leader Mummar Gaddafi, this initiative never started because John Garang was not to sit with Col Gaddafi due to his vision of Arabism and double standard. The eighth initiative was the Congolese's one President Mobutu Sese Seko of Zaire, it never stared but John Garang visited Mobutu to explore that proposal. The ninth initiative was the Organization of Africa Unity (OAU), under Dr. Salem Ahmed Salim, who proposed OAU to be the mediator between the Sudan government and SPLM/A. That never started. The tenth peace initiative was of Mr. Tiny Rowland the owner Lorhorn international Company, it never started. Other six peace initiatives, which did not start at all included; Ghanaian president Jerry Rawling's, Yoweri Museveni's of Uganda, Robert Mugabe's of Zimbabwe, the French's initiative, Bishop Desmond Tutu's among others.

THE PEACE PROCESS, 1985-2005

Abuja I and II Peace Talks

In 1992, the Nigerian Government of Ibrahim Babangada invited the warring parties to peace talks. The government of Sudan and the SPLM/A with it splinter group; the SPLM Nasir faction. They all attended the Abuja I peace talk but ended with no agreement. The SPLM/A introduced a demand for the self- determination for the people of Southern Sudan. The government of Sudan and SPLM/A met for the second time in the Nigerian Capital, Abuja but, the talk ended without a breakthrough because the government described the initiative as was written by the SPLM/A and signed by the Nigerian government. The IGAD Initiative was the last peace initiative that brought peace to the Sudan and ended the longest Africa civil war. The IGAD peace talks started in 1994 and dragged on until the Government and SPLM/A agreed on the declaration of the principle (DoP).

Resurrection of Saed al-Bandas Operation (RSBO), 2001

By 2001, the SPLA launched the military operation known as Resurrection of Saed al-Bandas Operation (RSBO) in Western Bahr el Ghazal. RSBO was commanded by officers who included Cdr Pieng Deng Kuol, Cdr Biar Kuol Ayuen aka Biar Jaw-Jaw, Cdr Santos Ayang Deng, among others. The RSBO liberated Rajah garrison and other four outposts of NIF forces which includes Dam Zubeir, the infamous slavery market during Turco-Egyptian rule in Sudan, Foso, Bor Medina and mineral-rich Kafia Kengi.

Operation Ngacigak Ngaciluk (ONN), 2002

After the signing of the Machakos Protocols in Kenya by the SPLM/SPLA and NIF/NGOS, mediated by IGAD on a framework for negotiated political settlement, in which the warring parties agreed on the three fundamental issues underlining the conflict : (1) right for self-determination, which was a choice for people of Southern Sudan to choose between (a) unity of the Sudan based on interim arrangements (b) secession or the independence of Southern Sudan from rest of Sudan (2) Religion and State, in which it was agreed there be three constitutions, one for Southern entity, one for Northern entity and one for the centre . Each entity should organize itself according to its constitution, the Northern Constitution may be based on Sharia according to their choice, while the Southern constitution shall be secular and democratic and the constitution for the centre as shall be negotiated by the warring parties, and shall not be based on any religion – in summary a separation of state and religion. (3) Interim Period Arrangement and Structures, in that issue, it was agreed that, "there will be a six years' interim periods, after which there will be an internationally monitored referendum on the self-determination for Southern Sudan, and there will be an Interim Government at the centre based on the interim constitution, power at the centre during the interim period will be divided fifty-fifty as shall be negotiated by the parties in the next round of talks".

As the warring parties were waiting for the next round of talk, each took the advantage to launch a military offensive or propaganda offensive in order to negotiate in the next round of talk from the position of strength. From the perspective, the SPLM/A launch the Operation Ngacigak Ngaciluk, meant to liberate Torit and finally Juba to encounter the NIF Peace from Within campaign, which had already started doing over the media, radio and Televisions.

Battle of Torit

On the 29th September, the SPLA attacked Labalwa, the rear-guard of Torit, overrunning it. On 1 October, the finally assault on Torit was launched, where the two positions of Nazziir and Ali Brigades were defeated in one-hour fiercest battle, that marked the second fall of Torit from NIF forces to the SPLA, the first fall of Torit to the SPLA was in 1989.

President Beshir ran amok with the fall of Torit, in his response to the news of Torit, he cancelled the peace talks with the SPLM/SPLA and he declared all-out war. He called the three forces; the Mujahedeen, Popular Defence Forces (PDF), Equatoria Defence Forces (EDF) and Southern militia groups, and SAF to go to teach SPLA or John Garang a lesson in Torit that he would never forget. As President Beshir said, SPLA was taught worst lesson by a combination of aerial bombardment and ground assault from Southern militia forcing the SPLA to tactically evacuate from Torit, one month after it was captured. The NIF forces attacked SPLA at Khor Doleib, a bridge 30 mile from Torit, with capture of Khor Doleib, there was panic in Torit, and it was evacuated without a fight. Two weeks from the evacuation from Torit, permanent ceasefire was declared, marking the end of 21-year civil war in the Sudan. Last frontlines of the SPLA around Southern Sudan were; Tindilo-Juba road, Aruu-Juba road, Terekaka-Juba road, Kiyala-Torit road, Mile 40 Yei- Juba road.

Yei – Nairobi Crisis

When the peace was around corner, there was crisis a last crisis that almost destroyed and failed SPLM/A in 2003. As saying goes 'what goes around comes around '. After John Garang and Salva Kiir did away with the other five founding members of SPLM/SPLA, for disagreeing because of one reason or another, their time also came for themselves to do away with each other. The history of doing away went like this; in 1985, Martin Majier and Joseph Oduho differed with the SPLA/SPLM leadership. John Garang, Kerubino Kaunyin, William Nyuon, Salva Kiir and Arok Thon did away with them by arresting Majier and Oduho. In 1987, Cdr Kerubino Kuanyin differed with movement leadership. John Garang, Willam Nyuon, Salva Kiir and Arok Thon did away with him by arresting Kerubino Kaunyin. In 1988, Arok Thon differed with SPLM leadership. John Garang, William Nyuon and Salva Kiir did away with him by arresting Arok. In 1992, William Nyuon ran away from Pageri after he heard rumours of his eminent doing away, he declared a rebellion.

In 2003, a time came for John Garang and Salva Kiir to do away with themselves, there was no more permanent members of Political Military High Command, where one could unite against the other. Everyone was alone. Garang was alone and so did Salva. Each one was planning to do away with the other. Thank God, the doing away plan ended happily in win – win. Indeed, both men would have cut each other throats in the no man's land between Nairobi and Yei. John Garang beckoned Salva Kiir, 'Kiir mawaa, if you are really a Tiger, you meet me in Ramciel, on the other hand, Salva Kiir beckoned John Garang, Ayaa Garang, if you are BSC-1989, let us meet in Malual Akon.

Kuol Manyang and Pagan Amum said no one would either go Ramciel or Malual Akon but rather all of us had to meet in Rumbek, the capital of New Sudan. It was discovered all threatening messages that Garang and Kiir were issuing were not by themselves but the interest group, who would have benefited from the fighting of the two men. In famous Rumbek Meeting, a problem between John Garang and Salva Kiir was resolved amicably.

Comprehensive Peace Agreement (CPA)

At last, peace was reached between the SPLM/A and National Congress party (NCP) in a Comprehensive Peace Agreement signed in Naivasha, Kenya. As a result of CPA, John Garang was appointed the first Vice President of Republic of the Sudan in Transitional Government of National Unity (TGoNU) in Khartoum and President of Government of South Sudan (GOSS) in Juba. After taking oath of office on July 9, 2005, he returned to SPLM/A headquarters of New Site in East Equatoria.

Demise of Dr John Garang de Mabior

Before, he could come to Juba, he paid short visit to Kampala, Uganda. When he was returning from Kampala, the helicopter he was travelling crashed on July 30, 2005, killing John Garang all on board. John Garang was sixth SPLM/A senior member to die, other who died before him were; Joseph Oduho Awero, Martin Majier Gai, William Nyuon Bany, Arok Thon Arok and Kerubino Kuanyin Bol. John Garang, too, was fourth permanent member of five permanent members of SPLM/A to die, other three members who died before him were; William Nyuon Bany, Arok Thon Arok and Kerubino Kuanyin. John Garang was mourned bitterly and 500 tributes were written about him around the world by journalists and other writers. One of those who paid their tribute in writing was his closest ally Elijah Malok Aleng:

DR JOHN GARANG: THE DEATH OF PATRIOT, THE DEATH OF A HERO

Perhaps one of the first devastating blows to the implementation of the CPA was the sudden and mysterious death of Col. Dr. John Garang de Mabior Atem on Sunday, 30 July 2005 in an air crash in South Sudan. His death came only twenty-one days after he took the oath of office as the First Vice President of the Republic of Sudan in Khartoum on Saturday, 9

THE PEACE PROCESS, 1985-2005

July 2005. He was buried on Saturday 6 August, 2005. Strangely, Saturday seemed to be a special day for Dr John Garang, probably the day of his historical destiny! He was possible born on a Saturday, he left Juba for the national struggle on a Saturday, he took the oath of office on a Saturday, he died on a Saturday and he was buried on a Saturday.

Upon his death, national government and states in Africa and the world, mourned him for three days. National flags in Tanzania, Kenya, Uganda, Ghana, Zimbabwe and Republic of South Africa, flew at half-mast for three days. The Foreign Affairs Minister of Republic of South Africa, paid a glowing tribute to him as the man who represented hope for the whole of the Africa continent. He is survived by his wife, Rebecca Nyadeng de Mabior, two sons – Mabior and Chol, and four daughters – Gak, Akuol, Kuir, and Atong.

While, we the family members, friends and well-wishers all over world continue to read and recite the eulogy of late Dr John Garang de Mabior, much still remained unknown about the number of times he missed a death during the years of the discharge of his duties at the war fronts. Between 1996 and 2000, he missed death four times when the military SPLA vehicles in which he was, or he would be, travelling hit landmines, in each of those encounters he would come out unharmed. In 2000 also, he missed death, together with two other SPLM/SPLA leaders, when they aborted their travel to Abidjan in ill-fated Kenyan Airways flight that crushed off the coast of Ivory Coast (Cote d'iviore).

On this occasion, Dr. John Garang, the commander Kuol Manyang Juuk and Commander Nhial Deng Nhial were scheduled to travel to Abidjan where they see the Ivoirian President that evening, and take the same KQ flight back the following morning. However, there was a hitch at Jomo Kenyatta International Airport where a Kenyan security officer refused to let them board the plane for Abidjan, as he had no instructions and knowledge of that Dr John Garang was flying out of Kenya; that the security authorities had not alerted their agents at the airport that a VIP was travelling so that they could board him and see him off. He was therefore not allowed to fly. Unfortunately, on return flight, the KQ plane crashed into the sea killing all on board. Dr John Garang was scheduled to return on the same plane. Even as Dr Garang kept missing deaths, he once remarked 'I have been commanding the SPLA officers and men of various rank in this war, many of them have paid the ultimate sacrifice. If my turn comes to pay the ultimate sacrifice, and indeed it comes, then be it. We are in this war to win or die for national goals and objective we believe in. I am just an officer; a commander in chief of a patriotic army and one officer just like any of you. If death comes my way, I shall die like many of compatriots who have already laid down their lives in this war ''. Dr John Garang stated this, fully aware that the struggle for justice and equality in the Sudan was not an easy one and that all those who were carrying arms, including him, could pay the ultimate price. On Saturday, 30 July, he too paid the ultimate price.

However, Dr John Garang 's enemies wanted the world to believe that without him, Southern Sudan would be better governed under some of them and that the basic rights of the silenced minorities all over the Sudan would not only be protected by CPA, but that the CPA would be executed in letter and spirit. Little wonder that when Dr John Garang died, some Southern 'nationalists ' continued to vomit their political dirt on his 'shoes' . There emerged large talk not just that without Dr John Garang the unity of the South would be achieved and that the inter- South dialogue would result in an unconditional unity within the South, but also that those Southerners who were carrying arms fighting Dr John Garang as a person, and that now he is gone, all the militiamen would be become a part of the patriotic South . If this were truth, then why do some militiamen continue to carrying arms against the South? From whom is the South being defended? Since peace came to Southern Sudan as a result of the CPA. Who is now threatening the South?

Indeed, personalised hatred against Dr John Garang in some limited quarters had always been intense and persistent. During the Nasir Rebellion, its leaders decided not only to kill him, but also to pierce his heart. In last two years before his death, his enemies did declare that they would work to hire assassins to eliminate him, while others conspired with his real enemies arguing that it was only by eliminating him that the guns in South would become silence in the manner of Jonas Savimbi and UNITA rebel in Angola.

THE PEACE PROCESS, 1985-2005

In fact, some of those who swore to eliminate Dr John Garang are now well placed in the structures of the governments that they were formed as a result of CPA. Some of these people did not join and physically fight for the liberation of the people of the Marginalised Areas, as Dr John Garang did for twenty-one years, some of them stayed away in foreign capitals hiding themselves from perils of war, only to surface and get constitutional portfolios as a result of the CPA that was brought about by the nationalist struggle that was led by Dr John Garang. After Dr John Garang brought honourable peace, they then conspired against him. Indeed, while the body of Dr John Garang was being lowered into grave, some of the traitors who wanted to see Dr John Garang dead came very close to the grave just to make sure that indeed, Dr John Garang was buried.

If indeed the crash of the fateful plane that killed Dr John Garang was not an accident but a foul play that was meant to kill him, who would be the main suspect? My suspicion falls on three groups. One, the Southern Sudanese traitors who always felt overshadowed by the political and military might of Dr John Garang. These are people who wanted to rule south but had no ability to lead the people during the terrible years of the armed struggle. They are peacetime heroes who had to work to kill Dr John Garang in the hope that the real enemy of the South would reward them by surrendering the leadership of the South to them once Dr John Garang was dead and buried. Two, is the strong Northern Sudan political establishment, comprising of groups that has never believed in the basic liberties of any other Sudanese other than themselves. It is a group that wants to rule whole Sudan on the paradigm of an Arab-Islamic state, a group that always became desperate when its political hegemony is challenged.

It is this group that conspired to kill, and indeed killed, William Deng Nhial in 1967 when he, politically and intellectually, challenged the narrow-minded definition of the identity of the Sudan as an Arab-Islamic Nation. This junta could have conspired to physically eliminate Dr John Garang because he had worked for the total liberation of all the Sudanese nationalities, people and communities. It is a group that could have felt threatened when Dr John Garang was given a tumultuous welcome when he arrived in Khartoum on July 9 2005 to take up his position as the First

Vice President of Republic of Sudan, a welcome that was shared by all Sudanese of all nationalities. In fact, my assumption is that, some Arabised leaders of the Sudan could not stomach such popularity in their midst let alone such huge national reception. Three, there was a group that fronted for the international economic.

Apparently, Dr John Garang had become a target of the international wealth barons, because he did not give in to external economic pressures that wanted to exploit the resources of Southern Sudan. But, my strong suspicion is that all these three groups – the Southern traitors, some Northern Sudanese Arabised political establishment and international economic interest – all united to kill Dr John Garang. Whatever the suspicion, Uncle Dr John Garang de Mabior, the warrior and a hero, fell with his spears and shield in the defence of the marginalised Sudan. He fought and died for a nationalist cause and he never looked behind when cowards, quisling and weaklings contemplated defeat and surrender. He was always in front leading the advance team in direction of true enemy of the people. He had always shunned his Southern Sudanese detractors because they were the huddles that did not understand the mission of liberty.

The CPA that he signed into law is now the mausoleum in which all hopes of majority of Sudanese are sanctified: it is a living document, a testimony to his national achievement upon which generation of men and women will attest to the will to be free in one's country, the will to resist tyranny, the will to enjoy freedom with justice and the will to participate in the affairs of one's country. These are the fruits that will fall from the tree that was planted on the eternal grave in which not only Dr John Garang, but also the millions of our compatriots, who paid the ultimate sacrifice, are buried.[1]

Another tribute to John Garang come from Panluel Wel, a South Sudanese columnist and blogger, who edited Panluel Blog, entitle:

THE LEGACY OF DR JOHN GARANG

The historical significance of Garang from the time he authored his famous letter in January 1972 to the time he died in July 2005 is that he had, more than any other South Sudanese leader (and Sudanese leader for that matter) within that brief span of time, shaken the entire edifice of power in Khartoum. True to his declaration, Sudan has not been the same since and will never be again.

Garang believed that the state policy of Arab-Islamism was a direct assault on Sudan-ness, what he called Sudanism is the idea that the Sudanese people should first and foremost be Sudanese before becoming Christians or Muslims, Africans or Arabs, Southerners or Northerners and so on. Garang believed that the endeavour of seeking an outside identity to subsume Sudanism conflict with the sacred values of democracy, justice, freedom and long lasting peace in the Sudan.

The contrived Arab-Islamism identity, strange and foreign as it was and thus largely unacceptable to most Sudanese, had to be imposed and sustained by force, and it was a force that engendered equal opposition from the disadvantaged majority Sudanese who responded in kind to the injustice meted upon them by the ruling clique in Khartoum. It was to right this injustice that Garang dedicated his entire life from the time he burst on the South Sudanese political scene with his 1972 letter to his boss, Joseph Lagu, throughout the war of liberation, and until he died in July 2005 after the signing of the CPA.

Garang understood that the Sudan's richness and diversity in cultures, languages, religion, and politics was more of an asset than a liability, yet it had been victimized and dilapidated by the chauvinistic policy of Arab-islamism. The solution, in his view, was for Southerners to seek refuge in numbers- the combined forces of the marginalized people of the Sudan. It is difficult to appreciate Garang's achievement if we do not understand that his dilemma was that he saw both the need for and danger of seeking refuge in numbers- the New Sudan vision.

On the other hand, he had the conviction that the only effective way to restructure the center of power in Khartoum was through the New Sudan Vision. If only the combined energies of the marginalized people were spent fighting the central government, then these groups could collectively finish off the dragon and then, freely and without coercion could decide to remain together in one voluntary union by consensus rather than by force

Alternatively, if they so wished and preferred, they could decide to break up the union free and peacefully, each going her own way to form independent amicable sister nation-states.

SPLM/SPLA: History of Liberation (1983-2005)

Although this was evidently a plausible vision, the stark reality was that Southerners had over the years, cultivated and internalized a culture of secessionism. So strong and entrenched was the pursuit of Southern independence that any alternative view, the New Sudan Vision, for example, was taken as an act of betrayal of the dissenting tradition.

Indeed, Garang's vision proved to be too threatening to both sides. Ardent Southern separatists saw it was at the best a dangerous distraction, at worst in outright betrayal of their long pursued dream of independence. On the other hand, Northerners saw it as existential threat to their discrimination ideology of Arab Islamism. Ironically, Garang ended up alarming and offending everyone, the victims and the oppressors alike. War broke out among Southerners —partly over the objective for the war and partly over leadership —and it was not until Garang defeated Southern "separatists" that he began his war of liberation against Khartoum.

The effectiveness and viability of the New Sudan Vision explains the irony of the Anyanya One movement that started out as a secessionist movement, only to end up signing a unionist agreement in contrast to the SPLM/A that commenced as unionist movement but ended up signing an accord that brought the independence of South Sudan. Truly, as the old saying among the SPLM/A cadres attests, they knew what they were fighting for—Ke Tharku angicku.

Thus, in retrospect, it was only opinions tactics that differentiated Garang from his pioneering predecessors of the Southern nationalism, for all had held the same overriding aim —freedom and liberty to their beleaguered region. Garang secured that wider support precisely because he promised the world of freedom and liberty for all Sudanese people, with new government based on mutual consensus rather than by force or coercion, of which all marginalized people dreamt. His vision implied a complete and extensive restructuring of the center of power, just distribution of national resources and equal and fair political representation in the central government.

But the very possibility of his vision, the near realization of the tenets of the New Sudan Vision, might have been behind the sudden and mysterious death of Garang in Helicopter crash in 2005. His vision, however, still excites South Sudanese socioeconomic and political imaginations- the tantalizing prospects of political freedom, economic prosperity, and social progress. It still beckons them to manifest the New Sudan Vision in the new Republic of South Sudan- to provide a democratic and pluralistic society where freedom and liberty are guaranteed to all regardless of race, gender, political affiliation, tribe, religion or region. And it imbues them with the conviction that the two Sudan could prosper and shine as beacon of hope for the rest of the African continent.

Garang's vision was not only that the freedom of the people of the marginalized regions would herald the true freedom and peace for the whole Sudan (southerners' freedom will make Northerners freedom possible but also that the vision of the New Sudan could be a template to solving continental issues, wherever marginalization and exploitation of the peripheral regions by a central government is experienced.

There is this pervading phrase nowadays in all corners of South Sudan, wherever there is an overwhelming national quandary: "if only John Garang was alive." Yet, critics of Garang have been quick to interpose that Garang would never have voted for an independent South Sudan. Implied therein is the supposition that Garang was a power hungry man who wanted to rule whole Sudan at the expense of the aspirations of South Sudan people.

Yet, back in 1992 during his conversation with Steven Wondu in Nairobi, Kenya, Garang told Wondu that he knew about the aspirations of the South Sudanese as much as the Nassir group: " I know as much as they do that the South feels strongly about its quest for independence. There are valid reasons for their wish but the strength of passion is not the same as the practicality of the proposition at this time. We must base our approach on the objective realities facing us.

Garang also knew that if given a chance to vote in the free and fair referendum, South Sudanese would vote almost 100% for independence" and knowing this, he told Riek Machar (after Riek had signed the Khartoum peace agreement) that if Khartoum was serious about letting the South go, he (Riek) should let Khartoum withdraw their forces from Juba, Wau and Malakal and conduct the referendum.

Garang's unambiguous prediction of the January 2011 South Sudan's referendum outcomes, coupled with his "Rumbek Exhortation" in which he had urged South Sudanese not to be second class citizens in their own country, hardly leave any room for doubt regarding his intent and political stance had he been alive to vote during the referendum on South Sudan Independence.

Garang was the right man at the right time; as Steve Wondu succinctly observed: "I felt that Southern Sudan was blessed to have him at its hour of most need and that those Southerners who sought to bring him down were making grievous mistakes." But in the cruelest irony of fate, Garang who had "single-handedly kept the hopes of the black Africans in the Sudan and the man who "fought for the freedom and justice of the Southern Sudan for over 20 years was suddenly killed in a mysterious helicopter crash on his way back from Uganda.

Today, there is no bigger honour that South Sudanese people can accord Garang than to ensure that the vision of the liberationary struggle that he led and for which he paid the ultimate price is actualized in the new Republic of South Sudan.

Anything less will be ultimate betrayal, not just of Garang, but also of all the pioneering fathers and all the martyrs-men and women without whose blood and flesh this country would have never been freed.

The greatest legacy of Garang over and above his comrades- the pioneering fathers of Southern Sudanese liberationary struggle- will always be (as Francis Mading Deng decorously recognizes) the extent to which he shifted the Southern outlook from that of a minority, struggling for recognition and a degree of autonomy in a marginalized corner of the country, to one of self-assertiveness, pride and dignity in the struggle for a democratic Sudan.

Although Dr. John Garang De Mabior, "the most visionary and incisive revolutionary thinker of Africa and undying martyr of South Sudan," died physically on 30 July 2005, "his vision will continue to inspire many peace loving people around the globe.

Indeed; it will be said of him that he did better than Biblical Moses. At least he stepped in the Promised Land, albeit for only three weeks. As the scriptures might say, he tasted of the wine, but never drank of it. But let it be said of Garang; few men ever made a finer political brew than he died" Return in peace (R.I.P) John Garang![2]

THE PEACE PROCESS, 1985-2005

Notes
1. Panluel Wel, 2012, Bor, South Sudan, The Genius of Dr John Garang: Tributes to the Late SPLM/A's Leader p. VI
2. Ibid pp. 180-183

CHAPTER 9

A GLIMPSE OF HISTORY OF SPLM/A, 1983-2005

Sudan People's Liberation Movement /Army (SPLM/A) was one of the most successful revolutionary armed struggles in African history. Under the stewardship of saltiest and sugariest Col. Dr John Garang de Mabior, and his entire fraternity of bravest field officers and political cadres and men who wished for timely death, and indeed died timely in thousand, fought the longest civil war for the unity of the Sudan. Although, the SPLM/A was categorically fighting for the democratic, socialist, united, New Sudan as an object of the war for 21 years, there was, however, a subtle and veiled changes made, through many years of the struggle, in the objectives in which the war was fought upon. Through those difficult years of struggle, unity became actually unattractive in its all aspect, and secession turned out to be one of the fall back options. Therefore, throughout the last six year of transitional period, unity was just continued to be used not as an end itself but rather craftily and merely as means of achieving separation of Southern Sudan, as it became the case in 2011, when South Sudan got the independence from the Sudan through referendum vote.

In the beginning, SPLM/A got its support from the communist bloc, because, the communist by then, had a global agenda of helping the oppressed people around the world to free themselves from bourgeois capitalism. After the collapsing of communism, Christianity became second agenda and the only strong reason, why SPLA was supported by Western World; USA, Norway and many others.

The SPLM/A in its war effort, from 1983 to 2005, had trained more than 60,000 soldiers four countries, Ethiopia, Sudan, Eritrea and Uganda, who were organized into divisions, battalions and task forces,which included; New Battalion 105/4 (1983), Jamus Battalion (1984), Tiger Battalion (1984), Timsah Battalion (1984), Koryom Division (1984), Muor Muor Division (1985), Kazuk Division (1986), Zalzal Division (1987), Infijar Task Forces (1988), Intifada Task Forces (1989),Intisar Task forces (1990), Red Army (1991), Ignas Task Forces (1994), Panda Oyee Task Forces (1996) . From 1983 to 2002, SPLA had initiated and carrying out more than 1000 raids and attacks, laid more than 1000 ambushes, fought more than 50 major battles, and more than 1000 skirmishes. At the same period, SPLA fought and withstood more than 10 campaigns and operations initiated and launched by Sudan Armed Forces (SAF). The major convoys, the campaigns and operations of Sudan army (SPDF, SAF and Mujahedeen) encountered by the SPLA were; Saga Sudan 1984, Mazalat (1984), Ajana (1985), Zubur Zaida (1985), Liwa Radar (1987), Yarmuk (1989), Junti Watan al Wahid (1990), Seif al Ubuur (1992), Fejeer al Sadiq (1992), Usud al Gaba (1993), Muhijideen (1999), Popular Defences Forces (1999), Dababin (2002). On the other hand, the SPLM/A had initiated and launched more than 10 military operations and campaigns ; Rainbow Operation (1986), Unity Campaign (1989) Bright Star Campaigns-BSC (1989), Kon Anok Campaign-KAC (1989), New Funj Campaign-NFC (1989), Operation Jungle Storm-OJS (1992),Operation Black Fox-OBF (1996), Operation Thunderbolt–OTB(1997), Operation Deng Nhial - ODN (1997), Operation Final Lapse (1997), Resurrection of Saed Bandas Operation-RSBO (2000) and Operation Ngacigak Nyaculuk – ONN (2002). Throughout the 21-year civil war, the SPLA lost more than 10,000 fallen heroes and had suffered more than 20,000 wounded heroes. The SPLA had shot down 45 planes, both military and passenger ones and these planes were shot down by sharp shooters like; Cde Garang Akook Adut, Cde Mamer Mum, Cde Garang Ayor, Cde Simon Okan, Cde Majier

SPLM/SPLA: History of Liberation (1983-2005)

Mayom, Cde Duoth Dejul Kuny, Cde Akuoch Miyong and Cde Wundit Mawien and many others. SPLA had also destroyed more than 100 tanks and more than 2000 other military and civilian trucks.

The success of SPLM/A as a national liberation was attributed to number of factors and reasons: (1) SPLM/A used judiciously the mistakes and bitter experiences of the first Anya Nya I war, as point of references, in fighting the new war, to achieve its objectives and aims (2) charismatic character of John Garang, who was fullest of truth, correct reasons and beliefs, and concrete analysis of situation (3) national forest of Southern Sudan, which the SPLA used for hiding places, making it difficult for enemy to get them (4) Nile river that made it hardest for enemy to chase the SPLA with tanks easily (5) rural women, who were pounding and cooking food for soldiers (6) Mobile Radio 77 that was used by SPLA to communicate (7) chiefs, who were collecting food(bulls, goats, sheep, sorghum, cassava, maize, potatoes, honey, dried fishes, milk, lalop ..Etc) for the SPLA. For 21 years, the SPLM/A had been walking on foot around whole Southern Sudan, and Southern Blue Nile, Southern Kordufan, Darfur and Port Sudan in North of the country.

Sudan, historically, got its independence from Britain in 1956. Before celebrating the Independence Day, a civil war broke out in August 1955, in the Southern part of the country, that war ravaged the country for 17 years until Addis Abba Agreement (AAA) of 1972 was signed. Twelve years later on, another civil war, a worst one, broke out in 1983, devastating the country for another 21 years until Comprehensive Peace Agreement (CPA) of 2005 was signed. Therefore, the title, the Glimpse of History of SPLM/A is ontologically summation of the history of politic, war and peace in the Sudan, that was made by two archenemies, the Government of Sudan (GOS) and the armed rebel Sudan People's Liberation Movement /Army (SPLM/A). The two principal rivals, in the beginning, had vowed to wipe off one another in battlefields, but they were all indestructible to one another as shown in many occasions, in which one had attempted to destroy the other. Those attempts of annihilation one another were started from Bor Uprising in 1983, through the first Battle of Malual Goath in November 1983, to the last Battle of Torit in October 2002, until the time the peace salvaged the two, on January 9, 2005, when the two signed CPA in Naivasha, Kenya. After more than 25,000 soldiers died timely in the battlefields and another 1 Million people died of hunger, disease and other war related causes, on both side of the war, the two changed their extreme views and positions, moderating their positions, from the far left and far right, in order to settle the dispute not through military means, but, through negotiation, concession and political settlement.

The genesis of the civil war in the Sudan was rooted in deteriorating ideological differences among the citizens, according to Emmanuel Mabut Ajieth, a freedom fighter and teacher who taught thousands of pupils in SPLM/A liberated area. Basing his argument on his past experiences as student, who witnessed at first hand President Nimieri's political gambling, leading to the outbreak of war in 1983, he said, in many countries around the world, for example, there are segments of population whose members feel very strongly that their beliefs should not be dominated by those differing from them, and that the land they occupy or section of a country should not come into the control of others, and if indeed, it happened they are dominated or controlled by others, they can become very hostile to central government that they feel they don't control . And definitely, these ideological differences can result in problems, if the members of the other group, they do not share the same views with, are not willing to adjust some of their ideas, to allow those differing from them to meet some of their special needs or aspirations. Undesirably, these cultural, economic or political variations among the citizens of a country, who are not willing to cooperate with one another in solving their problems can lead to armed conflict. And that was, exactly what happened with the Muslim Arab Northern Sudanese, who were not ready to adjust some of their Islamic and Arabic views in order for Christian and Black Southern Sudanese to meet their aspirations in the secular and united Sudan as shown by underlying and immediate causes of SPLM/A revolution in 1983. The immediate and the underlying causes of the war in 1983 were: (1) Southern Sudanese had been calling for federation since 1956, and that call for federal system had long been opposed by Northern Sudan elites, on the ground, it would weaken the unity of state, and impede the process of Arabisation and Islamization in country. Thus, answering the Southerners' call for federal system through lip services, ruling SSU of President Nimieri came up

SPLM/SPLA: HISTORY OF LIBERATION (1983-2005)

with decentralisation policy, in which the autonomous region of Southern Sudan was divided into three regions of Equatoria, Upper Nile and Bahr el Ghazal. Here the Southerners wanted federal system but Northerners never cooperated with them, in solving their demand for federation, they rejected it, and introducing decentralization instead. As a result, the decentralisation weaken the Southerners' unity and it strengthened national unity of the Sudan (2) implementation versus abrogation of Addis Abba Agreement(AAA), Southerners wanted the fullest implementation of AAA in letter and spirit in order to meet the special needs or aspiration as spelled in it, but the Arab abrogated the agreement so that Southerners could not benefit from it (3) through the state of emergency, President Nimieri unveiled the new Map of Sudan, in which regions of newly discovered oilfields and other fertile land in Upper Nile and Bahr el Ghazal were carved out and annexed to the North of the country. That new map was protested and rejected by Southerners. Realising, it was impossible to take the oil by default, President Nimieri had to substitute it with building of the oil refinery at Port Sudan in North, far away from where the oil is drilled in order to benefit north of the country and deprive the South of the country (4) the transfer of Battalion 105 to North, the Southern Command of Sudan army in Juba, which was dominated by the northern senior officers, ordered the transfer of Battalion 105, which was manned by only Southern of ex-Anya Nya I soldiers to North. Battalion 105 refused the transfer and gave many reasons, why, they could not go to the north. That defying of orders, was considered as indiscipline and treacherous itself. And therefore Battalion 105, according to Sadiq al Banna, had to be disciplined militarily. As a result of that, military discipline got out of hand and became a civil war, lasting for 21 years and killing more than 30, 000 soldiers on both sides of the war. There were two different versions and different reasons given of why the forces refused the transfer to the North.

In 1983, the Sudan's army was one of cleanest institution in the country in term of military administering, inspecting, accounting and auditing. There was no corruption in army. Every soldier got his salary on the 28 of every month, with all his allowances of night duty's, mosquito's, expedition's, operation's, sick's'...etc. Every soldier had 30 Day annual leave, and 30 bullets he would fire in annual military exercises or war game. 12-month food ration and 12-month fuel for the armoured and transport trucks. All annual food items, fuel and money were kept by Special Sergeant Major (SM) under oversight supervision of Battalion commander.

In 1981/2, a team of inspectors and auditors came to Malual Chat Barrack in Bor to inspect and audit the ammunitions, fuel, food items and finances of Battalion 105. The team found that, there was embezzlement of a lot of money, there was misappropriation of the army food and fuels. The committee found that Major Kerubino Kuanyin Bol, the acting Commander of the Battalion 105 and SM Yusif Keer Tangkier, the Battalion Administrative Sergeant Major, were responsible for embezzlement and misappropriation. It was discovered Major Kerubino and SM Yusif Tang Keer used to request the money for almost a Brigade, when the force was actually a Battalion of about 700 soldiers, because, it was formed in 1972, there had, not a single death, been reported for 12 years and no single absentee reported at the same period. The Southern Division Command in Juba decided that, in order, to get Major Kerubino and his Yusif red-handed, they had to be transferred from Bor to Shendi in the North. When Major Kerubino and SM Yusif heard that, they incited their soldiers not to accept the transfer to north, lest, they would be liquidated there. That was one reason of what caused Bor mutiny or uprising.

As there were three different reasons given of why the soldiers were transferred to North and as a result were refusing to go the North, which were: (1) the soldiers were ordered to be transferred to the north as part of long due integration into national army as stipulated in AAA of 1972 (2) the soldiers were ordered to be transferred to the North as means of screening, after they had embezzled a lot of money, and (3) the soldiers were ordered to be transferred to North, because, it was discovered that they were planning to rebel or stage a coup. Whatever the reason why they disobeyed the orders, more than five committees were formed, to persuade refusing soldiers to move to North.

Although, there were five different committees formed to negotiate and persuade the soldiers to move to the north, our focus would be on last committee led by First Lieutenant General Ahmed Hamad Sadiq al – Banna. When he arrived in Bor, a parade was called at Malual Chat and General al-Banna addressed soldiers, he told them point-blank, they had to go to the north as they were ordered by their command. And he would not listen to any complain from them before they had already moved to Shendi. After four hours of negotiation and persuasion, SM Yusif Keer stood and said:

'Saitek 'he called Gen. al –Banna

'Yes ', answered al- Banna, 'what is your name?'

'Sergeant Major Yusif Keer Tangkier'.

'Your words, Yusif ', said the General

'If gun fire at the hand of soldiers, what would you do?' Yusif asked

'Finish your words ', answered General al-Banna

'Well, if a gun fire in the hand of the soldier, two things always happen, you will hear the sound of gun by your ear, and you will see, where the bullet hit by your eyes, therefore, I can assure you, what is going on here in Battalion 105, you will not hear it by your ear, you will see by your eyes ', explained Yusif.

'Thank you, Yusif that is what I want, now Regimental Sergeant Major ', he called

'Yes ', answered Regimental sergeant Major.

'You fall out the parade for lunch, and we shall resume our negotiation at 2 o'clock.

Al Banna closed the meeting as if he were going to come back, but, he was camouflaging to escape, because, he had proven it, the soldiers had rebelled. He got in his car, when he was told to go to Dinning Hall for lunch, he told them, and he would go and eat lunch at Commissioner's house. On way, he told his driver, to turn to airport, because, his helicopter was already in air coming to Bor, it came and airlifting him immediately.

No sooner had al Banna arrived in Juba, he ordered forces under the command of Colonel Dominic Cassaino to go and attack Battalion 105. Colonel Cassiano went to Bor and returned to Juba without attacking them; instead, he went and left his forces in Langbar areas. At last, he sent another forces under the command of Colonel Stephen Ugut Obang, who went and dislodged 105 on May 16, 1983. During the fighting at Malual Chat, John Garang and vice President Abel Alier, for their own safety, they took refuge at Langbar, where the loyal forces that came with Colonel Dominic Kassiano were staying. After Battle of Bor, Colonel

A GLIMPSE OF THE HISTORY OF THE SPLM/A, 1983-2005

Dr John Garang de Mabior sneaked to Ethiopia with longest harboured plan to liberate marginalised people of Sudan, where he formed the Sudan People's Liberation Movement /Army through contradiction from Akuot Atem de Mayen and Samuel Gai Tut. John Garang and his group succeeded in forming national liberation movement because their concepts were truest, while Akuot Atem and his group failed in forming national liberation movement because their concepts were falsest as writer Leon Pompa's Philosophy of History argued:

[History is] interested not only in why people acted in certain ways but also in the success or the failure of their action. Hence, once the agent's reasons and beliefs are established, they must undergo further critical examination, since the success or failure of actions often depends upon the merits and defects of the beliefs and reasons behind them. Thus, it may be that although the agents action made good sense from his/her point of views, some of the relevant beliefs [may be] false1.

Dr John Garang won rightly over Akuot Atem and Samuel Gai and succeeded in forming the SPLM/A because he had good reasons and correct beliefs about the fundamental problems of the Sudan while Akuot Atem and Gai Tut failed because they had defect reasons and false beliefs about the fundamental problems of the Sudan, although their beliefs and reasons were making senses to them.

No sooner had John Garang and his group of Kerubino Kuanyin, William Nyuon, Salva Kiir, Martin Majier and Joseph Oduho finished forming the SPLM/A than they embarked on two immediate tasks of the reorganization of SPLA as formidable fighting forces, capable of destroying the Sudanese reactionary forces, and building of the SPLM as viable and vibrant national liberation movement. In reorganizing forces, Kerubino and William put into training all soldiers who rebelled on May 16 and others who deserted thereafter, while, John Garang and Martin Majier were writing SPLM Manifesto.

Thus, after finishing the writing of Manifesto and training of the soldiers, three immediate tasks were set out (1) launching of the war (2) mobilization of recruits (3) training of recruits. Kerubino Kuanyin was assigned the training of the youth who came to seek their freedom in bush, becoming Jamus Battalion. Captain Cigai Atem was sent to Bor to mobilize

SPLM/SPLA: History of Liberation (1983-2005)

the recruits to join the war effort. John Garang, William Nyuon and Salva Kiir, went and attacked Malual Goath. The aim of that attack was to launch officially the SPLM/SPLA as Sudan's national liberation movement. The Battle for Malual Goath, the first ever battle of the SPLA was fought on November 17, 1983, exactly six months after the Bor Uprising on May 16, 1983.

In the battle, a sharp shooter Comrade Garang Akook Adut shot down a helicopter gunship. Three weeks later on, the SPLA attacked Nasir garrison. Again, two helicopters were shot by the same Garang Akook. The first helicopter was shot down. When the second helicopter came to see the wreckage of first and it was also shot down. The shooting of the three helicopters by the newly formed SPLM/A brought a greatest scepticism. The government and the people in Khartoum were asking: Can Southerners who left five months ago shoot down a plane by a missile? When did they learn firing missiles? Where did they get those missiles? In their analyses, they concluded the Sudan is under invasion by the Ethiopians, it is the Ethiopian, who shot the three helicopters down and then John Garang claimed the responsibility by announcing that his money embezzlers of Battalion 105 shot them down. President Nimieri played down the threat from SPLM/A of John Garang and he concluded, 'it is just a matter of losing one thousand soldiers and SPLM/A rebellion of John Garang is finished '. History proven President Nimeiri wrong, because, it took more than 10,000 soldiers dead to bring John Garang back 21 year later.

After returning from the frontlines, John Garang took Garang Akook Adut, the sharp shooter, to meet President Mengistu Haile Mariam. Mr Mengistu asked Garang of how he shot down a plane manually without using guided equipment. Garang narrated to him, how he brought down three helicopters, flying at 10,000 feet above sea level, using SAM 7 missile. In his words President Mengistu said, 'Garang Akook is first black man, ever, who shot down a plane in history'.

At the end of 1983, three missions were accomplished, the SPLM/A was launched by the attacks on Malual Goath and Nasir garrisons respectively. 8000 recruits were mobilized from Greater Bor areas, and were underway trekking to Bilpam in Ethiopia, later on becoming Koryom Division. Jamus Battalion was graduated, while Tiger and Timsah Battalions had just entered the trainings. Jamus Battalion was divided into two groups; Jamus-Wau and Jamus-Malakal. The two contingents were assigned two missions: (1) to conduct a war of propaganda through guerrilla warfare of hit and run operations (2) mobilization of new recruits. Jamus-Wau went to Bahr el Ghazal, where they mobilized 8000 recruits who later became Muor Muor Division as they were conducting guerrilla warfare of hit and run operations. Jamus-Malakal went to Upper Nile region, where they mobilized the recruits and conducting guerrilla warfare around Malakal areas.

In January 1984, Tiger and Timsah Battalions were graduated and they went to frontlines. While Koryom Division entered the training. Tiger and Timsah Battalions fought in Pochalla, Pibor, although they fought well some of their soldiers defected and joined the Anya Nya II. They later proceeded to Bentiu areas whereby they closed down the Chevron Oil Company that drilling oil. The well-achieved objective of Tiger and Timsah was closing down Cheveron Corporation in Sudan.

Through September 1984 to January 1985, Koryom Division, a mixture of primary pupils, secondary students and cattle camp youth, who went to bush to seek for their freedom from minority clique regime in Khartoum through barrel of guns, had graduated. Koryom, the first SPLA largest Division, with 12 strong Battalions; Hadid Battalion, Zindia Battalion, Raad Battalion, Cobra Battalion, Rhino Battalion, Agreb Battalion, Bilpam Battalion, Lion Battalion, Hippo Battalion, Elephant Battalion, Aquila Battalion and Katiba Banat (She-Company) were dispatched into different parts of the Sudan. Hadid went to Blue Nile, where it destroyed Ethiopian rebels at the border and carrying attacks around Maban areas, before returning back to participate in other operation. Zindia invaded Equatoria, there; it fought in many spaces and brought recruits, who were almost finished by thirst in Tingli desert, to join the movement. Rhino had made incursion to Bahr el Ghazal, where it fought a heaviest Battle for Yirol. Agreb moved and captured Boma, first garrison that was captured by SPLA. Four Battalions; Bilpam, Hippo, Lion, Elephant were sent to capture Jekou that became a disaster for the SPLM/A.

By April 1985, there had been deadliest war-fighting all over Southern Sudan. The Battle of Jekou went on for 3 months, although it ended with withdrawal of the SPLA, However, there were loss of men and material from the Sudan's army. In Second Front, President Nimieri organized a largest force from Northern Division known as Ajana Division in Atbara in the North to crush the SPLA. Those forces were airlifted to Juba. In Juba, they were combined with the forces of Thaka Sudan in operation Subur Zaida that had been ambushed and blocked by SPLA for five months between Juba and Bor. It lastly arrived in Bor after it was exhausted already in bush fighting. The three events; two fronts in Bor and Jekou coupled with economic crisis and caused the Popular Uprising that toppled President Nimieri in April 1985. After the fall of President Nimieri, a caretaker president Field Marshal Abdurrahman Hamed Sowar al Dadab took over power. The SPLM/A called Sowar al Dadab to return the country to democracy, it said the civilian control of the government must be basic tenet of the constitution, and the policy of the people's authority vested in more than one branch of the government, including an elected legislature had to be exercised.

From 1986 to 1990, the SPLA had trained more than 30,000 soldiers in five different Divisions of Kazuk, Zalzal I and II, Infijar, Intifada I and II, Intisar. The availability of those bulkiest forces, at the time, made the SPLA strategists to change strategy from guerrilla warfare to convention warfare. As a result of adopting conventional warfare, SPLA Group planned three campaigns in 1989: New Funj Campaign (NFC), Kon Anok Campaign (KAC) and Bright Star Campaign (BSC). NFC launched its campaign in Northern and Southern Blue that campaign achieved little in term of military gains. After unsuccessful attacking Kurmuk in July 1989, it died down and nothing was heard about it again. KAC assaulted Rumbek in July 1989, but after four days of heaviest fighting, the battle was called off after 600 men were lost in attempt to capture it. KAC died there and nothing was heard about it again. BSC was only campaign that achieved completely its objectives as it was planned. It liberated whole of Equatoria except Juba, Yei, Terekaka and Rokon. The whole of Upper Nile was also liberated except Malakal, Renk and Maban.

Throughout the hardest years of the armed revolutionary struggle, there were confusions, contradictions and failures. As the members sat down, to reviews failures and tried to make sense of what happened, and how did it happen, there were blame games and scapegoats. Resulting into purges, detentions and execution in the SPLM/A. As the result of all those problems and shortcomings among Political Military High Command (PMHC), some members left the movement voluntarily for one reason or another at different times under different circumstances. Some members even rebelled against movement because of the particular members. There were, indeed, some rebellions within the main rebellion. By 1995, there were two remaining members, out of seven most senior political and military leaders of movement. Out of the five members, four were detained and one rebelled. In detention 3 escaped and one remained in prison. There was banalisation of evil in that prison. Three Martins with other junior members of movement were executed and thrown in the River Nile.

When SPLA had almost defeated the government of Prime Minister Sadiq al-Mahdi by 1989, NIF party colluded with military; on pretext the government was not fighting the war to expectancy of Islamic religion and Arabic culture. There was a need for strong military leader to command the war against SPLA. Brigadier Omer Hassan al Beshir was, therefore, propped up in military coup to become the President of the Republic. In his first statement to the Sudanese nation at the time he became the president and in conjunction with Islamic fundamentalists, Mr Beshir redefined the war not as the civil war, but an eschatological war in order to appeal to the senses of Arab worlds. He called Sudanese people to be patience and as he dealt with road blocker and outlawed John Garang, in his own words, he said 'Bear with me, in next six months, in patience, I will deal soldier to soldier with John Garang '. In his response to him, John Garang said 'nothing to be feared from Beshir's threat within six months, in his words, he said 'War has to be mechanized and has to be prolonged '. After the spectacular success of the BSC, the SPLA was now planning Operation Final Lapse (OFL) that was meant to capture Juba, and in Juba, an independent country of Republic of South Sudan would have been declared.

Before starting OFL, two unexpected events occurred, which had serious consequences and setbacks on SPLM/A: (1) President Mengistu of Ethiopia was toppled from power in May 1991. The fall of Mengistu was most wicked event for SPLA because Ethiopia was (a) a gateway for the SPLM/A to get its support from the communist world (b) a safe haven and a training centre.

At first the fall of President Mengistu was worse, however, Nasir Declaration/coup became worst because it was a split in the rank and file of SPLM/A for the first time since its inception in 1983. The movement divided itself into SPLM/A Mainstream and SPLM/A Nasir. An aftermath, internecine fighting broke out between the two factions. The split disrupted the OFL. During the internecine fighting, the momentum to capture Juba was lost. President Beshir took the advantage of an internal weakness of the SPLA and scrupulously prepared the counteroffensive.

In January 1992, President Beshir launched Seif al Ubuur, a counteroffensive to SPLA BSC of 1989. It adapted blitzkrieg and schwererpunk method –the use of combine arms of artillery fire, tanks and rapid movement of the mechanized infantry to achieve a maximum success, in shortest time possible. Seif al Ubuur in its new tactic and moving and penetrating in straight line as its meaning implied in Arabic, retook all 17 main garrisons from SPLA within five months, from March to August 1992. Those 17 garrisons taken from them between 1989 and 1990.

As Seif al Ubuur was chasing the SPLA to all borders of Southern Sudan, the SPLA dived and attacked Juba in an operation known Operation Jungle Storm (OJS). The aims of the OJS were to attack enemy, where it least expect the attack and divert it attention. Despite the OJS objectives of diversion, SAF/NIF pushed away the SPLA from Juba. It chased the SPLA from Juba to Nimule at Uganda border.

In 1994, the SPLM/A held it's first national Convention. Thereafter the birth of New Sudan, comprised of five regions of Equatoria, Upper Nile, Bahr el Ghazal, Nuba Mountain, Southern Blue Nile was proclaimed. As there are many approaches or different solution to any problems, John Garang introduced his five solution modalities for solving the Sudan's conflict; New Sudan, Confederation Model, United Islamic Arab Sudan Model, United Secular Black African Model and Total Separation Model (at last total separation model won in 2011). At that time the war was redefined, according to one of the five modalities not as a civil war but as secessionist war.

In 1995, the SPLA got support from the United States for the first time in its history of fighting the Arab North, because the conservative Americans, during President George Bush's administration, argued that the Christian in Southern Sudan were being killed by Islamic Arab Northern Sudanese on religious ground. As the result of American support, SPLA launched six biggest military operations in 1996 to 2002, Operation Black Fox (OBF), Operation Thunderbolt (OTB), Operation Deng Nhial (ODN), Operation Final Lapse (OFL), Resurrection Saed Bandas Operation (RSBO) and Operation Ngacigak Nyaciluk (ONN). Among the six operations, OTB was the most successful operation, capturing more ten garrisons in west of Juba; Kaya, Bazi, Morobo, Alero, Keji Kaji, Lainya, Kagwada, Kargulu except in Mile 40. In Mile 40, SPLA got resisted, because enemy realised the SPLA had many battle tanks, so it had to dig tank ditches and Dababiin (tank killers), who destroyed 6 tanks from SPLA at Battle of Mile 40 on 28 March 1997, it was the first in history of the 21 year the SPLA lost six tanks in one battle.

From 1983 to 2005, the senior martyrs who paid the ultimate price in the battle fields were; Pareng Koi Kotjang, Faustino Puok, Geu Athorkuei, Francis Ngor Maciec, Ngacigak Ngaciluk, Majok Mach Aluong, Anyar Apiu, Thon Agot Akon, Kuai Kuei Kuai, Dhieu Warabek, Mayen Akuak Mayen, Alier Biar Akol, Ayasio Ayiti, Santino Longar Mourdit, Alier Aguto-Maker, Anyar Mayol, Pilot Caesar Madut Ring, Tito Tong Akol, ... the list is longest .

By 2005, the bravest freedom fighter who fought the war to the last were; two founding members of SPLM/A; John Garang de Mabior and Salva Kiir Mayardit, four best zonal commanders; James Wani Igga, Daniel Awet Akot, Kuol Manyang Juuk and Malik Agar and more than 100 top field commanders ; Oyai Deng Ajak, James Hoth Mai, Obuto Mamur Mete, Anthony Bol Madut, Paul Malong Awan, Salva Mathok Gengdit, Majak D'Agot Atem, Bior Ajang Duot, Gabriel Jok Riak, George Athor Deng, John Koang Nyuon, Wilson Deng Kuoirot, Bol Akot Bol, Pieng Deng Kuol, Gier Chuang Aluong, Malual Ayom Ador, Chol Thon Bolok, Thomas Chirilo Swaka, Agustine Jadhalla Wani, Peter Wal Athui, Biar Kuol Ayuen ....the list is longest . There were also more than 40 top political cadres ; Pagan Amum Okiech, Nhial Deng Nhial, Yasir Said Arman, Deng Alor Kuol, Justin Yach Arok, Paul Mayom Akech, Mark Nyipoch, Samson Kwaje, Elijah Malok Aleng,Michael Makuei Lueth, Stephen Wondu, Samuel Abu John....the list is longest.

SPLM/SPLA: History of Liberation (1983-2005)

From 1983 to 2002, SPLA/M had executed by fire squad more than 1500 officers, soldiers and civillians as part of imposing justices, civil administration and military discipline. If you kill someone, you are fire squad. If you rape a woman, you are fire squad, if you lose a gun, you are fire squad, if you desert, you are fire squad ...etc

As SPLM/A was a national movement with its internal problems, as members were disagreeing for one reason or another at different times, at different circumstances, there were many crisis that befallen SPLM/A as an entity, which almost led to its failing, however, SPLA/M as national movement fighting a just war for just cause overcame all those crises that included ; Itang-Jekou Crisis, Longkuei-Addis Abba Crisis, London-Addis Abba Crisis, Nasir Declaration/Coup, Pageri Crisis, Kaya Crisis and the amicably-solved Yei- Nairobi Crisis . The SPLM/A won all external and internal crisis not because of its strength but its righteousness and the innocence of the marginalised Southern Sudan who the SPLM/A swore to liberate. The just cause of Southern Sudanese made the SPLM/A won the war despite its banalisation of the evil on some incidents.

During the war, there had been peace talks between Sudan government and SPLM/A, starting in 1986 with Koka Declaration in Ethiopia, Abuja I and II Peace in Nigeria, Washington Declaration in October 1993 between SPLM/A and SPLM/A Nasir agreeing on the Right of Self Determination (RSD) . Finally, IGAD mediated Peace talks that brought SPLM/A and the ruling National Congress Party (NCP) on the negotiating table, which resulted into Comprehensive Peace Agreement (CPA) that was signed by Chairman and Commander in Chief of SPLM/A Colonel Dr John Garang de Mabior and by Sudan's vice president Ustaz Ali Osman Taha on behalf of President Omer Hassan el Beshir in Naivasha, Kenya on January 9, 2005.

Six month later a Transitional Government of National Unity (TGNU) was formed on July 9, 2005 and the Chairman and Commander in Chief of SPLM/A, Col. Dr John Garang de Mabior was sworn in as the First Vice President of Sudan and President of autonomous Government of Southern Sudan (GOSS). Unfortunately, John Garang died in plane crash on July 30, 2005. And his deputy Chairman and Deputy Commander in Chief, Salva Kiir Mayardit succeeded him as the Chairman and Commander in

Chief of SPLM/A and becoming the First Vice President of TGNU and President of GOSS for the six years of transitional period. At end of those six years, there was a referendum for right of self-determination (RSD) for people of Southern Sudan. In that referendum Southerners were asked to choose between separation and unity of the Sudan. Finally, Southerners voted for separation on July 9, 2011, and Southern Sudan became an independent, Republic of South Sudan, after 38 years of civil wars, out of 49 years of Sudan's independence from Britain.

Notes
1 Leon Pompa, Philosophy of History, The Blackwell Companion to Philosophy, Edited by Nicholas Bunnin and E P Tsui –James

APPENDIX

HISTORICAL ISSUES IN WHICH SOUTH SUDANESE DISAGREE UPON

In the history of South Sudan, there are some political and historical issues, in which South Sudanese disagree, argue, clash, insult and criticise one another but end up without a consensus. The issues in question are; Bor Mutiny versus Underground Movement, Definition of the Martyrs and Martyrs' Day and the Heroes and Heroes' Day and the Father of the Nation.

Some South Sudanese say, Bor Mutiny was an accident and spontaneous event that was never planned by anyone. Some South Sudanese say no, Bor Mutiny was planned by the underground movement. To put it candidly when John Garang and Kerubino were comrades in arm, SPLM/A was the result of Bor Mutiny led Kerubino Kuanyin, however, after they had fallen out, SPLM/A was the result of the Underground movement led by John Garang. Here the debate never comes to consensus.

Some South Sudanese say July 30th, 2005 is the Martyrs' Day because it is the Day, Dr John Garang died, Some South Sudanese say no, and July 30th, 2005 is not the Martyr's Day because it happened after the peace was signed on January 9th, 2005 by John Garang himself. They say Martyrs' Day must be a day within the period from May 16, 1983 to January 9th, 2005. They say The Martyrs' Day must be strictly and restricted to those who died in the particularly battle, for example, a Martyrs' Day can be the first day when a first martyr was killed after the founding of SPLM/A in

SPLM/SPLA: History of Liberation (1983-2005)

1983, or the last day when a last martyr was killed, that can be either the day Malual Goath was attacked in 1983 or the day Torit was attacked in 2002. Here the debates never come to consensus.

Some South Sudanese say Heroes are the most important people in SPLM/A during the war and after it. They are in categories, fallen Heroes and Living Heroes (Wounded Heroes and entire SPLM/SPLA). Fallen Heroes are those who died during the liberation struggle or after it but not in a particular battle, for example, Cdr Martin Manyiel Ayuel, Cdr Yusif Kwa Mekki, Dr John Garang ...etc. Therefore, July 30th 2005 can be Heroes' Day. Some other still says July 30th, 2005 must be Garang's Day alone, in which to celebrate Garang's achievements like Mandela's Day. Here the debate never comes to consensus.

Some South Sudanese's say Salva Kiir is the Father of the Nation. Some South Sudanese say no, John Garang is the Father of the Nation. Some South Sudanese still say no, John Garang, Kerubino Kuanyin, William Nyuon, Salva Kiir, Joseph Oduho and Martin Majier are the Fathers of Nation like in USA; because in USA, there is no father of Nation but fathers of nation. Here the debate never comes to consensus.

The actually debates need to come to consensus, it needs more research on time of events and reasons behind it, in order to draw a logical conclusion .Most arguments and conclusion are based on emotions, frustration, hatred and on current political situation in country and losing sight of the real history . These issues need to be revisited on rational basis by academics, publics and parliament, so that a logical consensus is reached.

BIBLIOGRAPHY

SPLM Manifesto, 31 July 1983.
Mohammad Omer Beshir, The Southern Problems: Background to the Conflict, London, 1968.
Lazarus Leek Mawut, Why South Go Back To Arms, Khartoum, 1985
Abel Alier, Too Many Agreement Dishonoured, London 1990,
James Bandi Shimanyula John Garang and SPLA, Nairobi, Africawide Network, 2005
Mohammad Amin al Khalifa, Making Peace in Sudan, Khartoum, 2003
Severino Fuli Boki Tombe Gale, Shaping a Free Southern Sudan: Memoirs of Our Struggle (1934-1985), Lou, South Sudan
P M Holt and M W Daly, A History of the Sudan: From the Coming of Islam to the Present Day, Pearson Education Limited, Edinburg, England
Lam Akol, SPLM/SPLA: Inside An African Revolution, Khartoum, 2009
Elijah Malok, The Southern Sudan: Struggle for Liberty, Kenway Publication, Nairobi 2009
Panluel Wel, The Genius of Dr John Garang: Tributes to the Late SPLM/A's Leader, Bor, Jonglei, South Sudan, 2015
Mathew LeRiche and Matthew Arnold, South Sudan: From Revolution to Independence, Hurst and Company, London, 2012
James Wani Igga, Southern Sudan: Battles Fought and The Secrecy of Diplomacy, Roberts & Brothers Printers, Kampala, 2008
Donald Petterson, Inside Sudan: Political, Conflict, and Catastrophe, Westview Press, Colorado, USA, 1999
Peter Aduok Nyaba, South Sudan: Politic of Liberation, Fountain

Publishers, Kampala, Uganda, 1998.

Hendrich Kanyance, James Hoth Mai and Kuol Deng Abot, Liberation Struggle in South Sudan

Deborah Scroggins, Emma's Wars, Pantheon, 2002

John Garang, Call for Democracy in Sudan edited by Mansour Khalid, 1992

Oystein H Rolander, Guerrilla Government in Southern Sudan, Nordic African Institute, 2005 .

ACKNOWLEDGEMENTS
(continued)

The information in this book was obtained through an interviews with SPLA officers and men, who deserve an honour of mentioning them; Garang Deng Along (Zal Zal Division), Akol Nyang Apet (Zal Zal), Mou Biar Mou (Eagle Battalion), Albino Atak Deng (Zal Zal), Akuei Maluk Kondok (Wolf Battalion, Muor Muor Division), Agoth Deng Wol (Tuek Tuek Battalion), Yel Deng Thon (Zal Zal), Joseph Dut Deng (Kazuk Division), Lt Johnson Thou Nhial (Koryom Division), Deng Mayen Machar (Ingas Task Forces), Wuoi Ayuel Mach (Red Army), Jok Riak Anyang (Red Army), Majak Mangar Riak aka Mangar Ayen (Hadid Battalion, Koryom), Magok Atem Dut (Red Army of Cuba), Kuol Athel Mach(Cobra Battalion), Chol Ajak Chol (Zidia Battalion, Koryom), Herjok Malual Kuorwel (Hadid, Koryom), Joh Majier (Zal Zal), Beer Manyuon Jok (Zal Zal), John Aguto Jool Aguto (Koryom), Gai Mabil Kur Ngang (Bilpam), Alier Agot Deng aka Alier – athoc (Rhino Battalion), Kuol Garang Deng (Agreb), Pandak Kuai Nai (Cobra Battalion), Lt Deng Wel Deng (Lion Battalion), Dot Nyang Akuei (Agreb Battalion), Akoi Garang Deng (Red Army), Ateny Patic Akau (Red Army), James Chol Bior (Red Army), Cdr Manyang Agok Aliet aka Khoor Mayual(Battalion 105), Cdr Michael Malith Lual aka Lual Niop (Battalion 105), Michael Wel Agot (Sudan armed forces) Joseph Maker Mareng (Rhino Battalion), Khamis Ayuen Lual (Koryom Division), Cdr Machar Thiong Ayuel (Commando), James Gai Nyok (Red Army), Cdr Reuben Thiong Tat (Battalion105), Akoi Geu Mach (Lion Battalion), Paul Garang Deng aka Garang Deng-amuor (Battalion 105), Majok Athethiei de Mabior (Red Army), Lt Deng Adol Deng (Koryom), Cdr Deng Bior aka Deng-athoo (Koryom), Honourable David Deng Athorbei (SPLM/ SPLA), Major Jok Aleer (Koryom Division), Cdr Akuoc Miyong aka Awath Jago(Tiger Battalion), Lt Majur Kot Thon (Zal Zal), Simon Okan Amon (sharp shooter that shot down a plane over Malakal, Tiger Battalion), Joseph Garang Yor (sharp shooter of planes, Shark Battalion, Muor Muor Division), John Kuol Jurkuch (Battalion104), Denis Kur Juach (Hadid Battalion), Majier Mayom (sharp shooter of planes, Tiger Battalion), John Bol Ajak (Red Army), Khoor Mangok Deng (Red Army), Jol Nyok Riak (Battalion 105, Kaji Kaji Company), Gong Kuol Ajieu (Intifada Division) Makuac Nyok Mabil, Cdr Bior Yuang Bior (Rhino Battalion, Koryom), Lt Bior Ajang Duot (MP Jonglei state), James Kuol Deng (SPLA), Lt Philip Yuot Maguet (Commando), Kon Ayom Riak (Zal Zal), Mabior Nyang Akuook (Red Army), Malith Chol Manyiel (Panda Oyee Task Force), Major Deng Anyuon (SPLA), Ayuen Garang Nhial (Sudan armed Forces), Khoor Lueth Ayom aka Khoor –aguk (Red Army), Herjok Deng -atharkuei (Red Army), Mamer Aguto Ayuen (SPLA), Mach Achiek Akuei aka Guanyak (Red Army), Nhiany Pur Abuoi (Hadid Battalion, Koryom Division), Bheer Ayuen Mayen(Cobra), Machola Mabior Majak (Red Army), Gabriel Gai Majak (Aquila Mnyuon Battalion, Koryom), Lt Adet Malek Kuereng (Zidia Battalion, Koryom Division), Cdr Chol Mabior Akuei (Battalion 105), Achan Malek Ayom (SPLA Katina Banat), Nyakor Athieng((Old Sudan Prison), Cdr Athou Anyieth-chek (the first Southern Sudan woman to give the plight of refugees to General Mesfin), Cdr Angau Juuk (Battalion 105), Cdr Gabriel Jok Riak (Battalion105), Col . Deng Mabior Deng aka Deng-jamaula., Brig Alier Malual, Brig Marial Thuc Malek,Cdr Michael Manoah Kot, Brig Ayuen Dot Thon, Cdr Wuoi Mayom Wuoi, Cdr Angelo Jongkuch Jool, Cdr Wilson Deng Kuoirot aka Deng-wek, Abraham Malak Mangok (Koryom Division), Cdr Kur Kuol Ajieu (Jamus Battalion), Cdr Awuou Aluong(Battalion 105), Cdr Ajith-Manyangdit (Battalion 105), Cdr Deng Kut (MP Jonglei state), Cdr Chol Gai Arou (Koryom), Cdr Alier-aguar, the first driver of SPLA barge, Brig . Lual Manyang, Kon Mawut Abuoi (Muor Muor), Deng Mach Deng aka Deng raar-nyang(Muor Muor), Abraham Kot (Zal Zal),

www.ingramcontent.com/pod-product-compliance
Lightning Source LLC
Chambersburg PA
CBHW030255010526
44107CB00053B/1716